BLAH BLAH BLAH

BLAH BLAH BLAH

What to Do When Words Don't Work

DAN ROAM

Portfolio / Penguin

PORTFOLIO / PENGUIN
Published by the Penguin Group
Penguin Group (USA) Inc., 375 Hudson Street, New York, New York 10014, U.S.A. • Penguin Group (Canada), 90 Eglinton Avenue East, Suite 700, Toronto, Ontario, Canada M4P 2Y3 (a division of Pearson Penguin Canada Inc.) • Penguin Books Ltd, 80 Strand, London WC2R 0RL, England • Penguin Ireland, 25 St. Stephen's Green, Dublin 2, Ireland (a division of Penguin Books Ltd) • Penguin Books Australia Ltd, 250 Camberwell Road, Camberwell, Victoria 3124, Australia (a division of Pearson Austra-lia Group Pty Ltd) • Penguin Books India Pvt Ltd, 11 Community Centre, Panchsheel Park, New Delhi – 110 017, India • Penguin Group (NZ), 67 Apollo Drive, Rosedale, Auckland 0632, New Zealand (a division of Pearson New Zealand Ltd) • Penguin Books (South Africa) (Pty) Ltd, 24 Sturdee Avenue, Rosebank, Johannesburg 2196, South Africa

Penguin Books Ltd, Registered Offices:
80 Strand, London WC2R 0RL, England

First published in 2011 by Portfolio / Penguin,
a member of Penguin Group (USA) Inc.

10 9 8 7 6 5 4 3 2

LIBRARY OF CONGRESS CATALOGING IN PUBLICATION DATA

Roam, Dan.
Blah blah blah : what to do when words don't work / Dan Roam.
p.   cm.
Includes bibliographical references and index.
ISBN 978-1-59184-459-4 (hardback)
1. Thought and thinking—Art. 2. Visual communication. 3. Communication. I. Title.
BF441.R58 2011
153.4—dc23   2011021787

Printed in the United States of America

Designed by Daniel Lagin

For Sophie and Celeste.
Watching you learn illuminates the world for me.

For Kay M. Roam.
Fly, Mom—fly!

CONTENTS

PART 1

The Blah-Blahmeter

PART 2

If I Draw, Am I Dumb? An Introduction to Vivid Thinking

PART 3

The Forest and the Trees:
The Seven Essentials of a Vivid Idea

PART 4

Conclusion

APPENDIXES

DRAMATIS PERSONAE

(CAST OF CHARACTERS)

In Order of Appearance

PART 1

	Me	Author searching for a better way to think about complex things		John Hersey	WWII journalist and lover of words
	You	Hello! It's a pleasure to have you along		Ted Geisel	World's bestselling author you've never heard of
	My Former Boss	Entrepreneur; sales genuius but no operational skills		General Petraeus	Commanding General of U.S. troops in Afghanistan, 2010
	Jon Stewart	TV personality; can't recall how many sides a "pentagon" has		Barack Obama	44th President of the United States of America
	Terry Gross	Radio personality; struggles to recall what she read yesterday		VitaminWater	A Coca-Cola product of uncertain character
	Chuck Townsend	CEO of Condé Nast; sends confusing memos		Captain Chesley Sullenberger	"Sully"; pilot's pilot and hero of the Hudson
	Mr. X	Department of Defense "Super User"; overwhelmed with information		Bernie Madoff	Wall Street charlatan, former high-flyer now in jail
	Miss Brown	My second grade teacher; likes ducks				

PART 2

	Albert Einstein	Twentieth century's greatest mind; known by his nanny as "Stupid"		A Fox	Clever, witty, linear, and a little smug: our verbal mind
	Oog and Aag	Missing links; early hominids with expanding minds		A Hummingbird	Quick, exuberant, spatial, and a little flighty: our visual mind
	Richard Feynman	Nuclear physicist; believed anyone could learn anything		Anonymous User	Mobile phone user, lost and in need of directions
	Michael Porter	Harvard professor; most influential business teacher ever		Your Grammar Teacher	Yikes! Yes: She's back . . .

PART 3

	Airline Ticket Agent	Trying to get you on your plane on time; harried and frustrated		Abraham Maslow	Doctor of Psychology; enjoys hierarchies
	Medieval Scholar	Trying to grasp the true shape of the earth		Renée Mauborgne and W. Chan Kim	INSEAD business professors; *Blue Ocean* explorers
	A PC and a Mac	Two computers masquerading as a couple geeks (or vice-versa?)		Leonardo da Vinci	Fifteenth-century visionary; inventor of the parachute
	The Rich and the Poor	Two groups trying to avoid taxes		Edwin Land	Father of Polaroid; America's 2nd-greatest inventor
	Leno and Conan	Late-night comedians; both funny but neither laughing		Will Wright	Creator of "The Sims"; games mastermind
	Niall Ferguson	Economic historian; believes in long-term trends		Lady Gaga	The latest pop sensation; wears sunglasses
	The Medicis and the Rothschilds	Big moneymen making the world go around		Martin Eberhard and Marc Tarpenning	Serial entrepreneurs; inventors of Tesla electric car

	Donella Meadows	MIT scientist; leading light in "systems thinking"		Dmitri Mendeleyev	Russian mad scientist; creator of world's most influential chart
	Tatsu Takeuchi	Virginia Tech assistant professor; a relativity genius		Michael Burry	Financial visionary; foresaw global economic crunch
	Navy Officer	Teacher of naval history; expert in no-BS explanations		Genrich Altshuller	Soviet scientist and gulag survivor; sees invisible patterns
	Pat O'Dea	CEO of Peet's Coffee and Teas; making coffee better		A Cloud	A once vague idea made distinct and memorable

BLAH
BLAH
BLAH

INTRODUCTION

Half of What We Think About Thinking Is Wrong

e think that thinking means stringing words together in a meaningful way. We think that talking is the best way to share an idea. We think that speaking well is the cornerstone of intelligence. We're only half right.

This book is about three things: blah, blah, and blah—three little words that are killing our ability to think, learn, work, and lead.

Blah-blah-blah is complexity, which kills our ability to think. This book introduces an easier way to think about complicated things.

Blah-blah-blah is misunderstanding, which kills our ability to lead. This book presents a simple way to better understand our ideas before, during, and after we share them with other people.

Blah-blah-blah is boredom, which kills our ability to care. This book lays out a way to make learning about complex ideas infinitely more engaging—and infinitely more fun. (Don't tell anyone about that last part; they'll think we're not serious.)

This book is about how to stop blah-blah-blah before it stops us.

This Book and Its Tools

This book is laid out in three parts. The first part introduces the three blahs.

Blah   **Blah-Blah**   **Blah-Blah-Blah**

The second part introduces an antidote to blah-blah-blah. It's called "Vivid thinking."

Verbal + Visual

Vivid = Visual + verbal + interdependent

The third part presents a map that gets us from one to the other.

Each of the three parts introduces a tool. First is the **blah-blahmeter,** a device that helps us detect incoming blah-blah-blah before it hits. The second tool is **Vivid Grammar,** a simple set of guidelines that show us how to avoid blah-blah-blah by engaging both our verbal and visual minds. The third tool is the **Vivid FOREST**, a map that shows us an easy-to-follow path to make sure our own ideas are vibrant, clear, and memorable.

Let's Meet Our Contestants

 Blah   Blah-Blah   Blah-Blah-Blah

Blah, blah, and blah are the overuse, misuse, and abuse of language—anything we say that interferes with our ability to convey ideas. Blah-blah-blah isn't just about being boring (although boring is often part of it), nor is blah-blah-blah about being intentionally misleading (although misleading is also often part of it). What blah-blah-blah really means is that we've become so enamored of our words that we've fooled ourselves into believing we understand things better than we actually do.

When words don't work, thinking doesn't work. Wonderful as words are, they cannot alone detect, describe, and defuse the multifaceted problems of today. That's bad, because words have become our default thinking tool. Even worse, for most of us words are our *only* thinking tool.

We need a new tool.

Sliding into the Land of Blah-Blah-Blah

Many years ago, I worked at a small consulting company. Our boss was a brilliant salesman but an operational disaster, a combination that ensured we always had more work than we could handle. Being busy was an advantage: Since we never had enough time, we constantly improvised—and in looking for quicker ways to solve old problems, we were surrounded by new ideas. While our days were long, we always went home feeling good about everything we'd gotten done.

After a few successful years, our company got big. New management came in, and before long all we did was go to meetings. *Here's the new company vision and values. Here's our new synergy-leveraging go-to-market strategy. Here's our new customer-centric restructuring plan. Blah-blah-blah.* Those days were also long, but they weren't satisfying. The more we talked, the fewer problems we solved. Before long, ideas stopped showing up, and our once respected little company became a permanent fixture in the land of blah-blah-blah.

I quit.

There's No Place Like Home

But I couldn't get away. None of us can.

In today's learning and working world, blah-blah-blah has become our home. Ever been to three meetings back to back? Welcome to blah-blah-blah. Ever left a meeting more confused than when you entered? Ever watched two hours of cable news and knew that you knew less about the world? Ever stifled another yawn during another conference-room bullet-point bonanza? You get the picture.

At least we're not alone.

We Know Too Much

Blah-blah-blah comes in a sliding scale, from too much information to too little information to negative information.

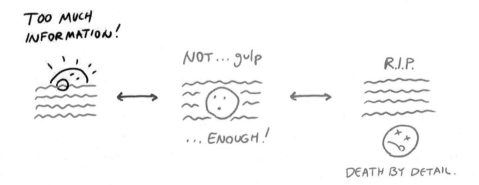

On the too-much-information side, blah-blah-blah overwhelms our capacity for recall: So much knowledge comes in that we've got no choice but to let most of it flow right back out. Case in point: Late last year, two of broadcast media's most well-read celebrities met on a New York stage to talk books—and ended up commiserating about how little of what they read they could remember.

Jon Stewart, host of the comedy news program *The Daily Show,* sat down with National Public Radio's interviewing legend Terry Gross to discuss Stewart's new book. Not long into the interview, Gross asked Stewart if he actually read all the books he reviewed. Stewart jokingly said yes—he always made a point of reading both the front *and* back covers. Then, momentarily serious, he continued:

Stewart: Some weeks we have four books, and they can be big ones, you know: historical nonfiction. But I read pretty quickly, and I try and read as much of the books as I possibly can and I have a pretty good ability to get through it, retaining a good deal of its information . . .

Then he paused for effect:

. . . for a four- to-six-hour period. And then it disappears from my brain for the rest of my life.

Gross: Do I know that feeling. I *so* know that feeling.

Stewart: I take it in and suddenly I'm an expert on the construction of the Pentagon . . . and then by eight o'clock that night I'm like, Really? I didn't know there was a building with five sides!

The scariest part of this exchange is that these are the *smart* people. If Jon Stewart and Terry Gross can't keep pace with everything they read, what hope is there for the rest of us?

We Know Nothing

Blah-blah-blah means sometimes we may be surrounded by lots of words but they contain no meaning.

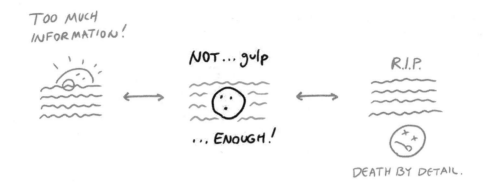

Condé Nast, publisher of the world's most prestigious collection of magazines (*Vogue, Glamour, Vanity Fair, Golf Digest, Wired, The New Yorker,* etc.), should know that: The company publishes millions of words every month that subscribers can't wait to read. Yet a recent e-mail sent by the CEO to all employees took five hundred words to say . . . well, nothing.

In his companywide note of Tuesday, October 5, 2010, Condé Nast CEO Chuck Townsend sought to clarify the thinking behind a number of changes the company was making in response to the Internet. His language was so full of corporate-speak that not even his employees could understand what he was telling them.

In July, we announced a strategic refocus of our Company and identified three clear priorities to ensure our future growth and success: a consumer-centric business model, a holistic brand management approach and the establishment of a multi-platform, integrated sales and marketing organization. Our commitment to consumer centricity is evident . . . To optimize brand revenue growth, we will shift responsibility for single-site, digital sales and marketing to the brand level. Publishers can now fully leverage their offerings across all platforms.

Huh?

According to the *New York Times*, one employee reacted by saying, "We all read it and have no idea what he was talking about. It's the kind of communication where there are no verbs and every other word is some kind of buzzy techno jargon."

When the head of a publisher can't make himself understood with words, we know that we're in big trouble.

We Know Less Than Nothing

At the other end of the scale, blah-blah-blah sometimes means we know less than nothing. When the depth of detail forced upon us kills our ability to comprehend, we end up receiving negative knowledge—*the more we hear, the less we know.*

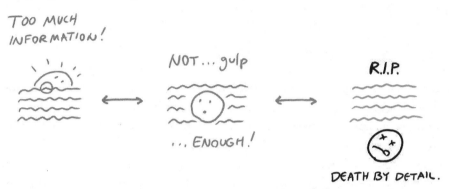

In early 2010, in a tiny, darkened room buried somewhere deep within the Pentagon (the one with five sides, Jon), a senior member of the United States Department of Defense sat down at a small desk. The desk was bare and his hands were empty. He was there for a briefing on projects under way in the war on terror. Although he was one of only a handful of people in the whole world privy to the full scope of our government's top-secret activities, he was not allowed to take notes.

Project slides flashed on the screen before him. A program name appeared, then a list of staff members and authors. Then a mission statement appeared, followed by a list of goals and objectives, then a list of tasks completed and not completed, then a list of resources and their current disposition, then a written schedule, then detailed agendas, then reference documents, then a budget overview, then supporting points for a request for supplemental funding, then a list of action items, then a partial list of associated programs.

When one program finished, another began. There were hundreds of programs to review that day.

Not long into the briefing, it dawned on this "super user" that he knew less than when he had started. "Stop!" he yelled, and walked out of the room. Then, according to the

Washington Post's two-year investigation of America's growing top-secret world, the super user flatly stated, "I'm not going to live long enough to be briefed on everything." The result, he added, was that it was impossible to tell whether this mind-boggling array of programs made our country any safer or not.

Let's think about that for a moment: The more the super user was briefed on the programs, the less he could tell whether they made our country safe. That sounds like as solid a definition of blah-blah-blah as we're ever going to get.

How Did We Get Here?

It's weird, isn't it? Everybody hates blah-blah-blah, yet here we are. None of us started out intending to make good ideas hard to find. Nobody decided up front that the best way to say one thing was to say everything else. Nobody began a career believing that the best way to get ahead is by making sure they're not understood.

With all the channels of instant communication available to us, we should understand each other better, not worse. With so much history accessible with the tap of a finger, we should find faster ways to solve problems, not quicker ways to assign blame. When we have a great idea, we should be able to share it more clearly than ever, not find it harder than ever to be heard.

The Treasure Map

We don't need more words. We need more ideas. We need them fast, and we need them to be good—and to know that they're good, we need them to be clear.

To tell the good ideas from the bad ones, the insightful from the ignorant, the creative from the creativity killing, we need to be able to *see* them. Yet seeing isn't something we can do here in the land of blah-blah-blah. This is the place to go to hide, obscure, divert, and spin. If we want to actually solve a problem, we have to get out of here.

That's where this book comes in. It offers an escape plan.

The escape comes in the form of a treasure map. It's a map we can use when we have a problem and we need to find a good idea to solve it, a map we can use when we're overwhelmed with words and we need to know what they really mean, and a map we can use when we see a great idea—and need other people to see it too.

What Makes a Useful Map

To be useful, any map must show three things: where we are now (in enough detail to decide whether that's a good place for us to stay), a better place to go (in enough detail to decide whether that place really does look more inviting), and a clearly marked path between the two (in enough detail to make sure we won't get lost along the way).

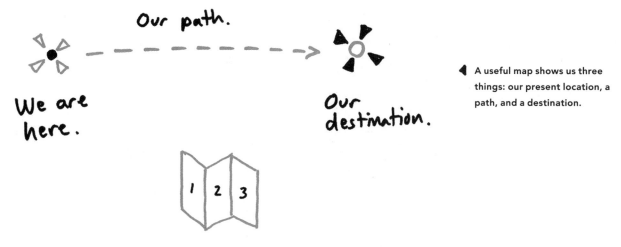

Our path.

We are here.

Our destination.

A useful map shows us three things: our present location, a path, and a destination.

Think of this book as a map that unfolds into three sections. The first describes our present location deep in the doo-doo of blah-blah-blah. The second describes a two-lane path that leads us out. The third describes a more desirable destination—a place where we know our ideas inside and out, trust that other people's ideas are worth our time, and are confident in our ability to see the big picture.

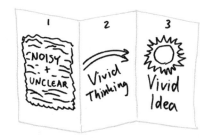

Before we embark, let's get familiar with our new map.

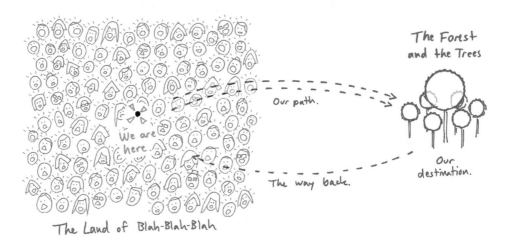

Our Treasure Map

The Forest and the Trees

Our path.

We are here

Our destination.

The way back.

The Land of Blah-Blah-Blah

This is our treasure map. ▶ Let's get familiar with it one section at a time.

We Are Here

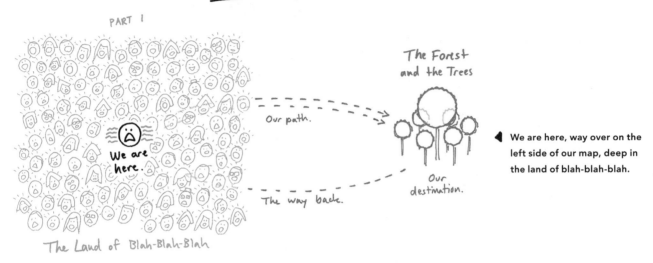

Our Treasure Map

PART I

We are here.

The Land of Blah-Blah-Blah

Our path.

The way back.

The Forest and the Trees

Our destination.

◀ We are here, way over on the left side of our map, deep in the land of blah-blah-blah.

On the left side of our map we see our present location, deep in the land of blah-blah-blah. As we know, it's a noisy place, full of activity and buzz. It's not necessarily a bad place—there is a lot going on here, and it can be thrilling to be in the middle of it all—but with all the talking and jostling, it's not a great place to try to think things through, and it's a nearly impossible place to get much attention.

In order to stand out in this crowd, one of us starts talking a little louder and a little faster. That works for a moment, but to compensate, all the rest of us start talking louder and faster, too. Things ratchet up until a new blah-blah-blah equilibrium is reached, at a volume, velocity, and quantity that make it difficult to know what's worth listening to. And that's the real danger here: With all our clamoring words, it's not long before we're so busy keeping up that we not only stop listening to anyone else—we stop listening to ourselves. Pretty soon we don't remember what our own idea was—or whether we even had one. All that matters is being heard.

A Path Out

Our Treasure Map

PART 2

Vivid Thinking

Our path.

The Forest and the Trees

We are here

The way back.

Our destination.

The Land of Blah-Blah-Blah

There is a two-lane path leading out—and we need to use both lanes. ▶

We could just stay here in blah-blah-blah; it's easy to do—and, in most ways, our trends and technology encourage us to do so. But if we really need a new idea, need it to be good, and need others to see it, we need a way out.

The path out of blah-blah-blah is simple to find, but it's not that easy to take. That's because the path has two lanes, and we've been taught about only one of them: the word path. This path we know well. It's the path of talking, writing, and reading, and our education has taught, trained, and tested us to rely on it.

The second path isn't secret; everyone knows that it's there. It's the picture path. As a thinking tool, pictures have been around much longer than writing. In fact, far in the past, long before anyone ever wrote a word on anything, pictures were the only path to take.

But somewhere between then and now we discovered writing, and most of us lost interest in the picture path. And now, because it's been so long since we have trekked it, the picture lane remains undiscovered and undeveloped—and a bit scary.*

So we stick to the path that we know—and we talk. The trouble is that, as much as we might want to leave blah-blah-blah behind, taking the word path always leads us right back in. Sadly, the second path—the picture path—isn't by itself much better. Even people who know this ancient path well tend to get lost when they try to use only pictures to explain themselves.

It's only by taking the two paths together that we can get where we need to go. To solve the problems of today, we need to see and hear, read and look, write and draw. And when we do—when we remember how to think verbally *and* visually—that's when we'll understand the power of Vivid Thinking.

Our Destination

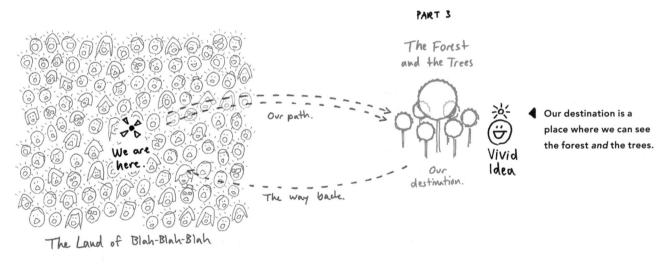

Our Treasure Map

PART 3

The Forest and the Trees

Our path.

We are here.

Our destination.

The way back.

The Land of Blah-Blah-Blah

Vivid Idea

◀ Our destination is a place where we can see the forest *and* the trees.

---

* If you're interested in how we lost the pictures, take a look at Appendix A, "How We Lost Half Our Mind."

On the right side of our map, we see our destination. It is a quiet little forest located far outside the land of blah-blah-blah. Here we can take a deep breath, enjoy a moment of quiet, and get a better look at what's really on our mind.

This isn't just any little forest. Although hushed at first, this forest isn't secluded; it's full of ideas—our own and those of others. After all the commotion of blah-blah-blah, it just takes a while to adjust our eyes and ears. But after a few moments we will begin to see more ideas out here, and we'll see exactly what they're made of. Out here, for the first time, we can see the forest *and* the trees.

A Way Back

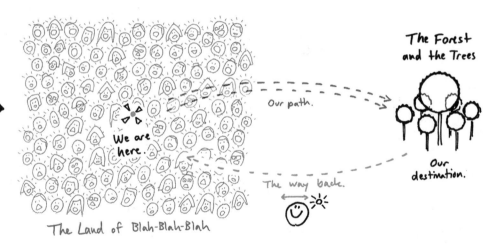

After our trip to the forest, ▶ we'll need to come back, only now we'll know how to cut through the blah-blah-blah.

Once we've visited the Vivid FOREST, we'll never look at the land of blah-blah-blah the same again. Of course, we'll eventually have to return, because that's where the action is, but it will be a different place for us. Because we'll know many new things about our own ideas, we'll share them differently. And knowing what we do, we'll also expect something different from the people sharing their ideas with us.

Enough Blah-Blah-Blah

That's it, this book in a nutshell: a section on the land of blah-blah-blah and how we got here, a section on the two-lane path out, and a section on a more vivid place to go.

Since we're going to start in blah-blah-blah, let's begin by understanding how we got here. And that's a story that begins with a picture.

Winging It

Way back in second grade, I drew what was to become one of the most important pictures of my life. It was a picture of a duck. I have no idea why I drew a duck, but I do remember the picture. In it, I captured the duck in midflight: nose out, tail back, legs tucked, wings stretched. He was a fast duck, and I drew him in profile so that I could add speed lines. I didn't know a lot about ducks, so I had to wing it. In the end, my duck looked like this:

◀ My fast duck, ca. 1970

A few days after I drew the duck, my teacher, Miss Brown, gave me a trophy. It said BEST DRAWING. I was surprised. I didn't even know that my duck had entered a contest.

I shouldn't have been surprised: My report card from the time, while complimenting my "creativity," also chastised me for talking too much in class. Miss Brown's specific words in the "Pays Attention in Class" section were "In need of improvement."

My report card also indicated that I was behind in reading. That, too, came as no surprise. I hated reading. Of all the things we got to do in class—draw, color, measure, cut and paste, build, talk—it was when instructed to read that I shrank. I said to myself that it was because reading was boring, lonely, and pointless, but the real reason was that reading was hard.

I was ashamed that reading was difficult for me, because I was considered among the smart kids in class. I sensed that as much as my side conversations irritated Miss Brown, she appreciated my participation. But when we had to read, I knew I was falling behind. When reading became the main reason for school, I lost my favorite reason to go.

This story could have ended badly. But right around that time, my dad brought home a book written by a doctor. I don't know if my dad knew I was having trouble reading, but he did know that Dr. Seuss's *Green Eggs and Ham* was funny. We started reading it together in the evenings. I was drawn in by the pictures and my dad's laughing, and after a time I also realized that the words on the page weren't so bad after all. They had only a few letters each, and those letters repeated in consistent patterns that were fun to sound out. After a few rounds of "Sam I am. I am Sam," the lightbulb in my head labeled "words" began to flicker, and when my dad and I moved up to the more complex *The Cat in the Hat*, that light began to burn bright. Thanks to Dr. Seuss, I learned to read.

Why Johnny Can't Read

So did hundreds of millions of other kids. By the time he died, in 1991, Dr. Seuss had written sixty books, which as of today have sold more than a quarter *billion* copies. According to *Publishers Weekly,* twenty-three of the 150 top-selling children's books of all time were written by Dr. Seuss. His approach to writing—half of which involved drawing—changed the way America learned to read.

But where did Dr. Seuss, with his funny words and goofy pictures, come from—and how did these seemingly simple books come to change so profoundly the way young students thought about reading? To know that story, we have to first meet John Hersey.

John Hersey didn't have the same troubles reading that I did. He loved words. As a correspondent during the Second World War, he wrote about the GIs landing on Sicily, the cold of the Russian front, and the heat of the Burmese jungles. While on duty in the Pacific, he survived a plane crash in the ocean. After swimming to the surface, the first thing he could think about was finding his writing—which he did, when his notebook floated up and bonked him on the head.

John Hersey's love of words was infectious. In 1946, he wrote the longest article ever published by *The New Yorker* magazine. His 31,000-word essay "Hiroshima" told of the devastation wrought by the first atomic bomb. (That's a lot of words for a magazine: 31,000 is more than half the length of the book you're holding in your hands.)

Hidden behind a lovely *New Yorker* cover cartoon showing a warm afternoon in Central Park, "Hiroshima" appeared in the magazine's August 31, 1946, issue. The sunny cover was a trick; the darkness of Hersey's article filled the entire magazine. For the first and (so far) only time, *The New Yorker* dedicated its contents to only one story—no cartoons, no news, no reviews; just "Hiroshima." It was among the magazine's most successful editions, selling out at the newsstands within hours. Later, "Hiroshima" was described by *Time* magazine as "the most celebrated piece of journalism to come out of World War II."

Clearly, John Hersey loved words, which makes it fascinating that when he later wrote an article for *Life* magazine about reading, he ended up writing mostly about pictures.

Pictures? Wait a second—wasn't Hersey a word guy? This discovery is so important to this story (and to the rest of this book) that I want to repeat it: *In writing an article about helping children learn to read, John Hersey focused more than anything else on the pictures that accompanied the words.*

Here's what happened.

By 1952, six years after his breakthrough *New Yorker* story, Hersey had become a successful novelist and professor of English. He had also become the father of five children, and in the interest of learning more about their education he joined a parent-teacher group called the Citizens' School Study Council of Fairfield. The goal of the study group was to help the Connecticut school district's principals, teachers, and parents understand why children weren't learning to read very well—something that Hersey, as a dedicated word guy, found particularly troubling.

As with today's concerns about how the Internet is affecting our brains, there was great concern sixty years ago that a new technology (television at that time) and a new teaching style (individualized teaching instead of group rote learning) were undermining public literacy. According to Hersey, the study council's goal was to answer the question "Are our young citizens learning to use our language well enough?"

To address this challenge, members of the study group attended school classes, read technical books, consulted educational experts, and learned everything they could about the art of learning to read. After two years of intense effort and research, Hersey concluded the study by writing another long article, this one appearing in *Life*.

"Why Do Students Bog Down on the First R?" appeared halfway through the magazine's May 24, 1954, issue. Surrounded by advertisements for cigarettes, sunglasses, and Greyhound bus vacations to Yellowstone, the article ran for a long ten pages. In the article, Hersey and the study group covered a lot of ground. They revealed that kids preferred to watch television over reading (no surprise there), that more emphasis was put on helping the slow learners than the fast learners (a bit of a surprise), and that decisions about the "right" way to educate were always going to be difficult because there was so little in education that could be meaningfully measured (a pretty big surprise).

But the biggest surprise of them all was also the simplest: The reason kids weren't learning to read was because their books *looked* boring.

Where There's a Will

Just looking at the pictures in the primers that the Fairfield students had been given, the study group could easily see why kids didn't want to read them. "In the classroom boys and girls are confronted with books that have insipid illustrations depicting slicked-up lives of unnaturally clean boys and girls."

Hersey became even more focused on the pictures: "Little boys trying to learn to read in Fairfield witness a lone boy named Tom condemned to play endlessly, and with unnatural control of his manners, with two syrupy girls, Betty and Susan. This frightful life that Tom leads is bound up inextricably with the first crucial stages of reading. It is not entirely surprising that some boys draw back from the experience."

What reading looked like in ▶
1954.

"Oh look," said Bobby.
"Look at the bird.
It is a nice bird."

"Oh yes," said Janey.
"You are right.
It is a very nice bird."

In summarizing their findings, the council concluded that the kids weren't learning to read because they didn't want to read the books they were given—and they didn't want to read those books *because they hated the pictures.*

Hersey ended his article with a plea to the textbook publishers. "In primary grade readers, pictures on each page give clues to virtually everything in the text. The child is helped to visualize the words, but he is helped by pictures that are uniform, bland, idealized and terribly literal. Why should they not have pictures that widen rather than narrow the associative richness the children give to the words they illustrate—drawings like those of the wonderfully imaginative geniuses among children's illustrators, Tenniel, Howard Pyle, Dr. Seuss, Walt Disney?"

Lucky for me many years later, one courageous textbook editor read the article.

The Lists

William Ellsworth Spaulding was an editor at Houghton Mifflin's textbook division in New York. He read Hersey's article and was inspired: Why *not* get one of those children's authors to write a school textbook? But of the illustrators Hersey mentioned, the options were limited. Sir John Tenniel, the original illustrator of *Alice in Wonderland,* had died forty years earlier, back in 1914. Howard Pyle, author and illustrator of *The Merry Adventures of Robin Hood,* had passed away even earlier, in 1911. And Walt Disney, while very much alive and kicking, was busy putting the finishing touches on a theme park in Los Angeles.

This left Ted Geisel, a moderately successful children's author who wrote and drew under his mother's maiden name, Seuss. Spaulding was familiar with Dr. Seuss and contacted his publisher, Bennett Cerf at Random House, to see if Cerf might be willing to loan the author out to try his hand at a textbook. Cerf agreed, as long as Random House could sell the bookstore version of anything Dr. Seuss wrote.

Agreement made, Spaulding approached Dr. Seuss. To ensure that whatever Dr. Seuss might write could serve as a textbook that teachers and school districts would buy, Spaulding gave Dr. Seuss three lists of words that experts had agreed were important for first-graders to read. Altogether, the lists contained 348 words.

Looking at the lists, Dr. Seuss thought the whole exercise ridiculous. But then he picked the first two words that rhymed: "cat" and "hat."

The Bet

It took Dr. Seuss nine months to write and illustrate *The Cat in the Hat*. (He used only 236 of the words.) The book changed the way teachers taught, how schools bought texts, how publishers thought about education, and—most important to *this* book—how people connected words and pictures.

The Cat in the Hat was so successful for Random House that Bennett Cerf decided to raise the stakes. He bet Dr. Seuss fifty dollars that Seuss couldn't pull off the feat again using only fifty words. This time the list contained "ham," "am," and "Sam." And this time it took Dr. Seuss just five months to write *Green Eggs and Ham*.

Pictures Make the Words Matter— and Vice Versa

And that's how I—and very likely you, and just about anyone we know who was born in America in the past fifty years—learned to read: by sounding out simple words that were interwoven with compelling pictures. The magic sauce that Dr. Seuss added to his books not only changed how America learned to read but changed how we think about books: The books that teach us stuff best are those that reach out to *both* our verbal and visual minds.

In the end, the magic sauce wasn't all that magic; it just made sense. One of the great insights of Hersey and the council's report was that experts and teachers agreed: *A child who really wants to learn something usually learns it.* "Some educators now believe beginners could absorb as many as 200 words in the first six months provided words are used that the children want to learn." And what's the best way to get a child to want to learn? Make it enjoyable to the whole mind.

What Happened to the Pictures?

From a combat correspondent's words to an inspired pair of publishers to an author who liked to draw to millions of children who decided reading wasn't so bad after all, it's a great story. Among many other things, it tells us that in learning to read, pictures matter as much as the words they accompany.

So here's the big question: If pictures make such a difference in attracting a young kid to an idea, why stop with kids? If pictures played such an important role in motivating us to *want* to undertake something as challenging as reading, why don't we use pictures today to motivate us to *want* to understand the problems we face as adults? If pictures gave us a good way to jump into the ideas then, why have we given up on the pictures now?

In business, as in politics, education, and life, we've left the picture path behind precisely at the time we need it most. Why?

Isn't "Thinking Different" Exactly What We're Looking For?

The biggest buzzword in business these days is *innovation*. The business press, business leaders, and business schools can't say it enough: "Innovation is the key to success." "We need to innovate our way out of this recession." "If we could emulate their ability to innovate, we could become the Apple of (insert industry here)."

When we're searching for innovation, aren't we simply seeking a different way of looking at the world? Let's ask the question of a moment ago again, but now from a different perspective. Why is it that at the moment in history when we most need to see the world differently, we don't force our mind to look at problems differently? If our goal is to *look* differently, where have all our pictures gone?

Why Johnny and Janey Can't Draw (the Real Reason We Can't Solve Problems to Save Our Butts)

◀ The reason we think we're not visual . . .

. . . is because just when we were starting to understand things . . . ▶

. . . they took the pictures away. ▶

Pictures Aren't Training Wheels

We all know the power of pictures as a learning tool. Before we learned to read, we were asked to draw. But then the pictures stopped. Our entire education system evolved to believe that pictures are like training wheels: They're useful only to get us started reading—and drawing should be discarded the moment we're able to write.

That is just so wrong. Pictures are the part of thinking that provides us with guidance and direction. It's the "big picture" that lets us see where we're going. Pictures aren't training wheels; *pictures are the front wheel.*

When it comes to thinking, talking, and solving problems, it's as if we're all riding around on mental unicycles. Sure, with enough training anyone can learn to ride one, but why bother: We'll always be faster and more stable with two wheels than one.

Blah-blah-blah. No wonder no one can explain the world. The rest of this book is going to get us back on both wheels.

PART 1

The Blah-Blahmeter

The Blah-Blahmeter

CHAPTER 1

Exploring the Land of Blah-Blah-Blah

ords can be used to describe anything.

But that does not mean words are the best way to describe everything.

What Is Blah-Blah-Blah?

Not all words are blah-blah-blah.

> *We hold these truths to be self-evident, that all men are created equal, that they are endowed by their Creator with certain unalienable Rights, that among these are Life, Liberty and the pursuit of Happiness.**

Words are magnificent. When used well, words help us think, make us feel, let us remember, tell us the truth, show us the way, help us understand, unravel the complex, gather us together, and give our lives meaning.

---

* The preamble to the Declaration of Independence, 1776.

Oh! I have slipped the surly bonds of Earth . . .
*Put out my hand and touched the Face of God.**

When words work, they not only change how we feel about the world; words change the world.

Yes we can.†

These are not the words we're talking about.

When Words Work

Words can do all these wonderful things because language is the single most sophisticated, finely developed, and important technology humanity has ever created. Using words is what makes us human.

But using words and using words *well* are not the same thing. That's because, wonderful as the technology of language is, it is also our easiest technology to mess up.

When Words Don't Work

When it comes to words, there are many ways we can break things. When we do, the result is blah-blah-blah: the overuse, misuse, or abuse of the technology of language.

Sometimes our blah-blah-blah comes from an honest mistake—we have a good idea to share, but we use the wrong words to describe it. Sometimes blah-blah-blah comes from not being clear in our own minds—because we're not certain that our idea is any good, we use words to dazzle up a lame idea or fog up a mediocre one. And sometimes blah-blah-blah is just plain evil—because we know our own idea is rotten, we use words to distract listeners from what we're really thinking.

Not all words are the same; not all blah-blah-blah is the same, either.

---

* From "High Flight," by John Gillespie Magee Jr., 1941.
† Eternal.

We are here.

The Land of Blah-Blah-Blah

Although the noise makes it difficult to tell, not all blah-blah-blah is the same.

Introducing the Blah-Blahmeter

Ernest Hemingway, the author most famously associated with keeping language as word-free as possible, once said the best thing an aspiring writer could do was to "develop a built-in bulls**t detector." What was true then is truer now: We need to pick up on when the bulls**t is heading toward us just as much as we need to be aware when we're the ones dishing it out.

One thing we know for sure about the world of blah-blah-blah is that it isn't uniform. There are all kinds of blah out there: too many words, the wrong words, unintelligible words, misleading words. We're going to need a lot more than a shovel to sift through it all.

How About a Built-in Blah-Blah-Blah Detector?

In a meeting, at a conference, in class, watching the news, tweeting—wouldn't it be great if we had a device to filter all the incoming words and quickly separate the signal from the noise? What we need is some kind of a blah-blah-blah detector, a quick way to identify what's worth listening to and what is not. Let's build one. Let's build a Blah-Blahmeter.

The Blah-Blahmeter is going to help us filter the incoming signal and noise into distinct levels.

The Blah-Blahmeter

What the Blah-Blahmeter Does

Our Blah-Blahmeter is a device that we'll use to detect which words are being used effectively and which are not.

When we point the Blah-Blahmeter at a verbal source, it will pick up the words and process them according to four distinct filters, then present the blah-blah-blah reading on a marked scale. Words that are used well—*words that have a clear message describing a sound idea delivered with good intent*—will register on the zero (or *"no blah-blah"*) side of the scale. Words that represent the worst abuse of language—*words delivering a misleading message intended to keep us from noticing a rotten idea*—will register on the maximum blah-blah-blah level. In between these two extremes we'll find words that are simply boring or unintentionally confusing.

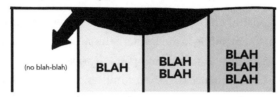

The Blah-Blahmeter

(no blah-blah)	**BLAH**	**BLAH BLAH**	**BLAH BLAH BLAH**

◀ The Blah-Blahmeter scale: *Zero blah* on one extreme, *blah cubed* on the other.

Depending on the measured result, we'll know whether or not we need to use the tools in this book to improve a particular set of words—and if so, which tools to apply to make sure the real message gets through and gets heard.

By the time we're done, we'll have the complete Blah-Blahmeter available to us and know how to use it. In full form, the Blah-Blahmeter looks like this:

The Blah-Blahmeter

	(no blah-blah)	**BLAH**	**BLAH BLAH**	**BLAH BLAH BLAH**
The message is . . .	Clear	Boring	Foggy	Misleading
The idea is . . .	Simple	Complicated	Missing	Rotten
The intent is to . . .	Clarify	Illuminate	Obfuscate	Divert
Vivid will . . .	Make crystalline	Unclutter and sharpen	Discover and develop	Debunk and dispel

◀ The complete Blah-Blahmeter. In this and the next chapter, we'll learn how to use all its features.

We'll build and test the full Blah-Blahmeter throughout this chapter and the next, but for now let's warm up our internal bulls**t detectors with a few sample quotes.

The "I Get It" Test

Below are five quotations taken from prominent newsmakers of the past few years. All five were originally stated in public forums where the speaker (or source) knew he would be listened to intently. All five describe important aspects of our lives and cover topics that we all agree are of consequence to us, our families, and our businesses.

These five quotations will serve as our first test of blah-blah-blah detection. Read through them, noting how each speaker uses words to convey an idea. To help you keep track of how well the speaker is doing, each quote is followed by an "understanding scale." Read each quote *only once* (we'll come back to them later), fill out the scale below it, then move on to the next.

One more thing you'll notice: I haven't named the speakers yet. We'll save that for the end.

Blah-Blah-Blah Test: Five Prominent Quotes from Recent Years

Ⓐ "Specially formulated with nutrients that enable the body to exert physical power by contributing to structural integrity of the musculoskeletal system, and by supporting optimal generation and utilization from food."

☐ I fully understand this ☐ I sort of understand this ☐ I don't understand this

Ⓑ "I would say, actually, we defined it [the health insurance 'public option'] fairly clearly in terms of what we thought would work best. What I said was, is that it shouldn't be something that's simply a taxpayer-subsidized system that wasn't accountable but rather had to be self-sustaining through premiums and that had to compete with private insurers. . . . Now, if you look at the results, the 80 percent of all the various bills that are out there that people have agreed to reflect our—most of the ideas from the start of this process. . . . But the 20 percent that right now is still the holdup would have been a holdup if we had put forward a plan, hadn't put forward a plan, had left it to Congress, had written it ourselves—because it represents some long-standing ideological divisions in our Congress and, frankly, in our society."

☐ I fully understand this   ☐ I sort of understand this   ☐ I don't understand this

Ⓒ "Typically, a position will consist of the ownership of 30–35 S&P 100 stocks, most correlated to that index, the sale of out-of-the-money calls on the index and the purchase of out-of-the-money puts on the index. The sale of the calls is designed to increase the rate of return, while allowing upward movement of the stock portfolio to the strike price of the calls. The puts, funded in large part by the sale of the calls, limit the portfolio's downside."

☐ I fully understand this   ☐ I sort of understand this   ☐ I don't understand this

Ⓓ " 'The oil spot,' if you will, is a, is a term in counterinsurgency literature that connotes a peaceful area, secure area. So what you're trying to do is to always extend that, to push that out. Of course, down in Helmand Province [Afghanistan] what we sought to do was to build an oil spot that would encompass the six central districts of Helmand Province, including Marjah and then others, and then to just keep pushing that out, ultimately to connect it over with the oil spot that is being developed around Kandahar City."

☐ I fully understand this   ☐ I sort of understand this   ☐ I don't understand this

Ⓔ "This is the captain. Brace for impact."

☐ I fully understand this   ☐ I sort of understand this   ☐ I don't understand this

Connect the Dots

Here are the five sources for the five quotes above. Write in the letter of each quote above with the appropriate source below:

General David Petraeus, describing Afghan war strategy on *Meet the Press,* August 10, 2010.

President Obama, discussing health care reform with *Time* magazine, August 10, 2009.

Text from the label on the Coca-Cola Company's Power-C VitaminWater product.

Madoff Securities Hedge-Fund Prospectus, *Barron's,* May 7, 2001.

Captain Chesley Sullenberger, to passengers aboard US Airways Flight 1549, January 15, 2009.

Plotting the Results

It's safe to assume that we will all have different levels of understanding of what each speaker was trying to say. But we will all agree that some of the quotes were quickly understandable and some were not. The first time I read (or heard) each, here is what I remember thinking:

(A) VitaminWater

☐ I fully understand this ☑ I sort of understand this ☐ I don't understand this

(B) Obama on health care

☐ I fully understand this ☐ I sort of understand this ☑ I don't understand this

(C) Madoff's investment strategy

☐ I fully understand this ☐ I sort of understand this ☑ I don't understand this

(D) Petraeus on Afghanistan

☑ I fully understand this ☐ I sort of understand this ☐ I don't understand this

(E) Sully on the Hudson

☑ I fully understand this ☐ I sort of understand this ☐ I don't understand this

In other words, of the five quotes (again, all delivered by prominent sources and all referring to critical aspects of contemporary life), only two—Petraeus and Sully—fit my personal criteria for the effective use of words: I understood them.

Oog and Aag and Why Understanding Matters

We're going to come back to these quotes and the Blah-Blahmeter in a moment, but before we do, it will help to understand something about our brains. To help us, let's meet two of our most ancient ancestors: Oog and Aag.*

Oog + Aag

◀ Our ancient ancestors.

All of us—Oog and Aag included—like to understand one another. We can't help it: Our brains are hardwired that way. Because confusion and uncertainty were dangerous to Oog and Aag, their brains evolved to take great pleasure in understanding things—especially

---

* We have no idea, of course, whether anyone named Oog or Aag ever lived, but we know *somebody* did—and we know that their brains evolved over millions of years. Giving even long-lost ancestors names and profiles helps us more vividly imagine what life must have been like for them.

each other. In fact, Oog's and Aag's brains rewarded them with a shot of feel-good dopamine each time they "got" an idea the other was trying to convey. (Ever feel that chill down the back of your neck when reading a thriller and you suddenly figured out whodunit? That's the feel-good stuff. Now imagine if you could get that every time your boss started talking.) We are so familiar with this feeling that we have a universal image to illustrate it.

The universal symbol for ▶ "I got it!"

Millions of years ago, out there on the savanna, *not knowing what was going on* was the fastest way for Oog and Aag to die. They had brains that helped them make sense of things, but keeping those brains going required a lot of energy. So during their millions of years of development, Oog's and Aag's bodies made a trade-off: They'd sacrifice some strength, speed, and endurance in exchange for being able to understand each other. In Oog and Aag's ancient world of constant life-and-death decisions, it proved to be worth the sacrifice.

Today, when we find ourselves in a death-by-PowerPoint meeting, it pays to remember Oog and Aag and to stop kicking ourselves when we can't stay focused. If we don't understand instantly what the presenter is saying—and if we can't figure out what to do about it and why it matters—we give up and look for something that will put our expensive-to-maintain brains to better use. But if we're stuck in a conference room, there's nothing else we can do. So our brains either start making stuff up (daydreaming and doodles) or go to sleep.

That's the real problem we face today: too many words with too little meaning coming at us too fast. This information rush interferes with our inner Oog and Aag and our ancient desire to understand one another. Either through boredom, befuddlement, or intentional distraction, any misuse of language that leads our brains to say "This is blah-blah-blah" must be avoided. At best, the blah-blah-blah puts us to sleep, and at worst it leaves us more confused than before.

With that in mind, let's get back to those five quotes and the Blah-Blahmeter.

Blah-Blahmeter Filter No. 1:
We "Get" the Message the First Time

Starting at the top, the first criterion on the Blah-Blahmeter scale is whether it picks up a signal at all: If the words are clear and effective, we'll be so busy absorbing them that we won't even see the needle budge. For example, Sully's seven-word study in concise language pegs the needle on the good side. *"This is the captain. Brace for impact"* is pure meaning. There is no blah-blah-blah here to detect.

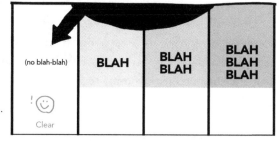

The Blah-Blahmeter

"This is the captain. Brace for impact." So clear that the needle doesn't budge. No blah-blah. Nothing more needed for the message to be heard and understood.

On my personal Blah-Blahmeter, this is also true of Petraeus's words. *"'The oil spot' is a term in counterinsurgency literature that connotes a peaceful area, secure area. So what you're trying to do is to always extend that."* *"The oil spot"** is a metaphor that requires no expertise

---

* Petraeus is correct: "Oil spot" is a term that has been used in counterinsurgency warfare since the late nineteenth century, when French general Hubert Lyautey coined the phrase to describe his strategy of securing, pacifying, and economically developing ever-larger territories in the French colonies of Algeria and Indochina. He called this approach *"tache d'huile"* because it looked like the spread of an oil droplet on a map.

in military planning to instantly *get*: The army's plan is to grow small secure areas in Afghanistan until they spread enough to link into larger secure areas. I don't know if that strategy will work or not, but I have no problem understanding the idea.

So let's leave Sully and Petraeus aside. No blah-blah-blah, no Blah-Blahmeter reading.

The Acid Test

It's when we *don't* get quick comprehension that the needle starts twitching. That's when we know one of two things: Either the message is beyond our understanding (in which case we need a more vivid explanation) or the technology of language is messed up.

One Blah = Just Boring

Once the Blah-Blahmeter needle starts jumping, the first stop on the scale is just plain "blah." One blah indicates the benign but ham-fisted overuse of words that makes interesting ideas boring. This is Grandpa telling war stories. By rights, his should be a fascinating tale, but somehow it ends up putting the family to sleep.

Grandpa telling war stories ▶ reads as one blah: He's got a great story to tell, but his overuse of words puts everyone to sleep.

The Blah-Blahmeter

	(no blah-blah)	BLAH	BLAH BLAH	BLAH BLAH BLAH
The message is . . .	! ☺ Clear	zᶻ 😐 Boring		

Let's go back and read the three remaining quotes again (recall that we've already discounted Sully and Petraeus as being too clear for the Blah-Blahmeter to detect). Read the three that remain (Coke, Obama, Madoff) and rank them again, only this time indicate your *immediate* response to each message, from bored to perplexed to mystified.

Read one more time through the quotes on pages 32–33. Here are my responses:*

Ⓐ VitaminWater

    ☐ I'm too bored to care   ☑ I guess there could be   ☐ What the—???
                                            something there

Ⓑ Obama on health care

    ☑ I'm too bored to care   ☐ I guess there could be   ☐ What the—???
                                            something there

Ⓒ Madoff on investing

    ☐ I'm too bored to care   ☐ I guess there could be   ☑ What the—???
                                            something there

Reading each quote a second time tells me that, of the three, President Obama's is the one most difficult to comprehend, because of its *quantity* of words. *"But the 20 percent that right now is still the holdup would have been a holdup if we had put forward a plan, hadn't put forward a plan, had left it to Congress, had written it ourselves . . ."* He's clearly talking about something important to him (health care), but he seems to have so many things to say about it that his ideas crash into one another, the same way an old typewriter snarls up when someone types too quickly.

In this case, my Blah-Blahmeter ranks Obama's quote as just "boring": a potentially interesting idea made unlistenable through broken language. Not intentionally foggy, not misleading, just too tiresome to follow.

Which leaves us with two quotes to go.

---

* Readings on our Blah-Blahmeters are of course a personal and subjective measure, and mine may be different from yours. Depending on our backgrounds, educations, expertise, and preconceptions, we may well have wildly different readings. That's fine—in fact, that's good: The whole point of the Blah-Blahmeter is to help us recognize for ourselves the messages that get through and those that don't.

Two Blahs = We're Fooling Ourselves

The next stop on the Blah-Blahmeter scale doubles the ante. As we add a second blah, we get *blah squared*. At this level, our device is picking up more than just boring delivery; on the contrary, at *blah squared* we often find the cleverest use of words. They have to be clever, because here the words are masking an idea that isn't there at all.

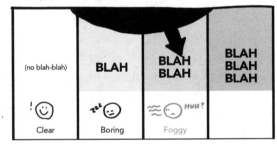

The lack of an idea masked by the fog of words bumps our scale up to the *blah-blah* level.

Quote A, the one referring to the drink that's *"specially formulated with nutrients that enable the body to exert physical power by contributing to structural integrity of the musculo-skeletal system,"* is from the Coca-Cola Company. It is from the label on its subsidiary Glacéau's Power-C VitaminWater bottle. This text was cited in a lawsuit brought against Coca-Cola by a consumer advocacy organization called the CSPI (Center for Science in the Public Interest).

The CSPI filed suit in 2010, maintaining that the labels on the VitaminWater products gave misleading information about the nutritional benefits of "enhanced water" products, which the group argued were nothing more than sugar water. The CSPI alleged that

Coca-Cola had knowingly created pseudoscientific language to intentionally delude consumers into believing that they were purchasing a product that was good for their health—when in fact the bottles contained more sugar than Coca-Cola itself.

In their legal response, Coca-Cola's lawyers defended the wording on the bottles by saying that the slogans printed on the bottles "describe only puffery" and that "no reasonable consumer could have been misled by VitaminWater's labeling."

In other words, Coca-Cola's own lawyers admitted that the company spent a lot of time and money writing words on their products that they never expected anyone to take seriously. Shameful? Yes. Surprising? Not really—after all, this is soda marketing.

This is true blah-blah: the intentional misuse of words to create a fog—a fog that masks the lack of an actual fact or idea. It's the same thing we've all done when we were supposed to have something intelligent to say but really didn't have a clue. It's the old "If you can't dazzle them with brilliance, blind them with bull***t" axiom come to life.

Blah squared emerges whenever we find ourselves at the morally neutral but intellectually dishonest position of verbally padding our thoughts in order to make ourselves sound smarter than we are. *Blah squared* isn't necessarily dangerous or malicious, but it is the beginning of a slippery slope of verbal self-delusion that, if unchecked, leads to the misguided belief that we understand an idea when in fact we don't.

Three Blahs = We're Fooling Everyone

At level three, three *blahs* appear—and now we're in the verbal danger zone, the place where words become weapons. *Blah cubed* is the worst of language distortion, where words serve their opposite purpose—where they are intentionally used to mislead us from grasping the speaker's real message.

The Blah-Blahmeter

(no blah-blah)	BLAH	BLAH BLAH	BLAH BLAH BLAH
Clear	Boring	Foggy	Misleading

The message is . . .

At full needle deflection, ▶ we're seeing words used as weapons: They intentionally misguide us.

We've only got one quote left and, challenging as it is, it is worth rereading if only for its sheer audacity. Through a brilliant mix of financial lingo and verbal sleight of hand equal to the best of magicians, Madoff Securities explained how the company's investment strategy "worked"—an investment strategy that in 2008 would be exposed as a $21 billion fraud.

> Typically, a position will consist of the ownership of 30–35 S&P 100 stocks, most correlated to that index, the sale of out-of-the-money calls on the index and the purchase of out-of-the-money puts on the index. The sale of the calls is designed to increase the rate of return, while allowing upward movement of the stock portfolio to the strike price of the calls. The puts, funded in large part by the sale of the calls, limit the portfolio's downside.

Founder and chairman Bernard Madoff, who seven years before his arrest (and sentencing to 150 years in federal prison) told *Barron's* magazine, "It's a proprietary strategy. I can't go into it in great detail," was a master of *blah cubed*. His is an unsubtle example of what is a well thought-through and highly nuanced abuse of language: Mask a rotten idea by using highly charged words that throw listeners to distraction.

The path to *blah cubed* is duplicity defined: Say whatever you want to say (no matter how vile, rotten, or wrong), but say it *by saying something else*. Here at the extreme edge of blah-blah-blah, words cease to serve as a means of clarification and instead become weapons of mass destruction.

Moving Down the Blah-Blahmeter Dial

That's the first horizontal span of our Blah-Blahmeter scale: From **Clear** to **Boring** to **Foggy** to **Misleading**, we've mapped out the dangers of increasing blah-blah-blah. But there's more. To make our Blah-Blahmeter useful not only in measuring incoming messages but also in improving our own, we're going to add three more filters in the next chapter. These filters will detect deeper meanings in the incoming message, giving us a greater sense of how to improve, illuminate, or disarm the speaker's real message—even if the speaker is us.

Especially if the speaker is us.

Blah-Blahmeter Basics

Those are the basics of the Blah-Blahmeter, enough to get started using it: We listen for someone's message, detect our immediate level of understanding, and plot it on the scale. If the message was clear, no problem: We take it in and prepare a response. If the message was unclear, at least now we have the means to figure out why—and understand what that lack of clarity means to the speaker and to us.

CHAPTER 2
Advanced Blah-Blahmeter Use

You Have a Choice . . .

This chapter dives into the complete Blah-Blahmeter in depth: what the remaining scales mean, the linkages between the different levels and the speaker's likely intent, and how the "Vivid Thinking" tools in the rest of this book can best be applied to clear things up.

If you'd like to learn much more about the Blah-Blahmeter and its uses, please keep reading. However, if you'd prefer to begin exploring what Vivid Thinking means and how it can keep all our ideas on the good side of the Blah-Blahmeter scale, go ahead and skip the rest of this section for now. You can always come back later.

The Full Blah-Blahmeter

When complete, our Blah-Blahmeter will contain sixteen measurements: the four we've already placed along the top of the scale, along with three sub-measurements below each. This combination will not only show how well we "got" the message to begin with (already accounted for along the top scale); it will also measure the clarity of the speaker's original idea, give us insight into the speaker's actual intention, and, lastly, illustrate how Vivid Thinking can help eliminate blah-blah-blah at any level.

The Blah-Blahmeter

	(no blah-blah)	BLAH	BLAH BLAH	BLAH BLAH BLAH
The message is . . .	Clear	Boring	Foggy	Misleading
The idea is . . .				
The intent is to . . .				
Vivid will . . .		Unclutter and sharpen	Discover and develop	Debunk and dispel

The full Blah-Blahmeter scale. When complete, we'll not only know whether we "got" the message or not; we'll also be clearer regarding the speaker's original idea, glean insight into the speaker's intent, and begin to see how Vivid Thinking is useful for eliminating any blah-blah-blah in our own messages.

Blah-Blahmeter Row 2: The Idea Is . . .

The fundamental premise of this book is that the purpose of language is to quickly and effectively convey ideas in a way that requires the least possible effort on the part of the recipient.* If language breaks along the way, it's a bad thing. If we can't "get" the speaker's idea, it doesn't matter how lovely his words might be—they're still the wrong words.

The second row on the Blah-Blahmeter scale reflects this. In direct correlation to the effectiveness of the speaker's message, we can deduce the nature of his original idea.

---

* My underlying rule (learned, occasionally very painfully, through years of business meetings and presentations) is that the more effort the originator of the idea puts into it in preparation, the less effort the receiver needs to—and the more likely the receiver will be motivated and pleased to understand. In other words: If an idea is worth the audience's time at all, it is worth all the time the presenter can invest in advance.

When a message is quickly clear to us, it is almost always a simple expression of a well thought-through idea.*

When a message is quickly clear, it is almost always expressed simply. ▶

On the other hand, when we become bored with an explanation, it's almost always because the presenter loses us in complication—an indication that the speaker either hasn't taken the time to simplify or that he doesn't understand his idea himself.

When a message is boring, it's almost always because the speaker hasn't taken the time to simplify. ▶

When a speaker's words are foggy, the first thing we should ask ourselves is whether we can detect a real idea buried in there at all; more often than not, the fog is an attempt to hide . . . nothing. Since there's nothing there, the speaker's only option is to turn on the blah-blah. In the hands of expert spinmeisters, in-over-their-heads creative directors, and on-twenty-four-hours-a-day cable news anchors, this intentional whipping up of steam can last for hours, leaving listeners so befuddled that we simply cave in.

A foggy message is a signal that there is likely no real idea within it. ▶

In other cases, especially with newcomers to the world of politics and business, the result is the painful process of watching gradually dawning ignorance. The speaker

---

* "Simple" is a relative term. If a group of kindergartners quickly understands our presentation on molecules, it's a guarantee we've come up with a simple way to describe introductory chemistry. If a group of biochemists quickly understands our thesis on alternative paths in the Krebs cycle, it's a safe bet we've come up with a "simple" way to illustrate advanced photosynthesis.

may start out smooth and convincing, her words confident and articulate. But as she continues, we realize that we're still waiting for the beef. At some point, our brains say it even before we do: "She has *no idea* what she's talking about." Literally: There's no idea there.

◀ When a message appears to mislead, be on the lookout for a truly rotten idea.

The last column is the worst. When the Blah-Blahmeter tells us we're being misdirected by someone's words—when the words just seem so far off or so far out that they can't possibly be taken at face value—we can be pretty sure that those words are intentionally masking a truly nasty idea, one so vile that even its originator can't quite stomach saying it aloud in public. What is a rotten idea? Just like the word implies for fruit or meat, a rotten idea is one whose time (if there ever was one) has come and long gone. If somebody is still trying to get us to take a bite, we better beware.

The Blah-Blahmeter

	(no blah-blah)	**BLAH**	**BLAH BLAH**	**BLAH BLAH BLAH**
The message is . . .	Clear	Boring	Foggy	Misleading
The idea is . . .	Simple	Complicated	Missing	Rotten

◀ The second row on the Blah-Blahmeter measures the nature of the idea itself, whether simple, complicated, missing, or just plain rotten.

Blah-Blahmeter Row 3: The *Intent* Is . . .

Another fundamental premise of this book is that the only reason to convey an idea at all is that we want it to become shared. If the creator of an idea does not intend to bring the idea to the light of day, there is no reason for her to wish to talk about it. If she voluntarily shares an idea, there must be some intention in doing so, from educating to selling to diverting. Understanding that intention is a powerful measure of whether words work or not.

The next row down on the Blah-Blahmeter scale helps us deduce that underlying intent by correlating the speaker's motivation back to the original quality of her message. The first column, for example, tells us that when a speaker delivers a simple message we "get" quickly, we can assume that at some level she meant to clarify.*

A simple message we quickly ▶ "get" indicates (usually) the speaker's desire to clarify.

In the second column, under "blah," we find the speaker whose desire is to illuminate her idea but who becomes boring when tripped up by her idea's complexity. Although her intent is good, her message quickly gets bogged down and becomes tiresome for the rest of us to follow.

Although her intent and ▶ desire are to illuminate an idea, the speaker who can't find a simple message quickly becomes boring.

Under the "blah squared" column, when we find ourselves getting lost in the fog of someone's message, we can be pretty sure that the speaker's intent was to obfuscate, either because he had no real idea to share or because he himself hadn't yet discovered what his own idea was. In either case, the best he can do is lead us (and perhaps himself as well) to believe there is a valid idea buried somewhere in his words and that the real problem is that we're too thick to see it. Foggy, befuddling delivery most likely indicates a desire on the speaker's part to intentionally get us lost—or at least dazzle us with enough bull that we no longer care.

---

* There are certainly cases where the most divertingly dangerous message is the one delivered the most simply and clearly. There we need to be especially careful since there is no measurable blah-blah-blah to indicate nasty intent. There will be more on using Vivid Thinking to uncover and avoid this verbal double cross in the final section of this book.

In the "blah cubed" column, intent becomes malicious. When the idea to be conveyed is a truly rotten one, an idea so distasteful that even the speaker is afraid to say it aloud, the speaker's only recourse is to intentionally divert the audience from the real message by substituting another. And that's when our Blah-Blahmeter should really be buzzing.

◄ When the message becomes increasingly foggy, we can be pretty sure the speaker's intent is to obfuscate.

◄ When an idea is truly rotten, the speaker's only option is to intentionally divert and misguide the audience.

Here's why. True "blah cubed" blah-blah-blah isn't like the other levels of language breakdown—and it's different because of the speaker's intent. With "blah," the speaker meant well but was just boring. With "blah-blah," the speaker was lost, but the worst we could say was that he wasn't up-front about it.

But at "blah cubed" we see someone become so enamored of his words that any real meaning the words once had washes away. And because the words themselves no longer contain meaning, the only option is to repeat them and twist them until they intentionally mislead. Then we've succumbed to the worst aspects of thoughtless words: We no longer care what our words mean; we care only that they provoke. Then we've all entered the land of verbal shock and awe—and that's when our real problems begin.

The Last Row: What We Can Do About All the Blah-Blah-Blah

The third fundamental premise of this book is that we don't need all the blah-blah-blah to get our message across. Regardless of what we want to say—whether simple or complex, reassuring or frightening, visionary or tactical, complimentary or critical—we can make any idea clear and compelling, both to our audience and to ourselves.

This is where Vivid Thinking comes into play. By encouraging us to actively use both our verbal mind (everything we've looked at so far in this section) and our visual mind (which we're going to explore in great detail in the next section), we're going to see that every quadrant on the Blah-Blahmeter can be improved. Every good idea can be made clearer, every missing idea can be found, and every rotten idea can be incinerated. All we need to do is think vividly.

One more time through the Blah-Blahmeter will show us how.

The Blah-Blahmeter

	(no blah-blah)	BLAH	BLAH BLAH	BLAH BLAH BLAH
The message is . . .	Clear	Boring	Foggy	Misleading
The idea is . . .	Simple	Complicated	Missing	Rotten
The intent is to . . .	Clarify	Illuminate	Obfuscate	Divert

Blah-Blahmeter Row 4: Vivid Will . . .

Vivid is simple. It's just a way to take what we've been well trained to do—to use words to think, critique, discover, and share—and combine that with our innate (yet neglected) ability to do the same things with pictures. The results of this combined approach will always be more powerful than using just one or the other.

Under each column of the Blah-Blahmeter, let's see how Vivid makes this happen.

The Blah-Blahmeter

	(no blah-blah)	**BLAH**	**BLAH BLAH**	**BLAH BLAH BLAH**
The message is . . .	Clear	Boring	Foggy	Misleading
The idea is . . .	Simple	Complicated	Missing	Rotten
The intent is to . . .	Clarify	Illuminate	Obfuscate	Divert
Vivid will . . .	Make crystalline	Unclutter and sharpen	Discover and develop	Debunk and dispel

The full Blah-Blahmeter: The message, the idea, the intent—and how Vivid will help clarify them all.

Let's start with the first column, "no blah-blah." If we have a good idea that we've thought through well enough to express simply with words, it's guaranteed that other people will get it. Could communication get any better than that?

Yes.

The mechanism for making good verbal communication great is to add the visual. Vivid will show us how to make an already clear verbal idea diamond sharp, something so refined that people won't be able to *not* understand it. A simple picture added to a simple statement makes a good idea become great, and a clear idea become crystal.

Adding the visual to the verbal makes a clear idea become crystal.

What about under the "blah" column: Can adding the visual help a message *not* be boring? Yes again—of course it can. Using simple pictures to work through a complicated idea always illuminates hidden simplicities and alternative perspectives, aspects of our original idea that remain invisible when words are our only tool. Vivid thinking gives us a way to bring those visual insights to the surface, where others can see them—and we'll never have to give a boring talk again.

Adding the visual to the ▶ complicated always illuminates hidden simplicities and always sharpens the picture.

Under the "blah-blah" column, the home of foggy messages masking barely conceived ideas, the visual helps, too. Nothing helps us see a vague idea more clearly than trying to draw it out. If we don't quite know our own idea or aren't even quite sure if we really have one, picking up a pen and making a mark on a piece of paper always gets the juices flowing.

The same is true when we're getting lost during someone else's foggy explanation of his own idea. If we can't draw it out, the likely problem is that there's nothing there. That's where Vivid comes in; as we'll see in the following sections, anyone can draw any idea, assuming that the idea *actually has shape**—all we usually need is a little help to get started.

Looking for the visual shape ▶ of a vague idea always helps bring the idea into focus, and always exposes a missing idea.

We've come to the final row and column of the Blah-Blahmeter—the end of the line, where words serve only to cause harm. Remember how we said a true "blah cubed" message is different from all others? When a message has become this far removed from having meaning, the only option is to counter the speaker's intent by exposing his underlying idea to the light of day. That's what Vivid pictures can do, far more effectively than any words. Curing "blah cubed" isn't something that we can do by ourselves. It requires the intervention of all involved—speaker, listener, and bystander—to take action and find the picture that debunks the idea, exposes the intent, and blows up the words.

---

* In the final section of this book, we'll see how important it is for a Vivid Idea to "have shape"—and we'll spend time finding ways to look for and draw the underlying shape of any idea.

◀ When the words hide a
malicious message, our only
choice is to find the picture
that blows the cover apart.

Putting Our Blah-Blahmeter to Use

For the rest of this book, we're going to use the Blah-Blahmeter to understand where, when, and how to use Vivid Thinking to best integrate our verbal and visual minds. The simplest way is to think of words and pictures like this:

If our message is clear, we'll use Vivid Thinking to make it shine.

Use Vivid to...

Make it shine.

The Blah-Blahmeter

	(no blah-blah)	BLAH	BLAH BLAH	BLAH BLAH BLAH
The message is . . .	Clear	Boring	Foggy	Misleading
The idea is . . .	Simple	Complicated	Missing	Rotten
The intent is to . . .	Clarify	Illuminate	Obfuscate	Divert
Vivid will . . .	Make crystalline	Unclutter and sharpen	Discover and develop	Debunk and dispel

◀ If we have a clear message,
Vivid will make it shine.

If our message is boring, we'll use Vivid to improve our delivery.

If we're boring, Vivid will improve our delivery.

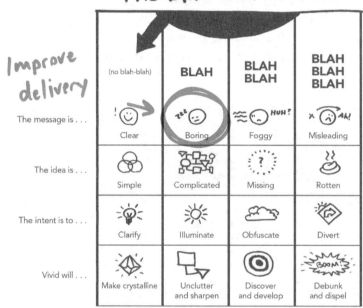

If our message is foggy, we'll use Vivid to explore our idea.

Use ViVid to...

Explore the idea

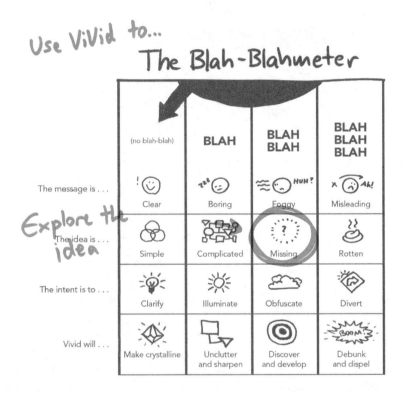

The Blah-Blahmeter

	(no blah-blah)	BLAH	BLAH BLAH	BLAH BLAH BLAH
The message is . . .	Clear	Boring	Foggy	Misleading
The idea is . . .	Simple	Complicated	Missing	Rotten
The intent is to . . .	Clarify	Illuminate	Obfuscate	Divert
Vivid will . . .	Make crystalline	Unclutter and sharpen	Discover and develop	Debunk and dispel

◀ If we're foggy, Vivid will help us explore our idea.

If our message is diverting, we'll use Vivid to expose our intent.

If we're misleading, Vivid will help us understand our intent.

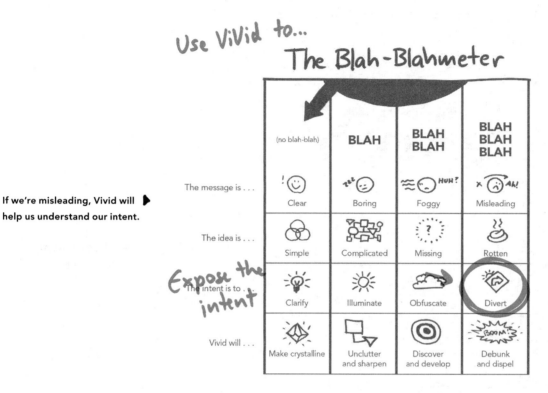

That's the Blah-Blahmeter: a tool we use to identify incoming blah-blah-blah and deduce the speaker's likely intent. But what if the speaker is us? That's where learning to think more vividly is going to help us make sure our ideas don't register any blah at all.

PART 2
If I Draw, Am I Dumb?

An Introduction to Vivid Thinking

verbal mind

visual mind

<u>Vivid</u> = **Vi**sual + **v**erbal + **i**nter**d**ependent

CHAPTER 3

Two Minds Are Better Than One

Blah-Blah-Blah Doesn't Mean Dumb

Most of the five quotes in the previous chapters were hard to understand. But that does not make the people who said them stupid. The president of the United States, the general in charge of the Afghan war, the captain of an airliner with forty thousand hours of flying in his logbook, a sophisticated marketer at the Coca-Cola Company, even a devious manipulator of money—all of these people are intelligent, well-read, and perfectly capable of making themselves understood.

But if they're so smart, what went wrong with their words?

Their problem isn't their words—their problem is that they used *only* words.

Einstein Was Stupid

Albert Einstein, universally regarded as one of the most brilliant people ever, didn't much like words. As an old scientist, reflecting on a lifetime of insight and discovery, he was quite clear about it: "These thoughts did not come in any verbal formulation. I rarely think in words at all."

Even as a toddler, Einstein wasn't much of a talker. Whereas most babies begin talking anywhere from nine months to two years old, young Albert didn't say a word until he was two and a half. His parents were so worried that they called in a doctor to see what was wrong. Finally, on the day his baby sister was born—a day that his mother promised would bring Albert a new "toy"—Albert pointed to the infant and asked in a perfectly formed sentence, "Where are the wheels?"

The problem wasn't that he couldn't speak; Albert just wanted to speak in complete thoughts.

Until he was eight, Albert composed his thoughts mentally, silently trying out the sounds while moving his lips, before finally verbalizing them in complete sentences. The Einsteins' maid had a word for that: She called Albert "stupid."

STUPID

A Tale of Two Minds

How would we today describe a person who at age six couldn't freely speak a complete sentence but could, while playing with a toy compass, discern the hidden forces of nature?* Which is it: Was Albert Einstein brilliant or stupid?

If we consider that each of us has two different ways of looking at the world—a "piece by piece" way and an "all at once" way—perhaps we can say that he was both.

---

* When Albert was six, he became seriously ill with influenza. Quarantined to his bedroom for weeks, he was brought by his father a toy compass to pass the time. It was while he lay there in bed, contemplating how the compass might work, that Einstein got his first glimpse of what he would later call "field theory," the basis of relativity.

As are we all.

Since the time of Oog and Aag and throughout the eons of human development, our ability to think* has evolved along two different paths. One path specialized in seeing the world as lots of little pieces, while the other path specialized in looking at the world as a whole.

Throughout the eons, we've pushed along two different "thinking" paths: One sees the world as lots of little pieces, the other sees the world as a whole.

The first path was useful because, by seeing the world as a collection of individual parts, we could choose which individual things to focus on. To a hunter like Oog, focus meant he could put all his attention on his prey, blocking out other distractions.

The bad news was that focusing forward on his prey meant Oog couldn't see the lion creeping up behind him. That's where the second path was useful. His all-at-once view relied on his peripheral vision (and movable eyes) to let him see the whole world, noting patterns and changes that were bigger than any one part.

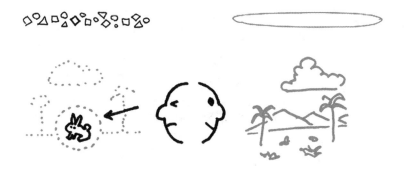

The first path lets us focus. The second path lets us see big patterns.

---

* This book focuses almost exclusively only on "descriptive" thinking. Without getting too blah-blah-blah about it, that means our uniquely human ability to give things characteristics and meaning that they don't actually possess. It is this that gives us the ability to think "about" things, as opposed to just reacting to them.

Double Vision

This ability to simultaneously see the world both piece by piece and all at once was a lifesaver. Thanks in large part to this double vision, Oog and Aag could think in new and remarkable ways, seeing things that other creatures could not, thinking about things in ways that other creatures could not—and surviving when other creatures did not.

Somewhere along this evolutionary chain, seeing both ways became so critical—but so mentally demanding—that the two hemispheres of our "thinking" brain, the *cerebrum*, split the tasks.* As neuroscientist John Medina describes it in his wonderful book *Brain Rules*, "the brain can be divided roughly into two hemispheres of unequal function." While both hemispheres shared most functions, each also specialized (in a variety of ways), supporting either the piece-by-piece view or the all-at-once view.

Over the past thirty years, an enormous amount of scientific and popular energy has been generated in pointing out the differences between the right and left hemispheres of the human brain—much to the excitement of the public and the chagrin of the scientific community. This notion of our having two brains—one verbal and linear, one visual and spatial—is so compelling that it has taken on the status of popular myth far beyond what the science actually knows or says.[†]

It's nowhere near as clear-cut ▶
as right brain versus left brain,
but our brain does see two
different pictures of the world
at the same time.

---

* All vertebrates have a bi-lobed brain. In all *except humans,* the two lobes perform functionally the same tasks. It is only in humans that the two lobes are functionally different.

† This near-hypnotic excitement about the split nature of the brain makes perfect sense. Any simple model that can be expressed so easily yet represents so much potential insight is catnip to our *entire* brain. It feels right precisely because it appeals readily to both our piece-by-piece mind and our all-at-once mind. We'll explore why in detail—and learn to use that simplicity to give our own ideas equally compelling shape—in the third section of this book.

Excitement aside, here is something we do know: Our single brain does have the ability to look at one scene, at one place, at one time, and yet still *descriptively* think about what it sees in two profoundly different ways.* One way sees the pieces while one way sees how the pieces fit together. Although the two pictures describe the same world, they do not look the same.

Words from the Pieces, Pictures from the Whole

As the eons passed, our two ways of seeing the world each became both more specialized and more complementary. As the two paths each got better in their respective roles, they also needed to rely increasingly on each other to fill in the evolving gaps. The big connections that the piece-by-piece path missed were picked up by the all-at-once path. The important details that the all-at-once path dismissed were detected by the piece-by-piece path.

◀ Our all-at-once path takes in the whole scene . . .

Over time, each path developed its own method for noting, recording, and passing along what it detected. The piece-by-piece path, being very good at looking at one thing

---

* There are other parts of the brain that "see" the world in other ways as well: Our *reptilian brain* makes instant "fight-or-flight" decisions long before our "rational" thinking parts kick in, and our *limbic brain* makes near-instant emotional decisions about how we feel about what we see. But when it comes to the process we call thinking, neither of these plays a role remotely equivalent to our *neocortex*.

at a time, developed a way to quickly assign each thing an abstract mental shorthand term that didn't require constant *looking* to recall what the thing was. That term became the object's name. (There's the *sun*, there's a *hill*, there's a *tree*, there's a *rabbit*.)

. . . and in order to account for many pieces *without needing to always be looking at them*, our piece-by-piece path assigns each piece a name.

☀ = "Sun"   ⛰ = "Hill"   🌳 = "Tree"   🐇 = "Rabbit"

By assigning names to the things it saw, the piece-by-piece path didn't have to keep everything in sight to know what was there; as long as nothing moved or changed, keeping track of the names alone proved an efficient way to keep track of the world—and make decisions about it. (The *sun* illuminates the *hill* behind the *tree* above the *rabbit*. *Now I see my lunch!*)

The Arrival of the Verbal Mind

Although both paths began by detecting things in the world around us, as the paths specialized, they diverged. The piece-by-piece mind, with its ability to use names, didn't need to see the "things" any longer in order to think about them. By using words, it didn't need pictures at all. This is how, over time, our piece-by-piece path became our verbal mind.

Eventually, the piece-by-piece path didn't need the pictures at all.

Sun, hill, tree, rabbit = lunch!

The Staying Power of the Visual Mind

But names had their limitations. First of all, our all-at-once path wasn't fooled: It knew that the name being used by the verbal mind wasn't actually *the thing*. Real things could move and change and disappear, only to reappear later in a different place and in a different form. Names struggled to account for that.

A second limitation of the word-only model was that it was linear. It had to be: For words to express a thought, they had to be strung together in a sequence. That meant that word ideas needed a beginning, a middle, and an end—something the visual mind knew to be false. (A landscape doesn't have a beginning and an end; it's all there all at once.) Precisely because it was *not* linear, the visual image remained necessary to account for the spatial reality of the world.

Sun, hill, tree, rabbit = lunch!

◀ While our piece-by-piece path was naming things, our all-at-once path kept the picture in mind.

Two Paths, Two Ways of Accounting for the World

It was a great system, and it stuck: two paths, two ways of seeing the world, two ways of recording it. The piece-by-piece path provided the words that became spoken language. The all-at-once path gave us the pictures that showed how it all fit together.

We are driving to the store.

◀ The piece-by-piece path gave us names, words, and language. The all-at-once path gave us pictures and vision. The two paths are equal (they see the same world) but not the same (they describe it in two different ways).

---

* To this day, one of the great mistakes of right-brain/left-brain thinking is that all language is located in only the left hemisphere. While it appears that most "words" are stored in this piece-by-piece brain, it is the right, all-at-once brain that is able to string them together, detect their combined meaning, and "read between the lines." The left brain sees the words; the right brain sees the paragraphs.

The two paths are not the same. Nor should they be: They see the same things in different ways. One provides one particular type of information about the world ("I see a *rabbit*") and the other provides a different type: 🐰 It is this difference that makes the two so valuable. As one path complements the other, they cover each other's limitations. As long as they stay in balance, the two work together to give a full account of the world—and that makes our whole brain happy.

When both paths are in ▶ balance, our brain is happy.

Three Examples of Our Two Minds at Work

Because these two paths coexist in each of us, we don't spend much time thinking about them. *Verbal mind, visual mind—so what? Isn't that just how our brains work?* But we should: We can learn a staggering amount about things we describe all the time simply by noticing the descriptive differences of our verbal and visual minds.

Let me show how with three increasingly complex examples.

Visual-Verbal Example No. 1: The Three-Legged Chair

You and I are businesspeople. I invite you over to my office for a discussion. When you arrive, my receptionist invites you into the conference room and asks you to take a seat while he calls me.

You step into the conference room. The first chair you see looks like this:

Do you sit on it?

No, you do not.

You don't need to think about that verbally to know that you won't. You've got millions of years of visual processing in your brain that takes an all-at-once look at that three-legged chair and rejects it as a safe place to sit. No words needed to be spoken. Your verbal mind did not need to say, "Oh—that chair only has three legs and is therefore unstable. If I sit on it, it is likely to tip forward, leaving me on the ground." (Your verbal mind might very well say that, and probably will, but that's an afterthought.*) Your visual mind picked up on the problem and made the decision not to sit long before any words had a chance to form. In other words, your visual mind did its job.

But then I come into the room. I'm so focused on meeting you that I don't look at the chair. When I go to sit down, you stop me by saying, "Wait! Don't sit on that chair—it's only got three legs!"

In the instant it takes me to turn around and look, my verbal mind (lacking any visual input from the actual chair) kicks into gear, thinking, "A three-legged chair? Is that bad?" My verbal mind might even have the time to pull up the words "three," "legged," and "chair" and call upon my visual mind to generate an image to go with them, perhaps coming up with an image that *was* safe:

---

* It is also an attempt by our verbal mind to "take credit" for a free gift from our visual mind, something that happens constantly as our two descriptive intelligences vie for authority. We'll cover this ongoing debate—and its amazing consequences—in the next chapter.

If I didn't look—if I relied entirely on the image conjured up from my verbal mind's words—I might very well go ahead and sit down anyway, hurting myself and embarrassing both of us.

So I look, see the problem with the three-legged chair, and pick another.

Verbal mind, visual mind: They see the same world, but they don't see it the same way.

Visual-Verbal Example No. 2: Shafted

Richard Feynman, a younger colleague of Einstein, was a Nobel Prize–winning physicist who played a key role in our understanding of how the universe works. When he was young, Richard spent a lot of time thinking about "thinking." He came to the conclusion that thinking means "having the ability to use words to walk through an idea in your head." He became so convinced of this approach that he spent years teaching himself to put the ideas he saw floating around in his mind into strings of words.

One day, when he was working on a project in the garage with his childhood friend Bernie Walker, Richard said what had to him become obvious: "Thinking is nothing but talking to yourself inside."

Bernie, himself a deep thinker, was shocked that his otherwise brilliant friend could be so deluded. "Oh, yeah?" Bernie said. "Do you know the crazy shape of the crankshaft in your car?"

"Yeah," replied Richard, "what of it?"

"Good. Now tell me: How did you describe it when you were talking to yourself?"

Although Richard could see the all-at-once image of the crankshaft in his mind, he struggled to find the right words to even begin to describe the image.

From then on Feynman knew that thoughts can be visual as well as verbal. It was to be a breakthrough insight for his work on the Manhattan Project, the U.S. government's Second World War–era program to develop the atomic bomb, and he became the most highly regarded physics professor in the world.

Richard Feynman never believed again that "thinking" was the same thing as stringing together words, which was what led him to create Feynman diagrams, the visual language used to this day to model subatomic particles.

Verbal mind, visual mind: They see the same world, but they don't see it the same way.

Visual-Verbal Example No. 3: Porter and the Five Forces (or: Shafted, Part B)

When Michael Porter arrived at the Harvard Business School as an MBA student in 1969, he'd just completed a degree in aerospace engineering at Princeton. He wanted to learn about something "more holistic" than the aerodynamic forces that drive airplanes, so he chose to study the market forces that drive business.

In those days, "business strategy" was mostly the study of "great men." When professors wanted to describe why one business succeeded and another failed, they would tell war stories of the gutsy decision making of GM's Alfred Sloan or the take-no-prisoners management style of IBM's Thomas Watson. But to Porter, that was like saying the Wright brothers' airplane flew because Wilbur had a strong personality. Porter wasn't interested in that approach; he wanted to see and map the larger competitive forces behind business success.

The problem was that Harvard Business School didn't look at business that way. So after getting his MBA in 1971, Porter jumped ship to join the Harvard Department of Economics (far removed from the business school both geographically and conceptually), and there he found what he was looking for. In the economics department, the professors of "industrial organization" modeled things. They didn't write business history; they created systems and developed frameworks that described the forces acting on the economy. Porter loved it.

For the next two years, he sketched out a model of his own, one that bridged the theoretical aspects of IO economics with the practical applications of business policy. When complete, Porter called his picture the Five Forces framework. A single chart that accounted for all the major forces acting on the competitiveness of a business, it was the "holistic" model Porter had long been seeking.

The framework "worked" by placing a company (*any* company, which was itself a breakthrough in business thought) at the center, then surrounding it with the five forces of competition: industry competitors, potential industry entrants, buyers, substitutes, and suppliers. Looked at this way, it became possible to see, all at once, everything that had a direct impact on a company's market position.

Michael Porter's Five Forces ▶ That Shape Industry Competition, the picture that turned business strategy (and the Harvard Business School) on its head.

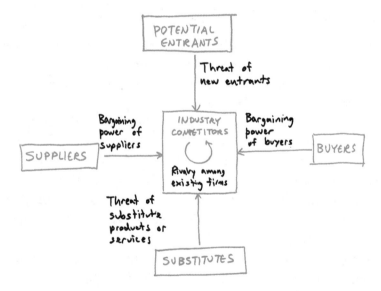

Michael Porter's "5 Forces"

Fig. 1-1 Forces Driving Industry Competition   p. 4

Competitive Strategy: Techniques for Analyzing Industries and Competitors
Michael E Porter   Free Press   1980

So radically did Porter's Five Forces framework upend the way economists thought about competition that the economics department awarded his work the prize for the best dissertation of 1973. And so radically did it upset the professors back at the business school that they rejected Porter's application for associate professor.

Shunned by the degree programs at the Harvard Business School, Porter spent the next three years teaching executive education, where he introduced real-world business managers to his Five Forces framework. His picture proved a breakthrough. As business historian Walter Kiechel describes students' responses in his book *The Lords of Strategy*, "Instead of walking away from class discussion wondering what they were supposed to have learned, they came away with charts, templates, lists that they could apply to the next strategic problem thrown at them."

If Porter wanted revenge, he got it. His "tons of takeaways" (chief among them his simple Five Forces picture*) made Porter's classes the most popular in the school. Big ideas about business—many new but many that had been discussed at length—became visible, and in so doing also became visceral. The Harvard Business School, no longer able to resist that visceral pull of Porter's thinking, instead made him a full professor—and there he still teaches today, the "most famous business school professor in history."

Verbal mind, visual mind: They see the same world, but they don't see it the same way.

Vivid Thinking Means Balanced Thinking

These two ways of looking at and describing the world are the two balanced sides of a scale. On one end, we have lots of important little pieces to note and recognize. On the other end, we have one big piece to pull it all together. The two sides "weigh" the same because they *are* the same—after all, they're the same world, just seen differently. As long as the scale stays in balance, we can think, lead, teach, and communicate well.

---

* Keep this picture in mind; we're going to see another equally influential picture of identical structure in Chapter 7—only that one will describe the forces that act on an airplane in flight. Coincidence? Given Porter's background in aeronautical engineering, I don't think so.

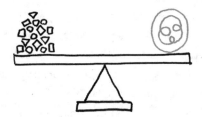

Our brain is happiest when we keep both halves in balance; the piece-by-piece view has equal weight to the all-at-once view.

This balance is generally stable. Because our brain has evolved to believe it's dangerous to only focus and equally dangerous to try to always see everything, our brain instinctively fights any tendency for the balance to tip.

But the balance can be tipped. If we spend too much time looking only at the big picture, we'll lose the elements that make it up. This is known as "having our heads in the clouds."

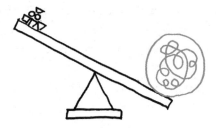

Having our heads in the clouds: If we spend too much time seeing only the biggest picture, we'll eventually lose our ability to recognize detail.

The balance can also tip the other direction. If we focus too much on the pieces, we'll collect so many details that we will lose the big picture. This is known as "getting lost in the weeds."

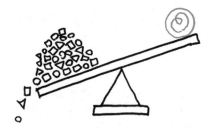

Getting lost in the weeds: Too much focus on the details and we'll lose both the big picture and, eventually, many of the details as well.

The Root of Blah-Blah-Blah

Now we come to it: the real reason we're so overwhelmed by the overuse, misuse, and abuse of words. Ready? The reason we are talking more and saying less, hearing more and listening less, learning more and knowing less is simple: *We've moved off the center of the balance.*

That's it. The reason for all the blah-blah-blah is that we've simply forgotten how to use both our minds. For thirty thousand years,* humans have been making marks on walls (then on paper, and more recently on touch screens) to reflect our thoughts. For twenty-five thousand of those years, we drew pictures. Only in the past five thousand did we begin the gradual shift to writing words. The problem is that now we've gone too far. As we've become increasingly enamored of and reliant upon words, our verbal minds have become heavier and heavier, while our visual minds have gotten lighter and lighter. The balance has shifted so subtly that we didn't even notice it. But now that we find ourselves facing some of the most difficult challenges of all time, we suddenly realize—oops!—that we've lost half our mind.

For the rest of this book, we're going to get our visual mind back, get both our piece-by-piece and all-at-once views working together, and get ourselves back on the center of the balance.

---

* For details on the long history of human drawing and writing, see Appendix A, "How We Lost Half Our Mind."

CHAPTER 4

Together Again: The Fox and the Hummingbird

Vivid Thinking Is Simple

Getting our balance back on center is simple: All we have to do is take a half-step back from our unshakable belief in the power of words and at the same time give our visual mind a kick in the pants. That's what "Vivid Thinking" does.

Vivid Thinking stands for *visual verbal interdependent thinking,* which means actively forcing our visual and verbal minds to work together when we are thinking, leading, teaching, and selling.

Here's a semi-wordy way to say that:

And here's a semi-pictorial way to look at that:

It's so simple to get our verbal and visual minds working together again that Vivid Thinking really has only three rules.* They are:

VIVID THINKING RULE NO. 1: When We Say a Word, We Should Draw a Picture (and Vice Versa)

Verbal + Visual

WORDS

---

* There are several substeps and many possible options within these rules, but for now let's start with the basics. Throughout the rest of this book, we'll take increasingly big steps as our overall Vivid Thinking confidence improves.

VIVID THINKING RULE NO. 2: If We Don't Know Which Picture to Draw, We Look to Vivid Grammar to Show Us the Way

VIVID THINKING RULE NO. 3: To Make Any Idea More Vivid, We Turn to the Seven Vivid Essentials

That's all there is to Vivid Thinking. Improving our thinking, teaching, and selling really is that simple: *(1) draw when we talk; (2) rely on a few basic rules of visual grammar; and (3) learn to visually identify the essentials of an idea.* Let's start with Rule No. 1. It's the simplest, and everything else originates from it.

Vivid Thinking Rule No. 1: When We Say a Word, We Should Draw a Picture (and Vice Versa)

Rule No. 1 tells us that the next time we have an idea, instead of just talking about it, we owe it to ourselves (and our audience) to draw it out, too. That's the essence of Vivid Thinking: *When we say a word, we should draw a picture.*

That's it. That simple little rule sums up well all we really need to do to become clearer in our own thinking, more effective in our teaching, and more persuasive in our selling. *When we say a word, we should draw a picture.* That step alone, actively engaging our *visual* mind each time our *verbal* mind kicks into gear, will take us far along the path away from blah-blah-blah.

But just because Vivid Thinking is simple, that does not mean it's easy at first: We've got a couple of speed bumps to cross before we hit the gas.

Vivid Thinking Speed Bump No. 1: We Forgot How to Draw

The proof that our visual mind has faded to the background is our inability to draw, or, more specifically, our *belief* that we can't draw. Every time I go into a business meeting,

I first ask everyone how comfortable they are with drawing. Almost without exception, three-quarters of the room says they can't.*

But it's an unfair question. Asking a roomful of professionals if they can draw is about the same as asking a roomful of kindergartners if they can read: *Of course they can't.* Learning to read takes a level of neurological development that most five-year-olds haven't attained and an intensity of training that they haven't received. Knowing how to read isn't something we were born with; we had to learn how—and that took years.

The same is true of adults and drawing: Even though 75 percent of our entire sensory processing capacity is dedicated to vision,† nobody has ever taught us how to use it. When it comes to expressing ourselves verbally, we've completed high school and college. When it comes to expressing ourselves visually, we never got out of preschool.

We all have the capacity to be excellent visual thinkers, but we've never been given the tools or motivation to try. Yet with the most basic of tools and a little encouragement, it doesn't take more than two minutes before the whole room stops thinking about *not* being able to draw and just does it. All we have to do is draw a circle.

Remember the example of the word *ball* and the picture ◯? Let's keep going with that for a minute.

First, let's add a bit more detail to our word. In the spirit of "When we say a word, we should draw a picture," let's add a corresponding increase in detail to our picture.

NOW SAY: NOW DRAW:

"beach ball"

---

* Although my workshops are not about "drawing," and I spend a lot of time making the distinction between being able to draw and being a good "visual thinker," our perceived inability to draw remains far and away our biggest hurdle in overcoming blah-blah-blah. There are many exceptions, of course: kindergartners, architects, and (some) engineers can't wait to start drawing. The kindergartners draw because they don't yet know how *not* to, and the architects and engineers draw because they were never allowed to forget—after all, you simply can't design a house or a device with words alone. Why we think we can design businesses, laws, and societies with words alone is the real mystery.

† Twenty times more than is devoted to touch and sixty times more than to hearing.

See? Vivid Thinking—making sure that our verbal and visual minds are working together—is the simplest thing in the world. We say a word, we draw a picture. The two halves of our mind have been working together for millions of years and know exactly how to do it. We're just out of practice. Let's try a few more.

SAY:	DRAW:
"sun"	
"car"	
"run"	
"love"	
"progress"	

Oops. Wait a minute: We were doing so well there, up until we hit a word that doesn't have an instant image associated with it. *Progress.* How can we draw a picture of that? If we think about it for a moment, we can probably come up with something. How about this:

| "progress" | |

Okay, fine picture, but that was hard. It was far easier to say the word and simply know what it meant than to rattle around in our mind's visual closet and come up with a corresponding picture. We can do it, but it takes a kind of thinking we're no longer used to.

Vivid Thinking Speed Bump No. 2: Concepts That Aren't "Visual"

Here's a problem common to those people in the conference room and Oog and Aag out on the savanna: Many of the ideas we have—especially abstract concepts, intuitive feelings, and complex arguments—don't lend themselves to simple corresponding pictures.

That's where names and words shine. A word is easy to recall, easy to say, easy to write, and easy to read. But how often does saying a word make us really think about what we mean? Coming up with the *ell* meant that we had to pause for a moment with that word *progress* and look at it in a new way. Reading the word and drawing the symbol are not the same: They don't trigger the same thoughts, don't stimulate the same processing centers, and don't make us feel the same things.

To get the words and pictures working together, we've got to get our whole mind working together—and that requires a new way of thinking about our mind.

The Fox and the Hummingbird: We're of Two Minds

Because all the terms we apply to our brain balance—*verbal versus visual, analytical versus synthesizing, linear versus spatial*—are *words*, they make sense to only half our mind. If we're going to wake up our visual mind (the half that wouldn't know a word if it fell over it), we're going to need a better way to *see* the balance.

Instead of getting tripped up with words-only distinctions, let's instead imagine that we've got two different (and very hungry) animals living in our head: a fox and a hummingbird.

As with our verbal mind and visual mind, these two animals have much in common: Both are high-energy creatures that require constant feeding to survive. Both are quick and agile, both are whip smart, and both are highly adapted to thrive in rapidly changing environments.

Fox

Hummingbird

◀ **High-energy creatures that must keep moving to survive, the fox and the hummingbird have much in common.**

These similarities are important. They help us see that, like the fox and the hummingbird, the verbal and visual sides of our mind aren't radically different creatures with little in common. On the contrary, it's their great commonality that links them together.

But it's the differences between the fox and the hummingbird that are more interesting—and that's why these two creatures make such a good metaphor for exploring what's going on inside our own heads.

THE FOX

The fox is sharp: Once he has spotted his prey, he advances step by step with laser-like focus. The fox is linear: With his objective clearly in mind, he stalks stealthily forward, shifting this way and that to avoid being seen yet always keeping his own eyes straight ahead. The fox is analytical: Noting that the direct path might put him in plain sight of his prey, the fox darts from point to point to take advantage of cover. The fox is patient: As long as he keeps his eye on the prize, he knows that he's got time on his side. The fox is clever: He tests the wind, calculates distance and velocities, and, at the precise moment . . . he strikes!

The fox is our president giving a speech, the CEO delivering the financial update, the lecturer teaching the class, the salesman giving the pitch. It's the *me-to-you, here-to-there, A-B-C-D, "I said it and I hope you got it—any questions?"* approach.

After successfully feeding (or speaking, delivering, teaching, or selling), the fox becomes a bit smug: Having achieved his objective, he kicks back to admire his own mastery of the forest. "Look how clear I am," says the fox. "I impress even myself." The fox is our verbal mind.

Fox

✓ Linear
✓ Analytical
✓ Patient
✓ Clever
✓ (a little smug)

Our verbal mind

Sharp, linear, analytical, ▶ patient, clever . . . and a bit smug: The fox is our verbal mind.

THE HUMMINGBIRD

The hummingbird is aware: With acute peripheral vision, she sees clearly in all directions at all times. The hummingbird is spatial: She sees her environment as a three-dimensional space with food potential everywhere; she can fly backward (and even upside down!) to get to the nearest flower. The hummingbird is spontaneous: She is so fast that she doesn't travel along a path from one flower to another—she just appears there. *Zip.* And there. *Zip.* And here. The hummingbird synthesizes: Touching and seeing everything, she builds a complete model of the forest in her mind.

The hummingbird is the accountant checking the books one more time, the CFO scanning the spreadsheets for the rounding error, the pilot preparing for landing at the busy airport, the architect reworking the facade on the drawings. It's the back-and-forth, up-and-down, rolling, scanning, *"I know it's here somewhere . . ."* approach.

The need to see so much so quickly makes the hummingbird flighty and easily distracted—not to mention exhausted. After expending bursts of energy scouring all corners of the forest, she needs frequent breaks—after all, tomorrow she'll cover it all again. "Whew!" she says, "All done . . . but wait: where did I put the keys?" The hummingbird is our visual mind.

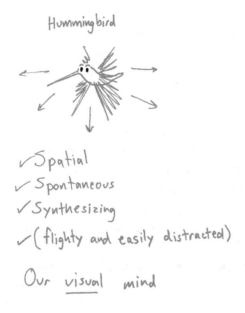

◀ Flighty and easily distracted: The hummingbird is our visual mind.

Seeing the World Both Ways

Verbal mind = *piece-by-piece mind* = *fox* mind. Visual mind = *all-at-once mind* = *hummingbird* mind. Let's see how they each see the world. The fox goes first.

Read the following sentence. (This is our fox talking.)

The beach ball rolls down the sand, picking up speed as it bounces over tufts of grass, getting higher and higher with each bounce until it finally leaves the sand altogether, a final leap sending it high over the foam and straight into the sea. Splash.

Now look at the following picture. (This is our inner hummingbird drawing.)

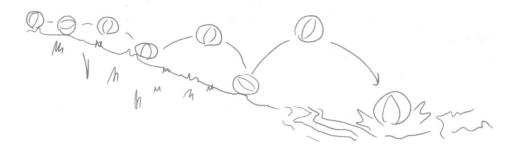

Let's go back and do that once again: Read the paragraph, then look at the picture. This time pay careful attention to how different your brain feels while "reading" and "seeing" the same scene as described in two different ways.

In reading the first description, the fox's view, we followed along the sequence of words in order, A-B-C-D, from beginning to end. We had to: The only way to process the words was to look at them one at a time and let our verbal brains piece them together to create the scene.

But in looking at the hummingbird's picture, something very different happened in our heads: We saw the entire image all at once, taking it all in near-instantaneously as our eyes rapidly zipped around searching for (and eventually finding) a meaningful sequence.

The Forest According to the Fox and the Hummingbird

The fox and the hummingbird both live in the same forest. Let's imagine how each of these creatures might see their home. The fox (our verbal, piece-by-piece mind) sees the forest as a set of landmarks linked together along a linear path that takes him from here to his prey. This path might not be straight—after all, he will need to shift from time to time to stay under cover—but it is a single line with a clear beginning and end. The forest according to the fox looks like this, a line from point A to B to C to D:

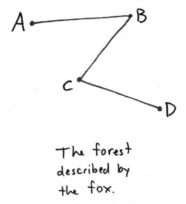

The forest described by the fox.

◀ The forest according to the fox: a linear path containing a series of landmarks that lead from here to there.

But the hummingbird's view of the forest is different. Because she is so fast and moves so freely in all dimensions, her path is an endlessly looping set of rings, nearly devoid of the constraints of time and sequence. Touching everything, her path has no particular beginning or end but rather builds a complete all-at-once sense of space. The forest according to the hummingbird looks like this, a series of overlapping swirls and circles that describe a space containing many areas of interest:

The forest described by the hummingbird.

◀ The forest according to the hummingbird: sets of interconnected rings with no beginning or end but a complete sense of space.

Both views of the forest are accurate and correct; both are complete as far as their respective critters are concerned. But both are missing something: They are both missing the insights that come from the other perspective. Clear as the fox's A-B-C-D line is, it misses the fact that the forest has height as well as distance. Sweeping as the hummingbird's circles are, there is no clear path through them.

What if We Combined Our Fox and Our Hummingbird?

To make our metaphor complete, let's imagine what we might see if we could get our fox and our hummingbird to work together. (Tricky, yes: As with our verbal mind's learned dominance over the visual, our fox has a powerful desire to eat the hummingbird. Until our fox sees the value in what our hummingbird has to offer, we're going to have to work to keep the fox firmly in check.)

Fox   Hummingbird

We need to be careful that ▶ **our fox doesn't immediately eat our hummingbird (which is precisely what our verbal mind has been taught to do).**

Let's say that we've got an idea, something we picked up in a meeting. If we wrote it down, we'd end up with a linear outline, a string of words taking us from the beginning of the idea to the end. Conceptually, it would look like the fox's view of the forest. We'd "get" it, but we might be left asking ourselves, "So what? How does this idea fit in with all the other ideas I have?"

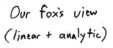

Our fox's view
(linear + analytic)

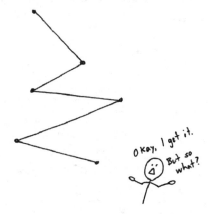

Okay, I get it. But so what?

◀ **Our fox's piece-by-piece view of our idea: We get it, but might ask, "So what?"**

If we sketched out the idea, we might end up with intersecting shapes and circles, a crude map of the many elements of the idea. It would look like the hummingbird's view of the forest. We'd probably be dazzled with what we'd drawn but have no idea how to approach it.

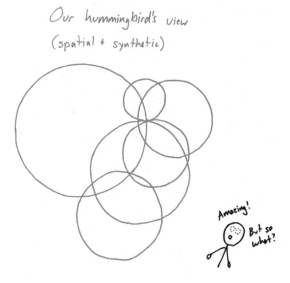

Our hummingbird's view
(spatial + synthetic)

Amazing! But so what?

◀ **Our hummingbird's all-at-once view of our idea: dazzling but impenetrable.**

If we could find a way to bring these two views together, we would have a singularly powerful idea—and who knows, we might even see something in it that neither individual view saw. Let's try it: If we superimpose our hummingbird map on our fox line, an entirely new picture emerges. . . .

As we superimpose our two ▶
views . . .

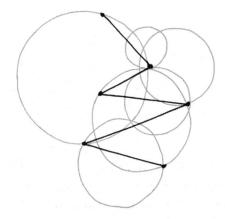

. . . a new view begins to ▶
emerge.

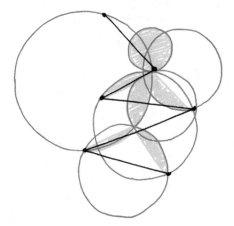

In this case, what was originally a zigzag line and a bunch of circles emerges as a person. Now we see the big picture:

Both woven together: our *Vivid* view.

AHA!
I see it!
I get it!

◀ Aha! Only by combining both views do we see the big picture.

What does all this mean in the real world of business, politics, and education? It means this: Most of us have been taught to capture, record, and present our ideas in the linear structure best suited to words. We have become pure fox. We end up with a long-winded document that was as much of a challenge for us to write as it will be for most people to read. (In other words, they won't.) We create explanations that move us from introduction to conclusion—but because words don't contain a map of the territory in between, we usually get lost somewhere along the way.

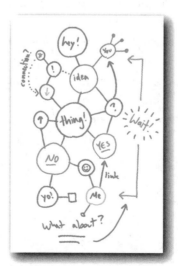

I. Blah
  A. Blah Blah
    1. Blah Blah Blah
    2. Blah Blah Blah
  B. Blah Blah
II. Blah
  A. Blah Blah
    1. Blah Blah Blah
    2. Blah Blah Blah
  B. Blah Blah
    1. Blah Blah Blah
    2. Blah Blah Blah
    3. Blah Blah Blah
III. Blah
  A. Blah Blah
  B. Blah Blah
  C. Blah Blah Blah

Our typical fox document: ▶
linear and tedious, more
likely to lose us than
illuminate us.

In recent years, there has been an admirable rise in recognizing the power of our inner hummingbird. Many people see the powerful capability of pictures in data visualization and mind mapping; both are visual ways to collect and represent context-rich and content-rich ideas. However, because these approaches open the door to such a breadth of possibilities, they often become—just like the hummingbird's view of the forest— impenetrable to anyone other than their original author.

Our typical hummingbird ▶
document: so rich with
connections and layers, it's
nearly impenetrable.

Either way—pure fox or pure hummingbird, long-winded narrative or complex picture—it's difficult for us to be sure that we've really nailed our idea, and even more difficult for anyone else to willingly approach it. There has to be a way that brings these two together. There is, and it starts here.

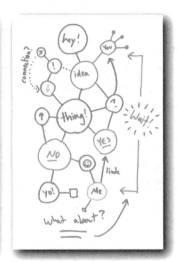

◀ Really: Who wants to approach either one of these ideas?

So Why Does Our Fox Seem Smarter?

Remember the first question I ask in a workshop? I ask the participants, usually well-educated professionals far along in their careers, about their comfort with drawing. Most express unease with, or in many cases outright hostility to, visually communicating an idea. There is something just plain wrong about using a picture to develop or explain a thought.

How could this be? On the surface, it doesn't make any sense. More of our brain's total processing capacity is dedicated to vision than to any other thing that we do—more than to memory, more than to rational thought, far more than to listening, and orders of magnitude more than to feeling—and yet most of us remain profoundly uncomfortable with visually expressing our ideas, *in spite of the fact that we perceive far more of the ideas in our heads as images than as words*. Why?

The answer is simple: grammar—or rather, the lack of it.

Asking a group of professionals to draw is as inappropriate as asking a group of kindergartners to read. They—*we, all of us*—haven't been taught the grammar yet.

The Training of Our Fox

Since we first entered kindergarten as five-year-olds, our teachers and parents have been feeding and training our verbal mind's fox: Group conversation (*Circle time! Show-and-tell! Family meeting!*) taught us the basic rules of talking. Then we learned to recognize and write the letters of the alphabet. Then came sentence structure and spelling, then basic grammar, then introductory writing, and finally critical reading.

Over many years of intense and thoughtful guidance, our fox grew and became ever more confident through rules, practice, and experience. We became literate. All along the way, we measured our fox's progress: From spelling tests in first grade through the SATs in high school to our dissertations in college, we taught, trained, and tested our verbal minds. And we were intelligent.

Neglecting Our Hummingbird

But what of our visual mind? What formal training did we give our hummingbird? Aside from a couple of art classes (which focused on creatively valuable but intellectually lame approaches to self-expression), nobody ever gave us anything visual that remotely demanded the level of rigor required to learn to read.*

what do I know?

What am I?

Think of the balance: By the time we left high school, we had hundreds of tools and a dozen years of word training behind us—and not one single tool to help us draw. No wonder our hummingbird is feeling a little uncertain.

Centering Our Brain Balance, Part 2

The goal of Vivid Thinking is to get our brain balance back to center, to make sure that our verbal fox mind isn't trying to eat our visual hummingbird mind, and then get them to work together. But as things stand now, that's impossible: Compared with our fox, our flitting hummingbird weighs nothing. As far as our verbal mind is concerned, our visual mind is out to lunch. So to make Vivid Thinking work, the first thing we've got to do is get our hummingbird back on the scale.

---

* Don't get me wrong: I love art classes—remember my duck drawing? But what I don't like is the lack of any sort of framework for the growth of our visual intellect. Why do we see the way we do? How can we think visually? How can we use our innate ability to draw in order to communicate complex ideas quickly? These are all subjects that are completely teachable, but none of them are taught. Visual literacy should be as required as verbal literacy.

How can we get our brain ▶
back in balance when our
hummingbird side is
weightless?

To coax our hummingbird down to a landing, we've got to provide two things: a perch for her to sit on (so we can carry her weight) and a wall around her (to keep the fox from eating her). What we need is a structure that provides our hummingbird a place to come down to earth and protects her from the hungry fox.

We need to provide our ▶
hummingbird with a
structure to sit on and
protect her; we need
to give her a perch.

That structure is the grammar of Vivid Thinking: a simple set of "How do I draw that concept?" guidelines. These guidelines give us the means to make the first rule of Vivid Thinking work: *When we say a word, we should draw a picture.*

What word? *That one.* What picture? *This one.* The first step toward getting our brain back in balance is to get both our creatures comfortably in place. Then avoiding blah-blah-blah becomes easy.

◀ **That's better.**

CHAPTER 5

The Grammar of Vivid Thinking

Grammar? Am I Out of My Mind?

Grammar. Everybody hates it.

It is a scientific fact that there is no faster way to get us to stop paying attention than to tell us we are going to study grammar. Brains freeze, eyes fade, ears shut, books close; it's the end of the lesson before it begins. There is something so dry and crusty about the word that only a real dummy would name a chapter of a business book "The Grammar of" anything.

So it's good we spent the past two chapters establishing that we're half-dumb. With our fear of that label behind us, we can take the time to explore the *grammar* of Vivid Thinking.

Visual Mind, Verbal Mind: One of These Things Is Not Like the Other

Quick review: Vivid Thinking stands for *visual verbal interdependent thinking,* which means getting our visual and verbal minds to work together again.

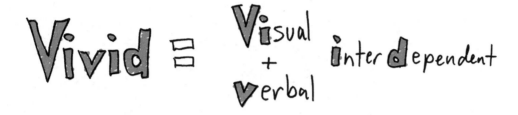

Actively combining our visual and verbal minds through Vivid Thinking means two things. First, "vivid" means that when it comes to thinking, two minds are better than one. Second, being "vivid" means that actively combining our visual mind with our verbal mind is the best possible way to avoid blah-blah-blah.

The second half (the *verbal* half) of the visual-and-verbal equation is well understood. We spent twelve long years in school learning the basics of verbal grammar. The fact that I am able to write this book and that you're able to read it proves that it wasn't a waste of time. The fact that it took so many years to learn verbal grammar also proves that it is complicated, nuanced, multilayered, arcane, and borderline unteachable.

But it doesn't need to be.

Verbal Grammar in Four Bullet Points and Two Pictures

In the end, all English grammar* boils down to a very few things. Since verbal grammar is our fox's domain, let's let him introduce it.

FOX GOES FIRST

Fox?

I thought you'd never ask.

Every thought that can be uttered in English, every sentence ever composed, and every paragraph on every page of every book ever written depends on the following short list of grammatical tools:

---

* The parallels I describe here apply precisely only to the grammar of spoken and written English. However, I have learned in my adult life to speak Russian (fluently enough to read the news and conduct business), French (well enough to make my way through a meal without completely embarrassing myself and, more important, my hosts), and Thai (badly enough to negotiate my way into and out of a Bangkok police station—twice), and in my nonacademic but road-tested understanding, the essentials of all are close enough to say that Vivid Grammar works just fine in those languages as well. I wait with bated breath for the linguists to start knocking heatedly on the door.

1. Every sentence demands at minimum only two elements: a subject and a predicate. *Something does something.* (It could be that *somebody* does something, or that somebody does something *to somebody else,* or that something happens *that triggers something else,* but those are all just variations on the essential subject-predicate theme.)

2. There are only eight "parts of speech": nouns, pronouns, adjectives, verbs, adverbs, prepositions, conjunctions, and interjections.

3. A separate and unique grammatical category called "tense" indicates *when* something happens.

4. The eight parts modify one another in various ways and, when combined with tense, account for all verbally describable aspects of anything: *what happened, how much it happened, where it happened, when it happened, how it happened, why it happened, and what to do about it.*

See how concisely I said all that? And now do you see why I am so intelligent?

Yes. Thank you, fox.

HUMMINGBIRD GOES NEXT

Concisely stated as that is, there still are a lot of bullets in our fox's list. Since our hummingbird excels at finding the connections between pieces, let's let her have a try.

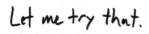

Hummingbird:

Pictorially, we can account for all those grammatical tools—and the ways they fit together—in a single picture like this:

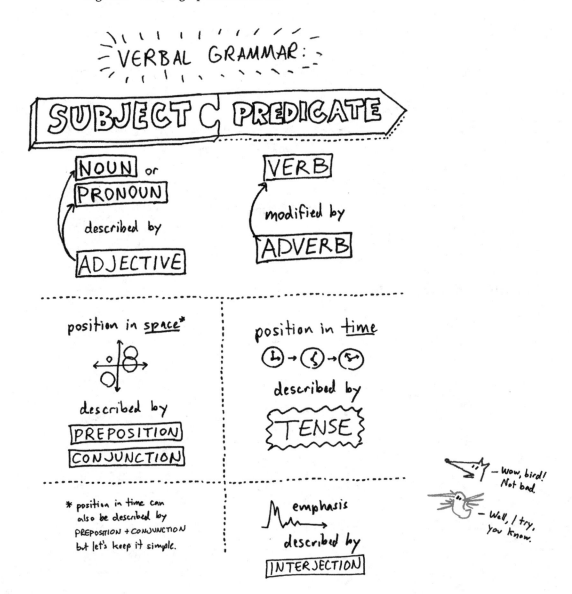

There. I think I got everything.

Nice job, hummingbird. Thank you, too.

That's it: The verbal grammar lesson is over. The visual grammar lesson is about to begin.

Verbal Grammar—Visual Grammar: It's a Two-Way Street

Here's why we needed a review of verbal grammar: Recall that our visual hummingbird has been taught no grammar, whereas our verbal fox has been doused with more than he can remember. Rather than run from what our fox already knows, we can use much of his verbal grammar as a starting point for creating a grammar to support our hummingbird's pictures.

This does not mean that a vivid description of an idea is simply the verbal description written in hieroglyphics. Such a description would not be "vivid" at all; it would just be a direct translation of sound symbols into some other kind of symbols—it might be an interesting academic exercise, but it wouldn't really get our hummingbird active.*

What it does mean is that for those of us who *don't* believe pictures can convey complex ideas well and *don't* believe we can draw, we can rely on the verbal grammar we do know as a starting point for our pictorial thinking. Once we see how simple it is to directly convert word thoughts into picture thoughts, it won't be long before we're comfortable going back and forth between the two—and that's when Vivid Thinking kicks in.

---

* Egyptian hieroglyphics—and the distinct but somewhat related pictograms of ancient Chinese—are a fascinating way to understand how people have used pictures to communicate throughout history. For an overview of how the ancients managed for thousands of years to marry our verbal and visual minds in written language, see Appendix A, "How We Lost Half Our Mind."

Rule No. 1, One More Time

Vivid Thinking Rule No. 1 told us that if we want to learn to actively engage our visual mind while we think, teach, and sell, the way to start is simple: *When we say a word, we should draw a picture.* That was easy for the first few pictures we drew, but then we bogged down. And consider this: The essence of the rule isn't just to get us to draw lots of individual words. Oh, no: The real purpose of the rule is to get us to draw entire *ideas*.

But if we struggle just drawing a picture of a basic word like *progress*, how on earth are we ever going to come up with a better vivid description of something as complex as an annual report, a sales pitch, a teaching curriculum, or an innovative technology?

Here's how: We're going to use the Verbal Grammar elements and rules we've just reviewed as a launchpad for an entirely new type of grammar—one that gives our hummingbird the same structural benefits that we gave our fox through all those years of training. And we're going to call it Vivid Grammar: the grammar of Vivid Thinking.

And that's where Vivid Thinking Rule No. 2 comes in. If we're working on an idea and we don't know how to draw it, we can use the six lessons on the following pages to get us started, no matter what our idea is about.

VIVID THINKING RULE NO. 2: If We Don't Know Which Picture to Draw, We Look to Vivid Grammar to Show Us the Way

Introducing Vivid Grammar

If verbal grammar is the set of rules we use to compose any spoken or written idea from a small set of word elements, then Vivid Grammar is the set of rules we'll use to compose any corresponding visual idea from an even smaller set of pictorial elements. Using this small set of visual "parts of seeing" means that when we say a word, we will know which picture to draw.

NOTE ON THE CONNECTION BACK TO *THE BACK OF THE NAPKIN*

Vivid Grammar is an evolution of (and complement to) a core visual thinking tool I call the "6 × 6 Rule," which I introduced in my previous book, *The Back of the Napkin*. The 6 × 6 Rule makes the connection between the six neurobiological "vision pathways" along which a visual signal travels in the brain and a set of six simple pictures that anyone can draw. Don't worry, though: Reading *The Back of the Napkin* isn't necessary for understanding Vivid Grammar. Vivid Grammar is a stand-alone concept whose meaning and application can be fully understood with no prior knowledge of that book.

If you have read *The Back of the Napkin*, you will notice the underlying similarities between Vivid Grammar and the 6 × 6 Rule—but please keep reading anyway. In the four years since 6 × 6 first appeared in print, I have had the chance to review it face-to-face with tens of thousands of people around the world, learning more about the "six W's" myself. Vivid Grammar is the result of my own continuing education, the ultimate expressive form of *who and what, how much, where, when, how,* and *why*.

If you are interested in the origin of Vivid Grammar, please look at Appendix B, "Connections Back to *The Back of the Napkin*."

The Six Elemental Pictures

Although our hummingbird does not see the world in the same way as our fox, all the pictures she sees are composed of just six elemental "parts of seeing" components, each of which corresponds directly to one or two of our fox's verbal "parts of speech." Listed in order of increasing complexity, the six elemental pictures of Vivid Grammar are: *portrait, chart, map, time line, flowchart,* and *multivariable plot.*

In their simplest forms, the Vivid Grammar "parts of seeing" align to the verbal grammar "parts of speech" in the following way:

THE SIX ELEMENTAL PICTURES OF VIVID GRAMMAR *(and Their Relationship to Verbal Grammar)*

(1) **Portraits** are the visual representation of nouns and pronouns.

☺ ⬡ ⛵ = NOUNS and PRONOUNS (and sometimes simple verbs and adjectives of "quality")

(2) **Charts** are the visual representation of adjectives **of quantity.**

Y ▮▯▮▯ = ADJECTIVES of quantity
A B C

(3) **Maps** are the visual representations of prepositions and conjunctions.

= PREPOSITIONS and CONJUNCTIONS

(4) **Timelines** are the visual representation of tense.

⇨⇨⇨ = TENSE

(5) **Flowcharts** are the visual representation of complex verbs.

▢ → ◯ = COMPLEX VERBS

(6) **Multivariable plots** are the visual representation of complex subjects.

Y = COMPLEX SUBJECTS
x

For the rest of this book, we're going to learn how to draw each of these six elemental pictures and then how to combine them to create vivid explanations of any idea we can come up with. That way we can be sure that our ideas will be so vivid that they won't show up on the Blah-Blahmeter at all—no matter how boring or convoluted they may seem when expressed with words alone.

Introducing the Vivid "Grammar Graph"

The six elemental pictures of Vivid Grammar are interlinked in the following way: We start with the most basic (the "portrait," which as we just saw serves as the *noun* or *pronoun* of our idea) and then add each upon the other within a simple framework as the six pictures become increasingly layered and meaningful.

Let's call this framework the "Grammar Graph." Because it provides a visual way to link together the six elemental pictures, it is a graph we will refer back to frequently throughout the rest of this book. Here it is, the framework of the six elemental pictures, aka the Grammar Graph.

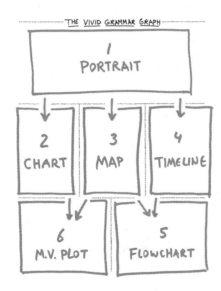

The Vivid Grammar Graph: the simple framework that accounts for and links together the six elemental pictures of Vivid Grammar.

For the rest of this chapter, we're going to run through the Grammar Graph quickly, just to get a sense of what the six elemental pictures show, how they parallel verbal grammar, and how they relate to one another.* Then, for the rest of the book, we'll put each of the elements through its paces.

① The *Nouns* of Our Ideas: Portraits

At the top of the Grammar Graph, we start with "portraits."

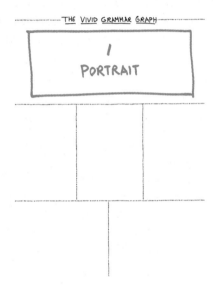

Portraits represent nouns and pronouns, the whos and whats of our ideas. At their simplest level, portraits show the "subject" of our thoughts: the person, place, or thing that we're talking about.

---

* For a deeper dive into the neurobiological, linguistic, and conceptual origins of these six elemental pictures, please see my previous book, *The Back of the Napkin: Solving Problems and Selling Ideas with Pictures.*

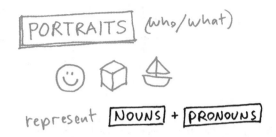

◀ Portraits (the whos and whats) of our idea represent nouns and pronouns.

When our fox says "face," our hummingbird draws a ☺. If our fox says "box," our hummingbird draws a ⬠. If our fox says "boat," our hummingbird draws a ⛵. Portraits are "vivid" because they let our hummingbird add visual meaning to the verbal names that our fox conjures up.

Since portraits represent the *subject* of our idea—they are the essential *thing* that is taking action, being described, being counted, being moved, being timed, or being modified—portraits are the initial building blocks of *anything* we want to vividly think through or describe.

For example, if we're thinking about developing a new piece of software, our fox might start by picking a word to identify the *person* who would use the software (the "user," says our fox), the digital *device* on which the software would run (a "mobile phone"), or our *software* itself (a "location-based application"). Summing things up, our fox might say, "The user has a mobile phone on which he runs a location-based application." It's a valid statement, it makes sense, and it gets our idea going. It's not blah-blah-blah—but neither is it vivid.

That's because our fox wasn't acting alone when making those words and stringing them together. The hummingbird was there all along, conjuring up images right alongside the fox's words. The hummingbird is just as active coming up with "user," "device," and "software," but she's seeing them, not saying them. Pictures give our hummingbird the chance to "speak" as well. That's where portraits come in.

To our hummingbird, all of those things—the user ☺, the device ✎, and the software ▦—can be represented with simple portraits. If we wanted to vividly describe our idea, we could simply start by drawing any one (or all) of them.

user

mobile device

location application

Drawing a simple portrait of ▶ any noun central to our idea is the beginning of a vivid description.

By engaging our hummingbird to draw those words as our fox says them, we make the "nouns" far richer in our own mind—and simultaneously vastly clearer to anyone who might be trying to read our mind. That's the essence of a vivid thought: *What is the best, fastest, richest, and most believable way to get an idea from my head into yours?* And that's just the beginning of what Vivid Thinking can do.

Portraits as Adjectives of Quality

If we add a few details to a basic portrait, they represent adjectives of *quality* as well. (What *kind* of person, what *type* of phone, what *sort* of software?) For example, if we add a few lines to a smiley face, we can visually describe many different kinds of faces.

With the addition of a few ▶ details, portraits also serve to describe *what kind* of person (or thing); they serve as adjectives of quality.

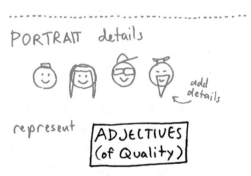

In this way, even a slightly detailed portrait is the visual equivalent of both a noun and the adjectives that describe its qualities. For example, we could say just "person" and draw ☺. But if we wanted to say "the person in the hat," we'd draw ☺, and if we wanted to say "the man in glasses wearing the hat," we'd draw ☺. See how efficient portraits can be? One picture can replace several nouns, pronouns, and adjectives.

Portraits as Simple Verbs

Once we get used to using portraits to visually represent the nouns and pronouns of our ideas, we will see that they can do one more great thing: Portraits can also represent simple actions and verbs. For example, we can represent "running" with 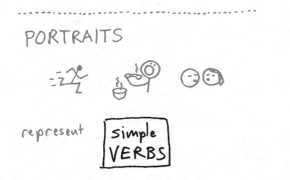, "eating" with, and "kissing" with.

Looked at this way, the potential of Visual Grammar becomes clear. Rather than saying, in a "piece-by-piece" way, the *subject* of a thought is over *here* and the *predicate* is way over *here*, we can combine both into a single "all-at-once" picture.

For example, we could say, "The dog ate my homework" like this:

Or we could say "Brace for impact" like this:

Or we could say "All men are created equal" like this:

A Portrait of the User as a Lost Man

With an initial portrait drawn, we can use visual grammar to expand our idea vividly in any direction. (By the way, that is the most important statement in this chapter, so let's say it again: *With an initial portrait drawn, we can use visual grammar to expand our idea vividly in any direction.*) This means that whenever we want to explore, teach, or sell a complex idea, all we need to do is identify *any* initial "subject" in the idea and draw its corresponding portrait. From that starting point alone, we can vividly expand our idea as far as our combined fox and hummingbird minds are willing to take us.

Let's jump ahead in the Visual Grammar Graph for a moment to complete our user-device-software example using a "time line." (We'll come right back to our step-by-step walk-through in a minute.)

In this "location-based application" software idea, we've identified one possible initial subject as a "user," so let's start with him. We draw his portrait.

A user. ▶

The reason this user is interesting to us is that he is unhappy—and therefore in need of our software. So let's add an "adjective of quality" (a frown) and draw him as an unhappy user.

An unhappy user. ▶

The reason this user is unhappy is that he is lost. With a few more simple "portraits" (a couple of boxes to sketchily represent buildings), we can draw that, too. Now we have a portrait of the user as a lost man.

Lost user

A portrait of the user as a lost man.

How do we help him become unlost? That's where our software helps. Imagine that our software runs on a device 📱 that our user already has with him—his mobile phone, for example. We can draw that, too.

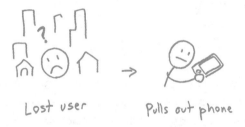

Lost user   Pulls out phone

Knowing he has a helpful application in his phone, he pulls it out of his pocket.

Now imagine if our software could determine our user's location based on his phone's internal GPS locator. Wouldn't that be cool: Just by having a phone in his pocket, our user already has a built-in location detector. How about if our software translates that internal location signal into a visual interface 🗺 that shows the user where he is on a map? We can draw that, too.

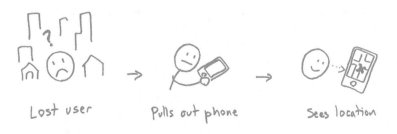

Lost user   Pulls out phone   Sees location

Our software translates the internal GPS signal into a visual map.

Look at that: With nothing more than a mobile phone running our software, our user knows exactly where he is! And now he's happy. And we can draw that, too. *(Cha-ching! Hey, nice software!)*

Look at that: Our ▶ software made our user happy!

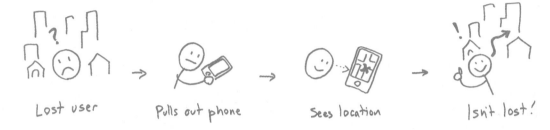

Lost user   Pulls out phone   Sees location   Isn't lost!

This is the role of a "portrait" in Vivid Thinking: By adding more portraits connected by arrows (the essence of Grammar Graph elemental picture number 4, the "time line," which we'll get to in a minute), a simple picture of any part of our idea becomes a starting point for vividly exploring the entire idea.

The Central Role of the Portrait

Portraits are key to everything else we're going to discuss in this chapter. Just as our fox's verbal grammar tells us that every sentence needs a *subject*, our hummingbird's visual grammar tells us that every picture needs a *portrait*. The "who" or "what" that first comes to mind when an idea begins to cook in our heads is what we draw first. We don't need to think about it any more than that: The first *thing* that comes to mind is the first *portrait* that we draw.

Because of this central role that portraits play in all Vivid Ideas, we're going to assign "portraits" a simple shorthand visual icon: the dotted circle ⬭. That way, when we talk about "portraits" as a category of pictures, this symbol will help us identify the key position they play. From now on, whenever we see an empty dotted-outline circle in a picture, map, chart, or diagram, we're going to know it means "a portrait belongs here."

In the rest of Visual ▶ Grammar, when we see a dotted-line circle, it means "a portrait goes here."

A PORTRAIT goes here.

As we explore the remaining five elemental "parts of seeing" that compose visual grammar, we'll see that empty circle again and again, reminding us that if we can draw a simple portrait, we can draw *anything*.

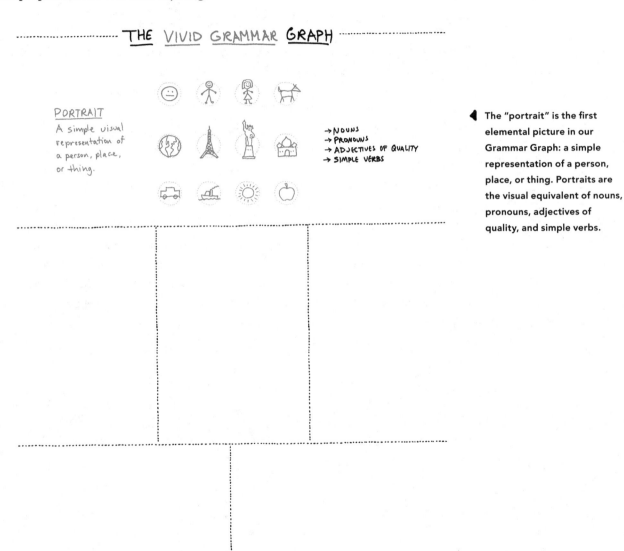

THE VIVID GRAMMAR GRAPH

PORTRAIT
A simple visual representation of a person, place, or thing.

→ NOUNS
→ PRONOUNS
→ ADJECTIVES OF QUALITY
→ SIMPLE VERBS

The "portrait" is the first elemental picture in our Grammar Graph: a simple representation of a person, place, or thing. Portraits are the visual equivalent of nouns, pronouns, adjectives of quality, and simple verbs.

Quick Break: Our Hummingbird Would Like to Remind Us of Three Things . . .

Before we go on, a word of reassurance. If any of us remain concerned about our ability to draw, our inner hummingbird can offer three soothing truths:

First, when it comes to Vivid Thinking, nobody cares "how good" our drawings look. Remember: The whole point of Vivid Thinking isn't to create a visual masterpiece; it's to get the pictures our hummingbird sees in our mind down on paper so other people (and our fox) can see them, too. And in most cases, the less refined they are, the better our inner fox likes them.

Second: Of all six elements of visual grammar, only the portrait requires any "artistic skill" at all—and we can learn that with minimal practice.

Third: In a pinch, if for whatever reason we just can't draw the right portrait—we can't draw the image well enough, we can't think of what the image might be, we don't want to get slowed down—a simple "word in a circle" can often serve as a workable temporary substitute. (But it's always worth coming back later to create the portrait; it's the visual thinking about what the "thing" really looks like that gives the portrait so much mental value.)

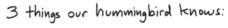

3 things our hummingbird knows:

① Nobody cares how "good" our pictures look.

② Of all visual grammar, only "portraits" are tricky to draw.

③ In a pinch, we can substitute a "word in a circle" for most portraits.

② The *Adjectives* of Our Ideas: Charts

The next picture type that occupies our Grammar Graph is the "chart," and it sits just below the portrait, on the left side.

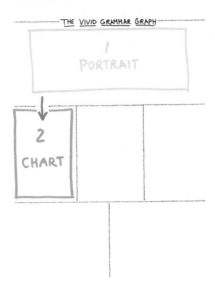

These pictures are called "charts," and they represent the numeric adjectives of our idea: Just as our portrait identified the person, place, or thing we had in mind, so the chart visually answers the question *"How many are there?"* In this way, charts represent the "how muchs" and "how manys" of our ideas.

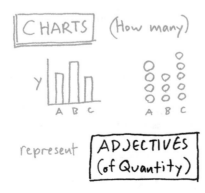

◀ Charts represent the number of objects we see; they are the visual adjectives of quantity.

Knowing how many of something there are is often critical to making decisions about it, especially when we want to compare the quantity of one thing to the quantity of another (books I have read versus books I haven't read, for example) or want to compare the quantity at one time with the quantity at another time. (For example, two years ago Apple was worth less than Microsoft, but today it's worth more.) That's why we see so many charts in education and in business: We want to see how things numerically stack up against one another. (Not to mention that stacks are really easy to draw.)

Charts show us how things ▶ stack up next to one another.

Although charts are the most common picture we see in education and business, the frequency with which we create them often masks what we're really supposed to see* when we look at them. As a visual representation of the quantity of something, the simplest chart is one that just shows exactly how many of that thing we have by representing its portrait that many times. If our fox says "three users," our hummingbird draws ☺☺☺. "Six mobile phones" becomes 📱📱📱📱📱📱.

The trouble with these kinds of portrait-quantity charts is that (as we can already see

---

* More often than not, charts are there only to show that *something* was measured, whether it has any real meaning or not. Don't get me wrong: Charts are great when it comes to showing numbers in a way that other people can "get." The problem is that we can easily get so enamored of our charts that we forget that other people need to make sense of them, too. We often swap axes, distort values, and switch coordinates in order to make things clear to ourselves, only to find that nobody knows what we're comparing anymore. That's why it's always a good idea to go back to our original portraits and make sure they appear in our charts.

here) they very quickly become unwieldy—if not outright unreadable. A better way to create a chart comparing many objects or large numbers is to first draw a portrait of the objects being counted and then add a box (or circle) around them to show relative quantity. The portrait helps our hummingbird see the difference between the types of objects being compared, and the chart helps see the quantity.

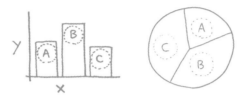

◀ The best way to create a chart is to first draw a portrait of each item being compared and then draw a box (or circle) to show the relative size or quantity of each.

Now when our fox says, "Ideally, every user should have two mobile phones and every mobile phone should have five of our software applications," our hummingbird can help everyone see clearly what that means.

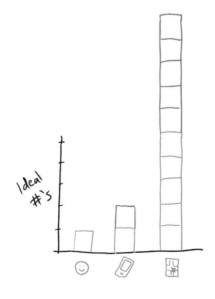

◀ This chart shows how much software we'd like to sell.

PORTRAIT
A simple visual representation of a person, place, or thing.

→ NOUNS
→ PRONOUNS
→ ADJECTIVES OF QUALITY
→ SIMPLE VERBS

How many?
⇓

The "Chart" occupies the second slot in our Grammar Graph: It is a visual representation of how many persons, places, or things we're thinking about. Charts are the visual equivalent of adjectives of quantity. ▶

CHART
Shows how many of those things there are.

→ ADJECTIVES OF QUANTITY

③ The *Prepositions* of Our Idea: Maps

The next picture in our Grammar Graph is the "map." "Maps" sit just below the portrait in the middle of the graph.

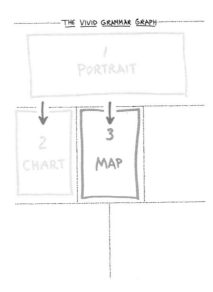

Like a chart, a map is another way of "packaging" portraits so that they show something new—in this case the *position* and *location* of the "things" the portraits represent. What a map does in visual grammar is identical to the role of a preposition in verbal grammar: It shows where one thing is in relation to another.

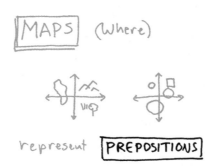

Maps represent the *prepositions* of our ideas, where one part of the idea sits in spatial relation to another part.

For example, verbal grammar tells our fox that if he wants to describe the fact that one circle is inside another circle, he has to use the preposition "inside." Our hummingbird instead draws the simplest conceivable "map," one circle inside another:

One circle is *inside* the other. ▶

As we might remember from the last time we slogged through grammar, sometimes a preposition takes a couple of words to describe (that's where "prepositional phrases" come from). If one person is "on the right" of another person, our fox has to use the prepositional phrase "on the right" to make that clear. Our hummingbird just draws the two portraits next to each other.

He is on her right. ▶

There are dozens of prepositions our fox uses to describe the spatial relationships of things*—and our hummingbird can easily show all of them:

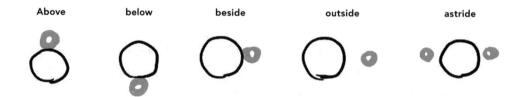

All a map does is use these visual positioning cues to show how far apart things are and in what direction. Like all elemental pictures, maps are easy to create if we start with a couple of portraits. We pick the things whose relative positions we want to compare and then draw them in those positions.

---

* There are also many prepositions that describe the temporal relationships of things—and we'll account for those in the next elemental picture, the "timeline."

◀ **This map shows that Little Red Riding Hood is still a safe distance from Grandmother's house.**

Simple maps like these also represent the visual equivalent of verbal conjunctions.

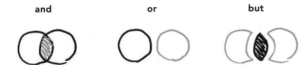

◀ **Maps also represent the conjunctions of our ideas.**

For example, our fox's verbal conjunctions, like "and," "or," and "but," become our hummingbird's visual equivalents:

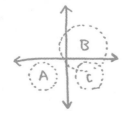

These kinds of simple maps are great when we want to show the position of things relative to each other, but if we want to show where our things are in relation to an absolute direction (like east versus west) or a conceptual ranking (like cheap versus expensive), we have to add something else: labeled coordinates.

In maps, labeled coordinates are two intersecting lines that explicitly show the dimensions against which we're mapping our items. (Labeled coordinates don't have to come in twos, but two makes the most visual sense when we're drawing on a flat surface.)

◀ **Labeled coordinates explicitly show the dimensions against which we're mapping our items.**

With only these elements—portraits plus positioning pictures plus labeled coordinates—we can draw maps of any *spatial* idea we can come up with.

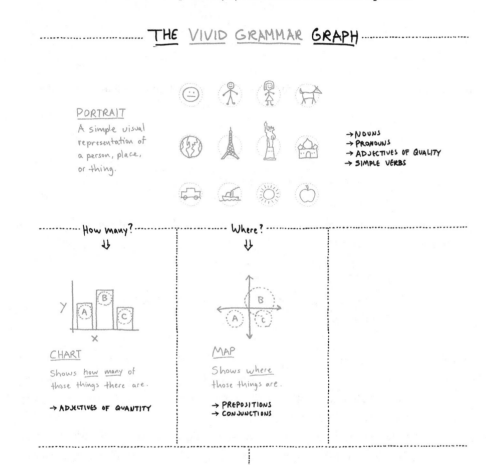

THE VIVID GRAMMAR GRAPH

PORTRAIT
A simple visual representation of a person, place, or thing.

→ NOUNS
→ PRONOUNS
→ ADJECTIVES OF QUALITY
→ SIMPLE VERBS

How many?

Where?

Maps give us the means to ▶ see where items are located within our ideas. Maps are the visual representation of prepositions and conjunctions.

CHART
Shows *how many* of those things there are.

→ ADJECTIVES OF QUANTITY

MAP
Shows *where* those things are.

→ PREPOSITIONS
→ CONJUNCTIONS

④ The *Tense* of Our Ideas: Timelines

The next picture type is the "timeline." In our Grammar Graph of elemental pictures, timelines also sit just below the portrait and to the right of the map.

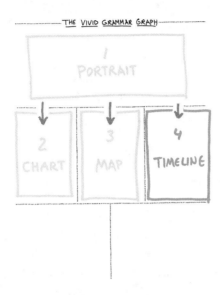

Just as **charts** showed the number of items in our ideas and **maps** showed those items' locations in space, so **timelines** show those items' positions in *time*. In visual grammar, timelines take the place of tense.

◀ Timelines represent the temporal relationships of the objects and events that we see. They are the visual equivalent of tense.

If our fox is feeling satiated and well rested, it's probably because yesterday he ate, last night he had a good snooze, today he is feeling chipper, and tomorrow he will need to do it all again. Whew: There's a lot of tense in that sentence. How would our hummingbird show it?

Ate, slept, feels chipper, will eat: Our fox lives a TENSE life. ▶

Timelines are easy to draw: As we saw in the first software example (back in "portraits"), all we need to do to create a timeline is draw a couple of sequential portraits and add an arrow between them.

A temporal sequence = a timeline. ▶

The key here is the *sequential* part: Since (as far as we humans can detect) time always appears to run in one direction, from past to present to future, all timelines must do the same. Unlike the arrows we used to create "labeled coordinates" in our map (which could point in any direction because they represented open space), the arrows in our timeline must always proceed in one direction, from *before* to *now* to *later*.

Before, now, later: Time is a one-way street. ▶

When we want to show "when things happen," we simply draw a timeline.

It's worth noting that as we translate verbal ideas into visuals, there is another way to express the relationships in *time* of our noun portraits: Some of the prepositions explored in the maps picture reflect temporal rather than spatial positions: *Before, during,* and *after* are prepositions that act in Vivid Grammar just like tense. We represent them with the same "*This first thing happened*" ⇒, "*That next thing happened*" ⇒, "*The last thing happened*" arrows ⇒ used in all timelines.

THE VIVID GRAMMAR GRAPH

PORTRAIT

A simple visual representation of a person, place, or thing.

→ NOUNS
→ PRONOUNS
→ ADJECTIVES OF QUALITY
→ SIMPLE VERBS

How many? ⇓

Where? ⇓

When? ⇓

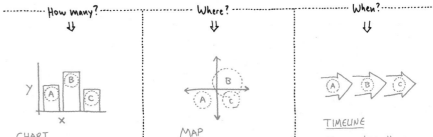

CHART

Shows <u>how many</u> of those things there are.

→ ADJECTIVES OF QUANTITY

MAP

Shows <u>where</u> those things are.

→ PREPOSITIONS
→ CONJUNCTIONS

TIMELINE

Shows <u>when</u> those things happen.

→ TENSE
(+ PREPOSITIONS + CONJUNCTIONS OF <u>TIME</u>)

◀ Timelines give us the means to see how the things in our idea fit together in time; what came first, what comes next, what will come tomorrow. Timelines are the visual representation of tense.

⑤ The Complex *Verbs* of Our Ideas: Flowcharts

The two remaining elemental pictures of Vivid Grammar are different from those we've seen so far. While we created charts, maps, and timelines by arranging portraits in uniquely different ways and kept the three resulting pictures independent, the next two pictures *require* us to mix things up.

The flowchart combines *nouns* and *prepositions* and *tense to* illustrate "how." ▶

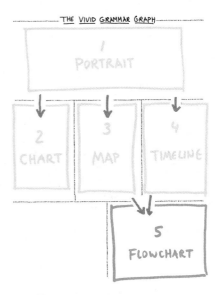

In our table of elemental pictures, number five, the "flowchart," sits below both maps and timelines. This is because this visual representation of complex verbs is created by combining aspects of the map and the timeline. By merging *nouns* (portraits) with *prepositions* (maps) with *tense* (timelines), flowcharts, like verbs, descriptively show *how* something happens.

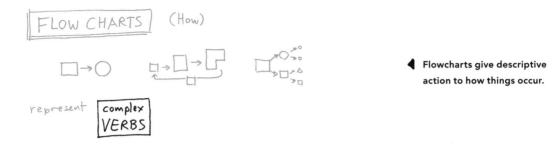

FLOW CHARTS (How)

represent complex VERBS

> Flowcharts give descriptive action to how things occur.

A more verbal, fox-like way to say that is, "The interaction of nouns plus prepositions plus tense gives us complex verbs"—or *who and what + where + when = how.*

NOUNS + PREPOSITIONS + TENSE ⟹ COMPLEX VERBS

> The interaction of nouns plus prepositions plus tense gives us complex verbs.

A more visual, hummingbird-like way to show that is:

who what + where + when = how

> *Who and what* portraits + *where* maps + *when* timelines = *how* flowcharts.

Both ways of describing flowcharts tell us the same thing: When our fox uses a sentence (or a paragraph or even an entire report) to describe a subtle cause-and-effect interaction, our hummingbird draws a corresponding flowchart.

For example, it has often been said that "the early bird gets the worm." As a graphic reminder that we should get up early and be diligent in our work, this statement can also be represented vividly like this:

The Early Bird Gets the Worm.

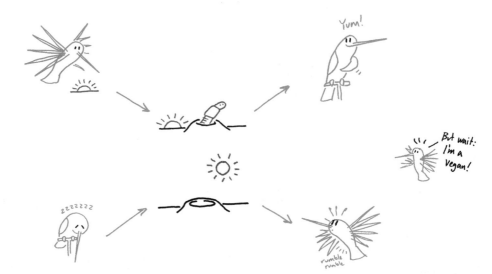

Birds, worms, timing, and ▶ location. They all combine to tell us to get up early.

Although this maxim talks explicitly about birds, worms, and time, what it's actually referring to is what happens when all three coincide,* resulting in a statement that tells us far more than how much someone gets to eat.

That's what happens when we let out hummingbird loose on a verbal expression that we've heard so many times that we don't think about it anymore. (Which is another good working definition of blah-blah-blah: *something we've heard so many times that we don't think about what it means anymore.*) When we force ourselves to create a visual representation of the words, the central idea becomes vividly clear.

Given the complexity of what happens in any multicomponent cause-and-effect relationship, we simply can't effectively wrap our heads around more than a few pieces at a time using words alone. That's the job of flowcharts: mapping out all the pieces of an interaction in one place so we can see them all at once.

---

* What it *actually* refers to, of course, has nothing to do with birds, worms, or even eating; as a metaphor, it uses those things as stand-ins for a whole set of items that would become pure blah-blah-blah spoken any other way. We'll spend a lot of time with the visual importance of such metaphors in the next part of this book.

⑥ The Interaction of the Complex Subjects of Our Ideas: Multivariable Plots

The sixth and last elemental picture in our Grammar Graph is the "multivariable plot." Otherwise known by the technical term "the kitchen sink," the multivariable plot is created by combining aspects of the **chart** (*who and what* portraits + *how many* of each) and the **map** (*where* are they located, both spatially and conceptually). As the term "multivariable" suggests, this last picture is the combination of all the elements of Vivid Grammar mapped together within a common frame.

When nouns, adjectives, prepositions, conjunctions, and tense come together in writing, we call them a *phrase;* when we add verbs, we call them a *sentence.* When they all come together in drawing, we call them a *plot.*

The best way to think about a multivariable plot (which for simplicity we'll call an "MVP" from now on) is to imagine it as a kind of visual stew of our ideas. We throw all the raw ingredients of our idea together into a pot and let them simmer. After several bubbly hours, the thicker meaty elements melt together at the bottom, the vegetables get friendly in the middle, the essential soup rises to the top, and the unnecessary details burn off as steam. From many ingredients comes together a single rich meal, tasty and fulfilling.

The essence of a multivariable plot: From many ingredients comes a rich stew. ▶

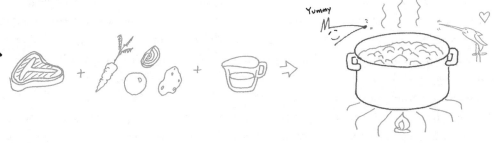

If we've selected good ingredients and cooked them together well, when we're done we'll have something tastier and more nutritious (not to mention more fulfilling) than any of the original components. That's the ideal MVP: a single picture that displays the rich interaction of multiple independent elements.

The ideal MVP: a rich display of multiple independent elements. ▶

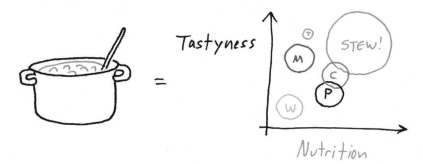

In this way, multivariable plots represent the interaction of all the previous pictures in the Grammar Graph: *who and what + how many + where + when + how = why.* Conceptually, multivariable plots can be said to represent the "whys" of our ideas in a vivid way.

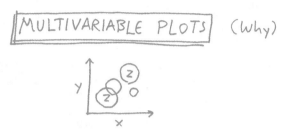

represent **entire sentences**

◀ MVPs present the interaction of all the preceeding pictures in the Grammar Graph.

Putting It All Together

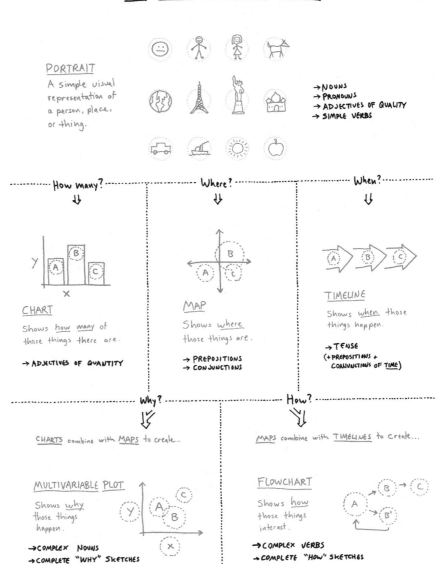

THE VIVID GRAMMAR GRAPH

PORTRAIT
A simple visual representation of a person, place, or thing.

→ NOUNS
→ PRONOUNS
→ ADJECTIVES OF QUALITY
→ SIMPLE VERBS

Our Grammar Graph is now complete. All six elemental pictures are accounted for, their relative positions established, and their linkages made clear. Let's put it to work.

How many?

CHART
Shows _how_ _many_ of those things there are.

→ ADJECTIVES OF QUANTITY

Where?

MAP
Shows _where_ those things are.

→ PREPOSITIONS
→ CONJUNCTIONS

When?

TIMELINE
Shows _when_ those things happen.

→ TENSE
(+ PREPOSITIONS + CONJUNCTIONS OF TIME)

Why?

CHARTS combine with MAPS to create...

MULTIVARIABLE PLOT
Shows _why_ those things happen.

→ COMPLEX NOUNS
→ COMPLETE "WHY" SKETCHES

How?

MAPS combine with TIMELINES to create...

FLOWCHART
Shows _how_ those things interact.

→ COMPLEX VERBS
→ COMPLETE "HOW" SKETCHES

Vivid Grammar Makes Visual Thinking Second Nature

There we have it: the six essentials of Vivid Grammar all pulled together into a single Grammar Graph. Using just these six elemental pictures, our hummingbird can create a complementary visual representation of any idea our fox can talk about. With Vivid Grammar, "When we say a word, we should draw a picture" not only becomes possible; it becomes simple—and, with a little practice, it becomes second nature. And why shouldn't it? After all, our visual hummingbird is just as legitimate and important a part of our mind as our verbal fox—and with Vivid Grammar, she now has the basic tools to express herself.

With Vivid Grammar, we've coaxed our visual mind back onto our mental balance. With both our piece-by-piece words and our all-at-once pictures ready to work together again, there is no blah-blah-blah we can't beat. Now let's put it all to work.

◀ With our verbal fox and our visual hummingbird lined up and ready to go, there is no blah-blah-blah we can't beat.

PART 3

The Forest and the Trees:

The Seven Essentials of a Vivid Idea

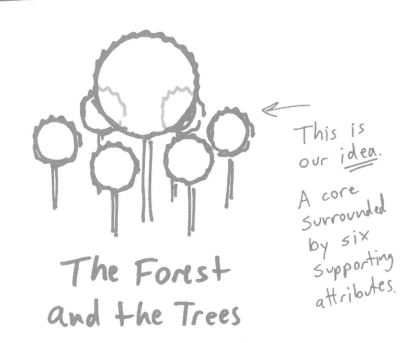

The Forest
and the Trees

This is
our idea.

A core
surrounded
by six
supporting
attributes.

CHAPTER 6

The Vivid F–O–R–E–S–T:
The Six Essentials of Vivid Ideas

Our Route so Far

Back in the introduction, I compared this book to a treasure map that unfolds into three panels. The first panel shows our present location, the second shows a path out, and the third shows our destination. So far, we've covered the first two.

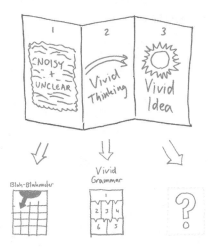

◀ This book is a three-panel map; we've now completed the first two.

Our Destination: The Forest and the Trees

Before we move on to the third panel, let's calibrate our bearings with a quick review of where we've been. Over on the left side we see blah-blah-blah, the starting point for this trip. To better understand that place and to help cut through the noise, we created the **Blah-Blahmeter,** a tool that showed us how spoken ideas can benefit from visual clarification and amplification.

Our way out of blah-blah-blah is a two-part path called **Vivid Thinking,** which runs from left to right across the center of the map. As we recall, Vivid Thinking is the active integration of our verbal and visual minds, where each increases the clarity of the other. To start down that path, we needed a way to reawaken long-dormant connections between the two, so we created **Vivid Grammar,** a tool that showed how to create illuminating pictures directly from our words (and vice versa). We visually summarized the essentials of that grammar on the **Grammar Graph.**

That's our route so far. We've come a long way—but we're not out of the woods yet. In fact, before we can complete this journey, we first need to go deeper into the woods. That's because the rules of Vivid Grammar take us to a place we've never visited before.

This new place is represented by the forest over on the right. When we bring our ideas into this forest, they are wordy, complex, and unclear—but when we take them back out, they will be vivid. During this trip through the woods, we'll get to know better than ever what our ideas sound like and look like. This next stop is the home of **Vivid Ideas**—a place where we will see the forest *and* the trees.

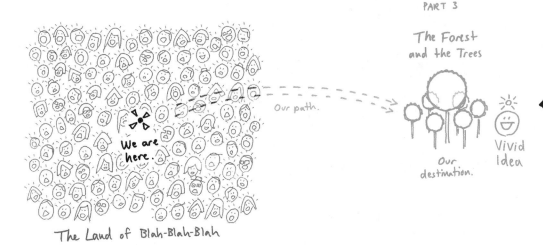

Our Treasure Map

PART 3

The Forest and the Trees

We are here.

The Land of Blah-Blah-Blah

Our path.

Our destination.

Vivid Idea

Our destination is a place where our ideas are so vivid that we can see both the forest *and* the trees.

It's a Forest Out There

Words are abstractions, the ultimate mental shorthand. When we know what they mean, words instantly call to mind ideas, images, feelings, and memories. When we all speak the same language, our words offer near-perfect communications efficiency. By lining up the right words in the right order, we can say so much by saying so little.

But the extraordinary verbal efficiency of words also has a steep downside. Like all abstractions, words are by definition distinct from the actual "things" they represent. If we are unclear in our own mind about which specific "thing" our word means or if we're unclear when we share words with other people, the whole system crashes.

Getting Above the Trees

Take the word *fly*, for example. It's a nice, simple word, only three letters long, and we all know what it means. Right? Right.

Think "fly." Got it, guys? ▶

Actually, wrong: We don't know. Without context, you don't know which "fly" I mean:

When I say "fly," I could mean the bug.　　　　= fly.

Or I could mean what a plane does.　　　　= fly.

Or I could mean how to pilot the plane.　　　　= fly.

Or I could mean what Superman does.　　　　= fly.

Or I could mean what a slugger does.　　　　= fly.

Or I could mean to get someplace quickly.　　　　= fly.

Point being, the abstraction of words ensures that even when we speak the same language, there is always vast room for interpreting *what we mean*. As much as we're taught to have faith in the precision of words, they are rarely anywhere near as clear as we'd like to believe. Instinctively we know that, of course, so we add context to clarify which meaning we mean. (Or we just let each other guess, which is how much of our blah-blah-blah is born.)

Context: Either More Trees or More Forest

There are two ways to add that context: Either we line up more words or we step back and add a picture. Usually, we do the first: We add context by adding words: *"I'd like to fly over the trees so I can get a better look at the whole forest."* Those extra words tell us which "fly" we're talking about, and the appropriate picture comes to mind.

◀ Think about "fly" as "being able to zoom around in the sky." Now we're talking.

There: Now we see the forest (the big picture) *and* the trees (the individual words), and the combination makes sense. But our verbal fox and visual hummingbird still aren't on the same page, because what I *really* wanted to convey was what that "fly" *feels* like—I wanted to share with you the "how-to," not just the dream-like fantasy.

As our hummingbird knows from personal experience, there's more to flying than jumping up and down and flapping. In fact, to her, "flying" is more like balancing a broom on a finger while running than it is like zooming around with outstretched arms—and that difference can be described only partially with words. She knows that adding a picture to those words is necessary to *show* all that is involved.

Flying is more like balancing than leaping. To convey that, our hummingird needs a picture. ▶

The picture she draws gives visual form to another long string of words: *Flying means simultaneously balancing four competing forces: thrust, which pushes us forward through the air; drag, which holds us back; lift, which pushes us up; and weight, which pulls us down.**

Here's what her picture looks like:

Flight:

Our hummingbird knows that flying means balancing four separate and simultneaous forces—something that can be shown only by combining words with a picture. ▶

LIFT

DRAG ⇐　⇒ THRUST

WEIGHT

Actually, you're experiencing four simultaneous forces in dynamic balance... (Trust me.)

---

* This drawing of the four forces of flight is the first image any flying student is shown when he or she begins training. Since everything else a pilot will learn depends on this simple model, it is never left far behind.

Now we have a vivid description of *this interpretation* of the word *fly*. It took a moment to get here, but it was worth the effort. Because once we see this picture, we begin the shift from having an abstract idea of flying to having a specific, realistic idea of what is involved—which means that rather than just dreaming about it, we can actually do it.

Coming back down to earth, this means that Vivid Thinking gives us a way to make sure that everyone in our boardroom, classroom, sales call, and project planning session not only thinks they know what they're supposed to do—they really do know.

What to Draw?

Our hummingbird knew which "flying" picture to draw for one simple reason: experience. She's thought about flying her entire life and knows exactly what it looks like. Good for her: Now our fox has a clue about what's involved as well. But what about the rest of us? Although we may be experts in finance, education, human resources, social sciences, physical sciences, management, leadership, technology, psychology, sports, and trades of every kind, we haven't unleashed our hummingbird since kindergarten. How do we take the lessons of Vivid Grammar and use them to create the pictures that enrich our verbal ideas?

That's where the third and final rule of Vivid Thinking comes into play: If we don't know what to draw, we look to the seven essentials of Vivid Ideas.

VIVID THINKING RULE NO. 3: To Make Any Idea More Vivid, We Turn to the Seven Vivid Essentials

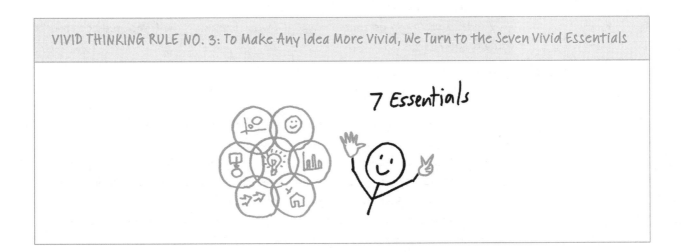

Making Thinking Simpler: The Seven Essentials of a Vivid Idea

The point of Vivid Thinking is to make it easier to think about complex ideas. Like Richard Feynman and his mental crankshaft, we've been taught to believe that the way to demonstrate knowledge of something is to talk about it. We've learned to rely on a single equation that reads like this: *More words = more clarity = more knowledge.* But as we now know, that equation is *at best* only half right.

Very often, we think we know something well because we have the words to describe it. But just as often, our words are missing vast chunks—or, even worse, obscure what's actually going on. Our usual response is to say more, but in reality these chunks can't be described and clarity can't be achieved no matter how many words we say. Our goal for the rest of this book is to help our visual mind pick up the slack to fill in those chunks and clear out that fog—with the added benefit that we'll always discover something new along the way.

Vivid Grammar got us started: *When we say a word, we should draw a picture. Say a noun, draw a portrait; say a preposition, draw a map; etc.* But that is just a start: Our ideas are far more complex than a few words strung together. Vivid Thinking is going to be useful only if it can help us translate entire thoughts into pictures.

Vivid Thinking can do that—and that's what exploring the forest and the trees is going to show us.

So Here's the Deal . . .

If we want to explore an idea solely with words, that's fine, but then we become pure fox and our thoughts need to be expressed as a long row of trees, everything lined up just so. If we explore an idea solely with pictures, that's also fine, but then we become pure hummingbird and our thoughts need to be expressed as a map, showing everything all at once.

Let's not be mistaken: Both options are useful and powerful. But both are flawed. In both cases we get *something* from the idea, but in both cases we don't *fully* "get" the idea. And that's not good enough in a world of blah-blah-blah.

The Vivid FOREST

Vivid Ideas really are like the proverbial forest: a big picture composed of lots of individual elements, each with its unique individual attributes. Put that into a picture and we see our first view of the Vivid FOREST: a tall central tree surrounded by six smaller trees.

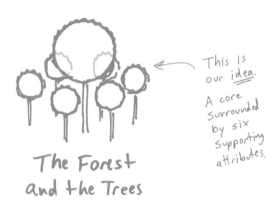

This is our idea. A core surrounded by six supporting attributes.

The Forest and the Trees

◀ Our first view of the Vivid FOREST: a central tall tree surrounded by six smaller trees.

The central tree represents the heart of our idea, in this case "*Vivid Ideas are both visual and verbal.*" The surrounding trees represent six supporting concepts: *Vivid Ideas have form, show only the essentials, are recognizable, keep evolving, span differences,* and *are targeted.* It's only when all are visible together that we can really think about our idea deeply enough to be able to express it fully.

To explore this forest, let's first send our hummingbird for a reconnaissance flyover from which she can create a quick map.

◀ First, our hummingbird goes out for a recon flight.

THE VIVID FOREST, HUMMINGBIRD VIEW

Our hummingbird returns from her aerial recon of the Vivid FOREST with a simple map. It shows seven intersecting circles, each containing a single essential concept, all linked together around the heart of the big idea. Nice map. Thank you, hummingbird.

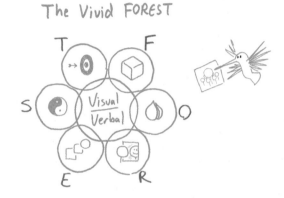

The hummingbird's map ▶ of the Vivid FOREST: The central visual/verbal idea is surrounded by six supporting ideas.

Although the seven trees are linked together, they do not appear to be in any particular linear order—we need our piece-by-piece fox for that. So let's send our fox into the forest to get the sequential order of things and bring us back a list.

Then our fox goes in for a list. ▶

Starting in the center, our fox runs from tree to tree taking notes, and here is his path:

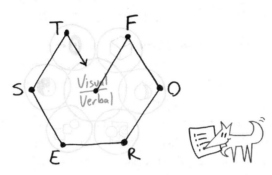

◀ As our fox runs through the forest, he notes the sequential position of each idea from the center out to the perimeter.

Having noted the sequence, our fox puts it into his favorite form: a list. Well, what do you know: The ideas surrounding the core spell out the mnemonic F-O-R-E-S-T. Thank you again, fox.

THE VIVID FOREST, FOX VIEW

- *Vivid: Vivid Ideas are expressed with words and pictures.*
- *F: Vivid Ideas have form.*
- *O: Vivid Ideas show only the essentials.*
- *R: Vivid Ideas are recognizable.*
- *E: Vivid Ideas are evolving.*
- *S: Vivid Ideas span differences.*
- *T: Vivid Ideas are targeted (especially to me).*

For the rest of this section, we're going to alternate back and forth between our hummingbird's map and our fox's mnemonic list as we explore all seven essentials of a Vivid Idea. When we're done, we'll know exactly what picture to draw, not just when we say a word but even when we want to express an entire idea.

The Heart of the Forest:
Vivid Ideas Are Visual and Verbal

Our tour of the forest begins in the center, at the heart of our idea. Every idea has this core, the central "thing" that the idea is really all about. Sometimes the core may be the first thing that crosses our mind: *"Hey, I could slice this bread!"* Sometimes it might take weeks or even years of grinding thought for it to appear: *"Wait a minute, maybe the earth isn't the center of the universe."* Either way, there is no way we can fully grasp an idea—and absolutely no hope that anyone else will—until we have found this core.

For many of us, the core of an idea is easier to find through talking or writing—but we need pictures as well. For many of us, the core is easier to find through just looking and drawing—but we need words as well. That's why we've got both a verbal and a visual mind—so we don't have to use only one.

The heart of this book: Vivid ▶ ideas are both visual and verbal.

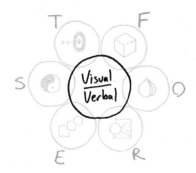

Lining Up to Board

Since we were just talking with our fox about lining things up, why don't we start with an example of lining up something else. How about airline passengers?

You'd think that after lining people up for nearly a century, airlines would have perfected the art of getting people on and off a plane. You'd also think that most of us, having boarded planes dozens (if not hundreds) of times, would know how to relate what we hear over the loudspeaker to the numbers and letters on the paper in our hand and know what we're supposed to do.

But neither of these is true. Airline boarding times are getting longer, Jetways are getting more crowded, passengers are getting more upset, and gate agents are just getting louder. An airline boarding announcement is the ultimate in blah-blah-blah: It can't really be heard, it says both too much and too little, and it's delivered in a way that no one wants to understand. It's no wonder that the most stressed we get while flying isn't during takeoff, turbulence, or landing—it's during the boarding process.

The airline boarding announcement: simultaneously too much information and too little, delivered in a way nobody wants to hear. The ultimate blah-blah-blah.

In 2008, Southwest Airlines, always a leader in doing things differently, introduced a new system to change all that. Already the most financially successful airline in history, Southwest had long ago addressed the boarding process in the simplest way possible—by getting rid of it. On Southwest, there were no assigned seats, so passengers just showed up at the gate and walked onto the plane in the order they arrived. That alone saved so much time that the airline consistently won points for the fastest gate turnarounds. But that wasn't enough.

Simple as the "just show up" approach was, it brought its own stress: Not knowing which good seats would be available, passengers learned to arrive at Southwest gates early. Before long, Southwest found itself in the same muddle as other airlines: vast crowds milling by the Jetway door, everyone jockeying for pole position.

Southwest saw a clear trend emerging in passenger surveys: The part of the airline experience that customers hated most was the chaos at the gate. Knowing they needed a long-term fix, Southwest representatives started looking differently at gate waiting areas—and, before long, saw a solution. Recognizing that people's stress is minimized when they can both see and hear what's going on, Southwest decided to make boarding a visual process.

In 2008, Southwest Airlines made the boarding process auditory *and* visual. It's already quick boarding speeded up by 30 percent.

Southwest made the waiting area visual, using tall numbered signs arrayed in order, to physically show boarding positions. Passengers could now confidently see these prominent indicators and know where and when to line up rather than anxiously wait for scratchy announcements. By visually finding their own boarding zone in the open space of the waiting lounge rather than jamming up by the Jetway, the passengers themselves took what was already the airline industry's fastest boarding process and sped it up by more than 30 percent.

All Vivid Ideas Start with Words and a Picture

There are many lessons to be learned from this example: Listening to customers is a good idea; it helps to look at existing problems in new ways; and nobody likes to be at the back of the line when they don't know what's going on. But we get the most important idea more quickly than reciting all that: Adding a visual element to a verbal process makes the process work better.

From now on, whether thinking, leading, teaching, or selling, we will say we really know an idea when we can both talk about it *and* draw it—and we'll know that other people really "get" our ideas when they both hear it *and* see it.

With that core in mind, let's do the same thing with ideas about business, education, finance, science, and communications. In other words, let's see what else is in this forest—we might be surprised by what we find in here.

CHAPTER 7

F · O · R · E · S · T

F Is for *Form:* Vivid Ideas Have Shape

 oo many ideas are like big fluffy clouds of words. We hear the sounds and know they're telling us something, but then *poof,* they're gone, only to be replaced by another big fluffy cloud. With little for our mind to grab on to, many ideas float past, never to be heard from again.

Question: Of all those clouds, which one are we going to remember?

Answer: We remember the cloud that has form.

◀ Ideas are fluffy clouds. Those we remember are those that have form.

Ideas that we remember are those that both our verbal mind and our visual mind can hold on to. Vivid Ideas are never vague or fluffy; the ideas we recall are always the ideas that have the most distinctive *form*.

Form: The First Tree in Our Forest

As we make our way around the Vivid FOREST, our first stop will be at *F*, which stands for "form." The first key to making our idea vivid is to find the idea's tangible form.

Form is the shape we give something to make it viscerally "graspable." Giving form to an idea takes it from the abstract to the concrete. Our fox's way of giving form to an idea is to put it into words. Our hummingbird's way to give form to an idea is to create an image.

Giving form to a vague notion is the single most important step we take in making our ideas vivid. The earth itself is a great example.

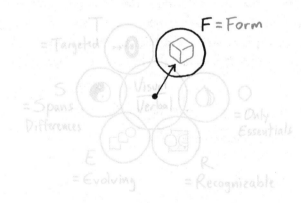

Our first stop is *F* for "form." ▶

Giving Form to the Earth

Throughout the Middle Ages, the scholars of Europe had little idea of what the world looked like beyond their own horizon. But through the exploits of adventurers and the retelling of stories from ancient cultures, some essentials were known. It was known, for example, that the world was composed of three landmasses: Europe, Africa, and Asia. It was known that the sun *oriēns* (rises) above Asia in the east and *occidēns* (falls) beyond Europe in the west. It was known that Jerusalem, the holiest of all places, was somewhere in the Asian part. It was also known that Jerusalem was far away and, worst of all, was under constant threat from people of many exotic shapes and colors.

To a well-educated European of the time, the concept of "the Orient" made sense: It was east, it was where the sun rose, and it needed to be saved. The trouble was, nobody really knew where it was. To save the Holy Land would require that vast numbers of people and vast sums of money find their way there. Something more than a vague concept was needed: What was needed was a shape that people could see. More than anything else, the medieval world needed *form*.

Thus was conjured the "T-O Map," the medieval map of the world. The name T-O comes from the map's form: a letter T drawn within a letter O.

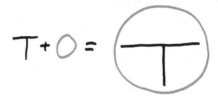

The medieval map of the whole earth was composed of a letter *T* drawn inside a letter *O*.

The T divided the O into three lands: Asia, Europe, and Africa. The largest land, Asia, sat on the top of the map, since that is where the sun rose (and, not coincidentally, was also the location of the eternally contested Holy Land). Europe and Africa occupied the bottom of the map, since that is where the sun set. Jerusalem sat at the intersection of the T.

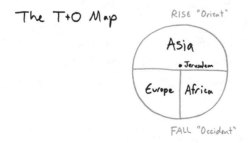

As the land over which the sun rose, Asia sat as the top of the map. As the lands beyond which the sun set, Europe and Africa sat at the bottom. Jerusalem was located at the intersection of the *T*.

This map did its job. It gave form to the previously vague idea of a single earth that could be navigated. In fact, the simple T-O Map did such a great job that it became the European map of the earth from about A.D. 1000 to 1500. The form of the T-O Map was so simple and its influence so great that whenever a medieval monarch or scholar wanted to demonstrate his grasp of the world, he would inevitably pick up a T-O globe.*

In paintings from the Middle Ages, whenever we see a monarch or scholar holding something, it is usually a T-O globe—clearly emphasizing his grasp of the world.

This simple form, composed of nothing more than the letters T and O, so clearly established the shape of the planet that it inspired countless new adventurers in their search for treasure. It was while looking at the T-O Map that Christopher Columbus got the notion that he could reach Asia by sailing downward instead of walking upward.† It was quite a mental leap, but as we look at a T-O Map today, we can see exactly what he was thinking.

How Do We Find the *Form* of Our Idea?

We know today that the earth is far more complicated than that, but the lesson still holds: When the form of an idea can be expressed clearly, the idea itself becomes clear. So how do we use Vivid Thinking to help us give our idea form? How can we come up with a T-O map of our own thoughts?

Simple: We remember Rule No. 1, *"When we say a word, we should draw a picture."* But instead of saying just one word, we're going to say many. And instead of drawing dozens of pictures to match those words, we're going to use the Vivid Grammar Graph to show

---

* Most "learned" medieval Europeans had believed since the time of Aristotle that the world was a sphere. It took the journeys of Columbus to prove that in the popular mind—another example of people not believing something until they could see it.

† Which of course led to the eventual "discovery" of an entirely new, fourth part of the world and a wholesale redrawing of the map. But that is another story.

us which *one picture* to draw. That picture will be the one that gives our idea its clearest form,* and it will become the foundation for all the other words and pictures to follow.

Rapid Review of the Grammar Graph

As we follow along the "form" picture selection process, we're going to refer frequently back to the Grammar Graph. Rather than flip back and forth, let's first create a portable version of the Grammar Graph to take with us as we go. Here it is: a simplified version of the complete Grammar Graph showing the six elemental pictures and their hierarchical relationships.

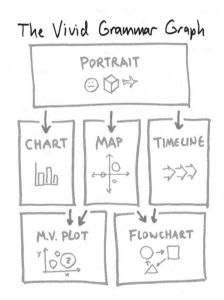

Our portable Vivid Grammar Graph: We'll take this with us for the rest of this section.

---

* To be clear, the first "form" picture we come up with might not end up being the best and, like the T-O Map, might turn out to be inaccurate as we collect more data. But all ideas start somewhere, and selecting a single starting picture—knowing full well we may need to select another later—is a wonderful way to get Vivid Thinking rolling.

Tricking Our Fox and Hummingbird into Finding "Form"

All Vivid Ideas have form. It doesn't matter what the idea is about—it could be the analysis of a complex financial transaction, an assessment of the market forces at work on a business, the process of systems dynamics, or an overview of our quarterly staff meeting—when we can find its fundamental form, the idea becomes thinkable. So how do we think up this form? Luckily, there is a simple set of six quick tricks that help us identify and vividly nail down any idea's essential form.

These Six Vivid Quick Tricks* help us find the form of an idea by forcing our fox and our hummingbird onto the same path whenever a new idea comes calling. Since both think the path is a one-way street—our fox is listening for the *words* and our hummingbird is looking for the *images*—we need to trick them into working together. The six tricks fool our fox and hummingbird into thinking they're the one in charge, when in fact they're bouncing their unique insights off each other. It's this active back-and-forth that propels an idea from a vague cloud into a distinct form. Jump-starting this back-and-forth bounce is where our six tricks come into play.

Both our fox and our hummingbird think that expressing an idea is a one-way street. We've got to trick them into helping each other find the form of the idea. ▶

What these six quick tricks will do is help us quickly convert the words that our fox hears into an image that our hummingbird can see. In other words, we're going to flop

---

* It's no coincidence that there are six quick tricks and six essential pictures; the tricks and the pictures are simply two different ways of identifying the core of an idea—two different ways of saying (and seeing) the same form.

Rule No. 1 for a minute: Instead of saying *"When we say a word, we should draw a picture,"* we're going to say, *"When we hear a word, we should see a picture."*

We start these tricks with our verbal fox for two reasons: First, in our world of blah-blah-blah, we've become so accustomed to ideas being expressed through words that it requires less trickery to get our fox engaged. He's already used to being hammered with words.

Our hummingbird is another story. Although back in Chapter 5 we gave her a grammar of her own, she's never had a formal structure before—so at first we have to trick her into using it. By letting our fox take the lead, we can casually guide our hummingbird to the Grammar Graph and let her think the whole thing is her idea—and then, as we'll see, once she's got the first image going, we'll have no trouble keeping her engaged.

Listening for the Verbal-Visual Triggers

All six Vivid Quick Tricks begin by identifying verbal-visual "trigger" phrases. This means that when a new idea first presents itself, we just listen. If it's someone else's idea, we listen carefully to their words.* If it's our own idea, we listen carefully to our own fox. Through this careful listening, what we're hoping to hear is one of a handful of key verbal-visual "trigger" phrases. These trigger phrases (we'll itemize them in a moment) are specific word combinations that give us an inkling of the essential form of the emerging idea.

Listen for verbal "triggers"...

◀ Through careful listening, our fox picks up a verbal "trigger" phrase.

Trigger phrases are specific verbal hints hidden within the blah-blah-blah, solid crystals of meaning buried within those clouds of words. Depending on the intent of the

---

* Think of "listen" here in the broadest possible sense. If we're in a lecture or a meeting or talking to a friend over coffee, I really do mean just *listen*. But if we're reading a book, blog, or magazine, I mean actively "listen" through our reading for the main idea of the author. If we're watching a movie or video, I mean "listen" for the key structural elements of what is going on and, above all, what is being said.

speaker (or our fox), these triggers may be stated clearly or buried deep. Either way, the beauty of these triggers is that if we listen carefully, they always come through—whether the speaker (or our fox) wants them to or not.

That's because a trigger phrase is simply the verbal expression of the underlying shape of an idea. It's the verbal clarification of the *who and what,* the *how much,* the *where,* the *when,* the *how,* and the *why.* When we listen for trigger phrases, all we're listening for is the building blocks of the idea, stripped of all other blah-blah-blah.

For example, one trigger phrase is hearing a person (the "subject" of the idea) being named: "There is this guy named *Big John,* and he blah-blah-blah . . ." There we have it: This idea is initially* about somebody named Big John. Another trigger phrase is hearing a big number stated: "Did you know that there are almost *seven billion* people on the planet and blah-blah-blah . . ." There we have it: This idea is initially about a big number.

Introducing the Six Vivid Quick Tricks

The Six Vivid Quick Tricks are the intersection of these verbal triggers and the pictures contained on the Grammar Graph. Normally, when we listen to an idea, our fox hears a trigger and makes a (verbal) mental note, then listens for the next words. The trick in Vivid Thinking is to get our fox to immediately hand off that trigger to our hummingbird so she can refer to the Grammar Graph and determine which picture best gives the idea visual form.

The trick in Vivid Thinking ▶ **is that our fox then hands off the "trigger phrase" to our hummingbird, who in turn refers to the Grammar Graph and knows which corresponding picture to draw.**

Listen for verbal "triggers"...

blah blah blah...

Grammar Graph

...which we can convert to visuals!

---

* When I introduced Vivid Grammar back in Chapter 5, I said that all we need to get any Vivid Idea started is an initial noun and its corresponding "portrait." That remains true here as well: Verbal triggers are the starting point.

As we recall, our Grammar Graph contains six pictures. And that's why there are Six Vivid Quick Tricks: one verbal trigger for each essential picture. Here they are.

The Six Vivid Quick Tricks are the intersection of the verbal triggers and the six elemental pictures of the Grammar Graph. In other words, if you hear *this*, you should draw *that*—and presto: Your idea has instant visual form.

The Six Once More, This Time in Detail

That's it: The key to giving any idea a memorable form is to listen for the verbal triggers, map them to the corresponding picture, then draw that picture. Presto: instant visual form. Will this first drawing be perfect? No. Will it contain every important aspect of the idea? No. Will it serve as a powerful starting point for further exploration of the idea? Absolutely, positively, and without exception, yes.

Here are the Six Vivid Quick Tricks, accompanied by a range of popular business, entertainment, finance, and science ideas—none of which are anywhere near as "formed" as their words might have fooled us into believing.

Vivid Quick Trick No. 1: Hear a *Name* = Draw a *Portrait*

What is in a name? As far as our fox is concerned, everything. As for our hummingbird, nothing.*

Names mean everything to ▶
our fox. And nothing to our
hummingbird.

---

* If we could ask William Shakespeare, the cleverest fox in the history of the English language, what's in a name, we know exactly what he would say: *Not much.* Juliet: "What's in a name? That which we call a rose by any other name would smell as sweet." In other words, the girl loves the boy regardless of what he might be called.

A name is our verbal mind's shorthand for a person, place, or thing, a cognitively efficient label applied by our fox so that we don't have to keep a full description in mind all the time. As a verbal stand-in, a name is a wonderful thing. But to give vivid form to a name, to think about *what it really is* and *what it really looks like*, demands our hummingbird's participation as well.

That's why our first quick trick says, *"When we hear a name (whether a person, an object, or a concept), we draw a portrait."* Giving the name form by drawing a picture makes the name sharper, more defined, more distinct, and much more memorable.

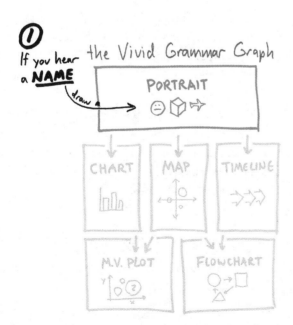

Which means more to us? This:

ARACHNIDA LATRODECTUS

Or this?

Shifting the thing we have in mind from a name to a picture (and vice versa) changes the way we think about it. This is true when we hear one name and want to know more about what makes that character unique. It is equally true when we hear two names and want to know what makes them distinct.

For example, let's look at one of the most loved (and despised) advertising campaigns in recent memory.

Imagine that we run a successful computer business. Our company has a great name—but also a great frustration: Although we make wonderful products, our market share has played second fiddle to a larger competitor for decades. It's doubly frustrating because, in spite of our competitor's financial success, we consider them unworthy in every other respect.

We believe that many customers would be happier switching to our computer brand—if only they knew us by more than just our name. As a name, we have everything going for us: We know that we make a better product than our competitor; we know that we have a more fiercely dedicated customer base than they do; and above all, we know we're much cooler than they will ever be. But we need more.

Question: What do we do? How can we get people who know us only by name to switch?

Answer: We draw portraits, of course. Two of them: an uncool portrait of him versus a cool portrait of us.

I'm a PC   I'm a Mac

How to distinguish between two similar things separated mostly by a name? Apple knew: Draw a portrait.

Our portrait of "PC": boring, plain, befuddled, confusing, prone to error, uncool.

Our portrait of "Mac": confident, at ease, simple, clear, lucky, cool (if not outright smug).

The message from Apple Computer's* initial 2006 "Get a Mac" ad campaign is unspoken but vivid: *Who would you rather be?* By the time the campaign ended four years later, sixty-seven ads had run, humoring, irritating, inspiring, and infuriating more geeks than any marketing campaign in history. Apple didn't care whether the reaction was good or bad; they just wanted their caricatures to get a reaction—and they did. By giving vivid form to a couple of names, the portraits worked, and Apple had a winner.

That's a profile: a stick-figure caricature that boils the essentials of one person (or group†) into the simplest of images. There's an underlying cognitive reason images resonate so powerfully in our minds: Whereas a name relies on memory to evoke associations, a portrait makes a visceral, real-time connection between an object and its most distinctive attributes. For a word to evoke a reaction, we have to already know and then recall the meaning of the word. For an image to evoke a reaction, we don't have to remember anything. It's all right there in front of us.

---

* By the time Apple discontinued the campaign four years later, there was no longer any need to compare the names "Mac" and "PC": Apple had successfully launched the iPhone and iPad, seen its stock price rise by a factor of six, and become the largest technology company on earth. Apple even dropped the word "computer" from the company name.

† Careful: What we're really talking about here is "profiling." The visual image of a name or idea is so powerful that when we draw a portrait, we should remain mindful of our own intent and what we choose to represent.

Vivid Quick Trick No. 2:
Hear *Numbers* = Draw a *Chart*

If we hear a series of numbers and want to find the form they signify, we draw a chart.

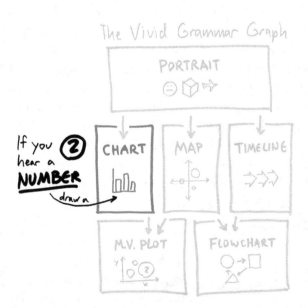

Numbers—long lists of them in particular—present a real processing challenge for most people. The problem isn't that the human brain is bad at understanding numbers—

it's not: The innate math skills of most of us are surprisingly good. The problem is that if we can't physically see the amounts in question laid out side by side, it's exceedingly difficult to get a sense of their relationships, especially when comparing vastly different amounts in quantity or over time.*

That's why, if we're hearing or thinking about an idea and lots of number triggers start firing, we should pick up a pencil and start drawing a chart. Otherwise we'll very likely miss the essential form of the idea—and come away believing that we've understood something numerically important when in fact we haven't got a clue.

In an article discussing the 2010 tax cut debate, *New Yorker* magazine economics correspondent James Surowiecki wrote the following:

> *The fight on Capitol Hill over whether to extend the Bush tax cuts is about many things: deficit reduction, economic stimulus, supply-side ideology. But at its core is a simple question: who counts as rich?*

That introduction makes the tax decision sound as if it boils down to simple numbers—which is encouraging for anyone who wants to have an informed opinion. But then Surowiecki continues:

> *Between 2002 and 2007, for instance, the bottom ninety-nine per cent of [American] incomes grew 1.3 per cent a year in real terms—while the incomes of the top one per cent grew ten per cent a year. That one percent accounted for two-thirds of all the income growth in those years. People in the ninety-fifth to the ninety-ninth percentiles of income have represented a fairly constant share of the national income for twenty-five years now. But in that period the top one per cent has seen its share of national income double; in 2007, it captured twenty-three per cent of the nation's total income.*

---

* This is why so many of us leave our fiscal decisions to other people: The way most numbers are taught and presented simply doesn't make sense. Bank accounts, investments, taxes, accounting, financial planning: These are the most important long-term decisions of our lives, and yet most of us glaze over within minutes when we have to think them through.

Wow. It's clear that Surowiecki has done a lot of research and discovered something critical to the tax debate, but from reading this I have no idea what it is. I hear time periods, years, income groups, income amounts, percentages, and growth—all solid, apparently meaningful numbers. But strung together like this, they have no coherent form. To his credit, Surowiecki sums everything up later by stating, "There's a yawning chasm between the professional and plutocratic classes, and the tax system should reflect that." But from the stream of numbers he laid on me, how would I know that—and what does it mean, anyway?

If I really wanted to grasp the form of Surowiecki's idea, by his second sentence my hummingbird should have recognized that his fox wasn't making any sense, and should have started drawing a chart. Since Surowiecki began by stating percentages of income, my hummingbird would begin by simply drawing one hundred American incomes, representing the proportions Surowiecki identified: the bottom 99 percent (including a subgroup of 95–99 percent) and the top 1 percent.

My hummingbird's pictorial ▶ response to Surowiecki's fox would begin by simply showing one hundred American incomes: the bottom 99 percent and the top 1 percent.

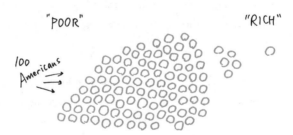

Then I'd add the income growth figures he cites for each group during the 2002–7 period: 1.3 percent growth for the bottom ninety-nine and 10 percent growth for the top one.

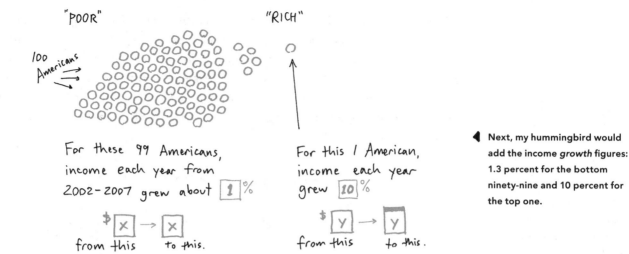

"POOR"

"RICH"

100 Americans →

For these 99 Americans, income each year from 2002-2007 grew about $\boxed{1}$%

$\$ \boxed{x} \rightarrow \boxed{x}$
from this   to this.

For this 1 American, income each year grew $\boxed{10}$%

$\$ \boxed{y} \rightarrow \boxed{y}$
from this   to this.

Next, my hummingbird would add the income *growth* figures: 1.3 percent for the bottom ninety-nine and 10 percent for the top one.

Looking at this, I think I'm beginning to detect the form of Surowiecki's idea: that the income at the top has grown ten times more than at the bottom—but then he shifts units, from income *growth* to total *share* of income, making it even more difficult to see what he's getting at. So I'll add his further details, including the verbally confusing and nonparallel units of "two-thirds," "ninety-fifth to ninety-ninth percentile," "twice the growth," and "twenty-three per cent."

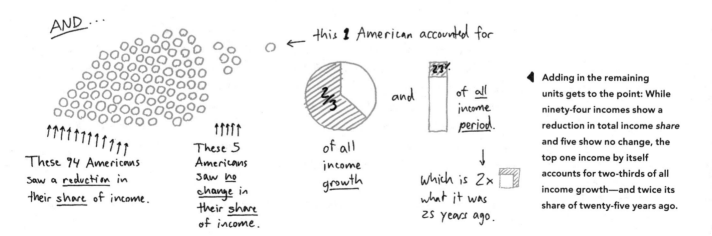

AND...

this 1 American accounted for

These 94 Americans saw a reduction in their share of income.

These 5 Americans saw no change in their share of income.

$\frac{2}{3}$

of all income growth

and

23%

of all income period.

which is 2x what it was 25 years ago.

Adding in the remaining units gets to the point: While ninety-four incomes show a reduction in total income *share* and five show no change, the top one income by itself accounts for two-thirds of all income growth—and twice its share of twenty-five years ago.

Now that we've really looked at the numbers by making a chart of them, we can finally see the essential form of Surowiecki's idea: *The income difference between the "poor" and the "rich" isn't growing much—but the difference between the "rich" and the "super-rich" is growing fast.* In pulling together his article, Surowiecki relied on words alone, which meant we had to take his conclusions on faith. Now that we see it, his idea has clear form—and by paring our chart back to *only its essentials* (which is the O of the next chapter), we make his idea vivid.

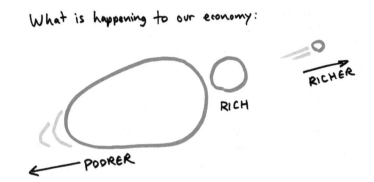

The vivid chart of Surowiecki's idea: While the income difference between the "poor" and the "rich" isn't growing much, the income difference between the "rich" and the "super-rich" is growing fast.

Vivid Quick Trick No. 3: Hear a *List* = Draw a *Map*

As we recall from quick trick number 1, when we hear a name we draw a portrait, and when we hear two names we draw two portraits. But what do we draw when the names keep on coming—how do we find the form of everyone in the Old Testament, for example, or—equally confusing—everyone on late-night TV?

The answer is we don't. When we hear four, five, six names or more, it should dawn on our fox and our hummingbird that this idea isn't about the differences between all the players but about the *relationships* between them. And as we further recall from the Grammar Graph, when we want to find the form of the relationships between multiple nouns (people, places, or things), we draw a map.

Which gives us quick trick 3: If we hear a *list* of names, objects, or concepts, we draw a map.

③ Hear a list → draw a map

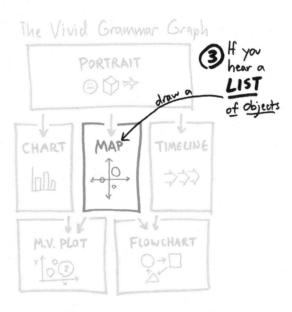

Here's an example. In mid-2010, two of the leading late-night comedians on American television switched time slots. In a simple move executed so seamlessly that few viewers even noticed, Conan O'Brien and Jay Leno changed showtimes.

Well, not exactly.

In his book *The War for Late Night,* Bill Carter tries to explain:

> Robert Morton had been David Letterman's producer at both NBC and CBS, from 1982 to 1996. He retained many friends in the late-night world, but none closer than Jeff Ross, Conan O'Brien's producer. The two men shared the shorthand of warriors who had

been in the trenches. Morty, with Letterman, had experienced the tumultuous ride from 12:35 to 11:35. Now, as 2009 was drawing to a close, his good buddy Jeff was in the middle of the same bumpy transition with Conan; naturally they had much to talk about.

Oops, my Blah-Blahmeter is twitching: Too many names are coming at me too fast. In one paragraph, Carter has introduced more characters than I can keep track of. My fox has to reread this just to figure out who is talking with whom. Hummingbird—you there? Better start with a map of the names we've heard so far: Robert Morton, David Letterman, Jeff Ross, Conan O'Brien, and Morty.

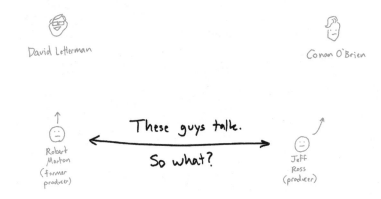

My map shows the relationship of the five names introduced so far: Letterman, his former producer Morton ("Morty"), Conan, and his producer Jeff. ▶

Okay: I see who is who so far. But that's just the first paragraph. Carter continues:

It had been only six months since Conan assumed the host chair at The Tonight Show, *the culmination of a five-year wait that began when NBC unexpectedly invoked term limits on Jay Leno in 2004, ordering an end to his long run at* Tonight *to make room for Conan, then following Jay on* Late Night . . . *NBC, fearing the financial consequences of Jay's likely move to ABC, came up with an alternative at the last minute: relocating Leno into prime time.*

Hold on—let me see if I got this: Conan got his *Tonight Show* on NBC from Jay, yet Jay has to make room for Conan or else move to ABC? Now my fox (no pun intended) is really losing it: This expanding cast of characters overlaps various networks, shows, and time periods. Before I get much further, I'm going to need a playbook.* I'd better read ahead† and add all the names to my map.

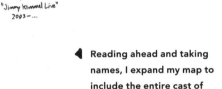

Reading ahead and taking names, I expand my map to include the entire cast of Carter's unfolding late-night drama.

---

* Wouldn't it be great if we could convert the disparaging comment "His idea is so convoluted we need a playbook to understand it!" into the compliment "He knew that what he wanted to explain was so convoluted that he gave us a playbook to follow along!"

† At this point there is no way I can follow the action without a list of the players—so I stop reading for meaning and skim ahead just to take down the names of this expanding Shakespearian drama. Creating a cast list (more on this later) is the best way to get ahead of the blah-blah-blah that comes with a long list of names.

Now I've got it: From Johnny Carson (the patron saint of late night) to CEO Jeff Zucker and his staff, all the characters are nailed down. The next step is to align them according to network and role. Reading ahead again, I note each character's various affiliations and time periods. When I superimpose those coordinates, I get a complete map of the underlying relationships that make up this story.

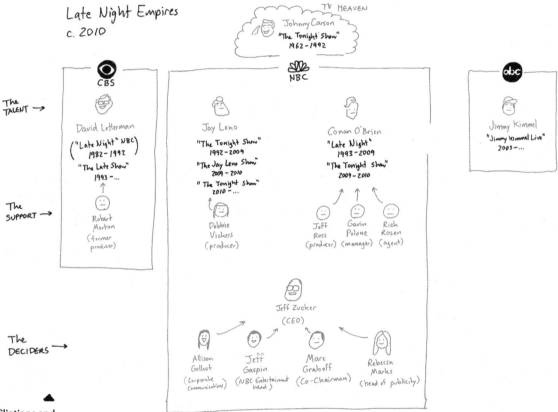

With network affiliations and time periods superimposed, my map shows the underlying relationships that make this an epic TV drama worth reading.

With this map in hand, I can now go back and enjoy the tears, broken hearts, and tragicomedy that make this an epic TV drama worth reading. Knowing that I can keep track of who is stabbing whom in the back has more than just entertainment value; it means that I can finally find the *form* of Carter's essential idea. Which is this: The "deciders" at NBC felt compelled to make Conan an offer he couldn't refuse. Because it was an offer that Conan believed would ruin his reverence for the iconic legacy of *The Tonight Show,* he did refuse. Rather than fight and destroy his dream, Conan left to start another show on another network, TBS.

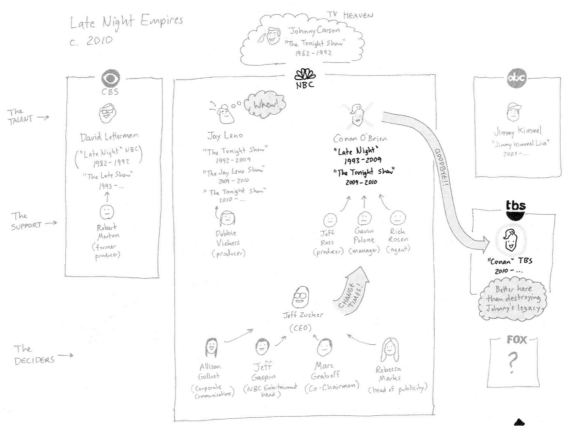

Late Night Empires c. 2010

TV HEAVEN

Johnny Carson "The Tonight Show" 1962 – 1992

CBS

The TALENT →

David Letterman ("Late Night" NBC) 1982 – 1992 "The Late Show" 1993 – ...

The SUPPORT →

Robert Morton (former producer)

NBC

Whew!

Jay Leno "The Tonight Show" 1992 – 2009 "The Jay Leno Show" 2009 – 2010 "The Tonight Show" 2010 – ...

Debbie Vickers (producer)

Conan O'Brien "Late Night" 1993 – 2009 "The Tonight Show" 2009 – 2010

GOODBYE!!

Jeff Ross (producer)   Gavin Polone (manager)   Rich Rosen (agent)

CHANGE TIMES!!

Jeff Zucker (CEO)

The DECIDERS →

Allison Gollust (Corporate communications)   Jeff Gaspin (NBC Entertainment head)   Marc Graboff (Co-Chairman)   Rebecca Marks (head of publicity)

abc

Jimmy Kimmel "Jimmy Kimmel Live" 2003 – ...

tbs

"Conan" TBS 2010 – ...

Better here than destroying Johnny's legacy

FOX

?

Vivid Quick Trick No. 4: Hear a *Story* = Draw a *Timeline*

A history is also a list, but instead of a list of names, it is a list of events. The point of history is to identify the things that happened in order to learn from them. If we can discern the form of the events and the patterns between them, we hope that we might repeat the good ones and avoid repeating the bad ones. To make that possible, the first thing any

▲

With my final map in hand, I can see the form of Carter's idea: Conan believed he had to leave NBC for TBS. Given the deal NBC offered him, it was the only way to not destroy his reverence for the iconic *Tonight Show.*

history must do is show us the events *in order*. Therefore, if we hear a story, we find the form by drawing a timeline.

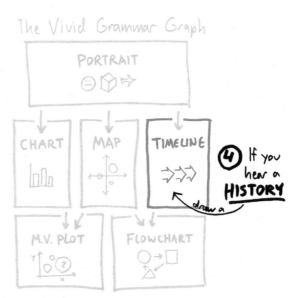

In 2008, the world economy came near to a complete shutdown. As wealth disappeared overnight, people the world around demanded to know what had happened—both to stop the financial hemorrhaging before the planet bled to death and to make sure it never happened again.

In his highly praised 2008 book *The Ascent of Money*, economic historian Niall Ferguson set out amid that chaos to make sense of the financial history of the world. Ferguson believes that the meltdown had more to do with history than anything else—or, rather, the lack of history. He states in his introduction, "I believe that today's crisis is in some measure to be explained by the ignorance of financial history—and not only among ordinary people. The 'masters of the universe' also paid far too little heed to the past, preferring to pin their hopes on elaborate mathematical models that proved to be false gods."

Describing the history of money as the ongoing process of creating wealth where before there was none, Ferguson lays out a set of six clearly defined historic steps that gave rise to today's integrated global economy: the rise of credit, the creation of banks to support that credit, the creation of bonds to extend that credit to nations, stocks to extend credit to business, insurance to extend credit to groups, and real estate to extend credit to individuals.

These six steps take us from an ancient time when money equaled metal (and wealth was limited to the few who possessed copper, silver, and gold) to our modern times, when money equals trust (and wealth is available to anyone who proves they can pay it back). "Credit," the world-changing invention at the heart of this monumental shift, is the critical mechanism in the spreading of wealth in ever-larger circles.

Yet clear as this model is (there is no question that *The Ascent of Money* is well written; even in the most detailed chapters, my Blah-Blahmeter barely twitched), it is not vivid. Although our fox is kept happy as Ferguson spells out and refers frequently back to his six steps, there is nothing for our hummingbird to see. Our ability to grasp the importance of what Ferguson has discovered is left to only half our mind.*

This is a shame, because in writing this enlightening history, Ferguson has already uncovered the essential form of his idea—and the visual aspect is right there, an idea ready to be seen. He just never drew it out.

Setting our own hummingbird to work, we will draw it for him. Recalling the six steps, we can easily create a timeline, an all-at-once picture that shows us the historic progression and lets our eyes dance across the entire idea in an instant. With this timeline, we

---

* This is typical of how history is taught: a verbally delivered linear progression of names, dates, and events, inherently limited to one-at-a-time presentation. Not only does this approach make it nearly impossible to detect parallel events; it makes the underlying form invisible. No wonder so few people find history engaging. It's not that the stories are boring—we just can't see how they connect.

don't have to remember exactly what Ferguson said three hundred pages back—all we have to do is look!

'CREDIT' is created.

In the beginning... Money = metal

Money exists w/out metal.

Banks → Bonds → Stocks → Insurance → Real Estate → Today... Money = Trust

Letting our hummingbird take a shot at Ferguson's six steps gives us a timeline we can see all at once. With this in hand, we don't have to remember every detail that came before as we learn more. We just look!

Of course, any history, no matter how important or well structured, is boring without the people who lived it and the adventures they had. Ferguson knows this better than most historians, and that's what makes his book so readable. In the banks section, we meet the Medicis, who funded the Renaissance by giving credit to kings. In the bonds section, we watch as the Rothschilds extend credit to nations and bet the world against Napoleon—and win. In the stocks section, we meet John Law, the first man to conceive of the market bubble. We don't want to lose these people; they are what makes the story come alive.

And now, with our timeline intact, we won't lose them; on the contrary, we now have a place to draw them in. (Remember "portraits"?)

The Vivid History of Money A visual interpretation of Niall Ferguson's "The Ascent of Money"

'CREDIT' is created.

In the beginning... Money = metal

Money exists w/out metal.

Banks → Bonds → Stocks → Insurance → Real Estate → Today... Money = Trust

Credit to KINGS — Medicis
Credit to NATIONS — Rothschilds
Credit to BUSINESS — John Law
Credit to GROUPS — Edward Lloyd
Credit to INDIVIDUALS — The New Deal

The form of money. Our hummingbird's visual take on Niall Ferguson's *The Ascent of Money*.

Putting it all together by combining his fox with our hummingbird—Ferguson's six steps, the stories he tells, the characters he introduces, and the timeline we drew—gives vivid form to his central idea: *Credit well managed is the creator of wealth; as credit extended from the few to the many, wealth spread around the world. Poverty doesn't come from nasty bankers stealing. It's just the opposite: Poverty comes from people's inability to access efficient (and trustworthy) financial institutions.*

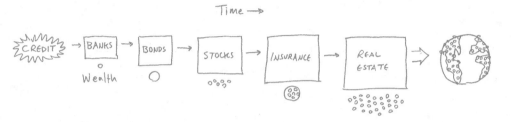

The real "Credit Line"...

CREDIT allows wealth to grow from the few to the many.

▶ The Vivid Idea: As credit has extended from the few to the many, wealth has spread around the world.

Vivid Quick Trick No. 5: Hear a Sequence = Draw a Flowchart

If we hear a cause-and-effect sequence, we draw a flowchart. Visually drawing out the interactions of the players in an event (or the components of a process) gives visceral form to the underlying causes and results.*

---

* Although initially similar to a history (which is a sequence of events), a flowchart shows more than a linear progression. Where a history can go in only one direction (and is easily misinterpreted to show causation), a flowchart can loop back on itself, run in many directions at the same time, and overtly show cause and effect. If we want to know "what steps took place," we create a history; if we want to know how one thing directly caused another and another, we create a flowchart.

"And when the two collided the whole thing exploded..."

⑤ Hear a sequence → draw a flowchart

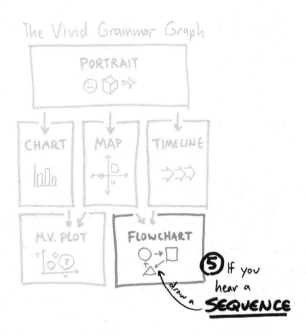

The Vivid Grammar Graph

PORTRAIT

CHART

MAP

TIMELINE

M.V. PLOT

FLOWCHART

⑤ If you hear a **SEQUENCE**

draw a

Any parent, teacher, or babysitter who has pried apart two battling children knows the universal lament "I hit him because he hit me"—and also knows the inevitable outcome of the process if it's left unchecked: more hitting, until everyone is in tears. The picture we draw to map out such a sequence does not need to be complex, but it still gives the sequence form: a spiraling loop with an unsurprising result.

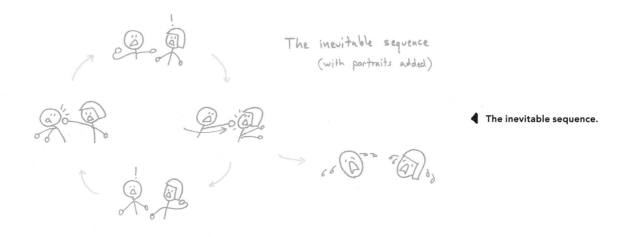

The inevitable sequence
(with portraits added)

◀ The inevitable sequence.

Even if we don't have time to draw the portraits (or believe we can't—remember the "words in a circle" fallback option discussed in Chapter 5?), we can still see the form of the sequence with a more basic flowchart.

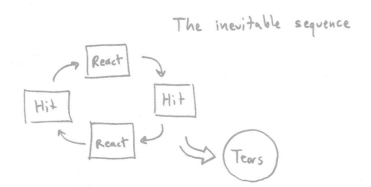

The inevitable sequence

◀ Even reduced to the most basic "words in a circle" picture, the flowchart shows clearly the essential form of the sequence.

Donella Meadows and her colleagues at the Massachusetts Institute of Technology had a more complex set of events they wanted to sequence: how our world works. In the early 1970s, many scientists and academics had begun to view the earth as a set of interlocking systems, from weather patterns to resource consumption to human dynamics. The result of this integrated approach to looking at the planet as a single big picture was given the name "systems dynamics," and Donella emerged as one of the new discipline's most insightful leaders.

In the early days of systems thinking, the entire approach was limited by the ways people talked about "systems." Since words were linear, they were fine for describing a simple A-B-C process but proved lacking when it came to describing the kinds of multi-dimensional relationships that occur when one process interacts with another. (Think of a cookbook: It can spell out perfectly well how to cook a chicken but fail miserably in explaining how to make a salad, potatoes, pie, and cocktails at the same time.) What was needed was a common way to look at any system by itself—and combine that system with any other.

Working with her husband, Dennis, and MIT colleague Jørgen Randers, Donella came up with something she called "the bathtub model" of systems dynamics. Her model said that we could look at any complex system as a "stock" (the bathtub) with an inflow (the spigot) and an outflow (the drain). The essential resources needed to fill the stock—water in the case of a bathtub, money in the case of a business, energy in the case of manufacturing—originate from some source, pass into the tub for some use, and eventually drain out into some dump (which, she was quick to point out, could well become another source for another tub).

Donella Meadows's "Bathtub" model of Systems Thinking

Donella Meadows's breakthrough model of systems thinking presents systems as a bathtub-like flowchart in which all inputs, outputs, and "stocks" are visually linked.

Some Source — Inflow — Stock — Outflow — Some Dump

* I added Donella, who did not appear in her original sketch.

This simple flowchart gave simple *form* to the incredibly complex concepts behind global systems dynamics and served as the breakthrough that brought systems thinking to the fore in environmental planning—and remains the foundation of today's emphasis on planned sustainability.

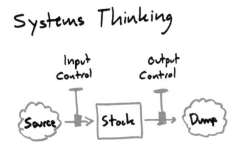

Systems Thinking

◀ The essential form of systems thinking: controlling what comes in and what goes out.

The simple form of that spigot-bathtub-drain flowchart was so powerful that once it was understood, it could be used as the basis for modeling almost any complex system. Indeed, Meadows and her team used the model for everything from sequencing resource consumption to the dynamics of global capital. In 1973, they used the bathtub approach to develop "World3," the first integrated computer simulation to model the impact of human activity on the planet. Reception to World3 was so positive that it prompted Meadows to write the book *The Limits of Growth,* which became one of the original calls to arms for today's environmental-sustainability movement.

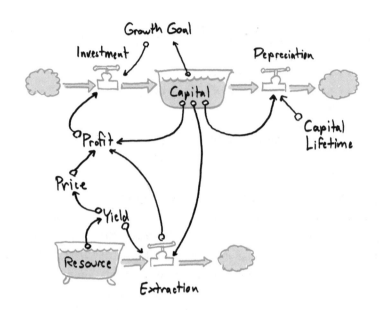

The Bathtub model applied to economic capital constrained by a nonrenewable resource

Growth Goal
Investment
Depreciation
Capital
Capital Lifetime
Profit
Price
Yield
Resource
Extraction

Once the basics of the bathtub model are understood, they can be used to give visible form to almost any complex system, such as the "Economic Capital Constrained by a Nonrenewable Resource" model shown here.

Vivid Quick Trick #6: Hear a Big Stew = Draw a *Multivariable Plot*

Our biggest information problem today is that we have too much of it. No matter what our daily work—calculating budgets, planning marketing campaigns, preparing presentations, designing software, studying new subjects—we rarely start with too little information. Invariably our first hurdle is figuring out what *not* to look at, an art that demands understanding the essential form of the incoming information.

When we're being overwhelmed with data and our verbal-visual triggers are all firing at the same time, our last-ditch hope is to create a single picture that shows everything and slows it down. So if we hear too many details bubbling up and it sounds like stew,

Vivid Grammar tells us that the picture we draw is a multivariable plot, which we'll shorthand here as an "MVP."

⑥ Hear a stew of details → draw a M.V. Plot

The MVP is the mother of all vivid pictures. By combining several distinct information variables on a common framework, an MVP reveals a more insightful picture than we would find by looking at the variables one by one. The purpose of the MVP is to give us a single pot in which to *try** to capture relationships that can't be accounted for with any of the previous "form" pictures.

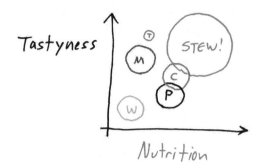

A multivariable plot is a ▶ picture that superimposes multiple types of information onto a common framework.

To see a couple MVPs in action, let's go big. We started this chapter watching ancient thinkers struggle to find the form of the earth. Let's close even bigger, watching other thinkers (some not so ancient) struggle to find the form of the entire *universe*. Along the way, we'll meet a couple influential MVPs.

The Universe

We'll start with something ▶ really big: the form of the universe.

In 300 B.C., the Greek mathematician Euclid postulated that the shape of the universe could be mapped out and measured through the geometry of triangles and intersecting planes. For all practical purposes, Euclid turned out to be right, and for well over

---

* Like a stew, cooking up a multivariable plot can be tricky. Since we're searching for a "form" that isn't immediately obvious, we can expect a lot of trial and error as we combine variables in new and unexpected ways.

two thousand years we've learned to do math and to build things using Euclidean geometry.

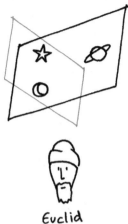

Euclid

◀ Two thousand years ago, Euclid showed that the universe could be mapped out and measured through the geometry of planes and triangles. For all practical purposes, he was right.

Then in 1644, the French philosopher René Descartes noted that if we add the labels *X* and *Y* to a flat Euclidean plane, we could mathematically describe the position and relationship of objects within it. For all practical purposes, Descartes was also right, and Cartesian coordinates provided the backbone for mapping out ideas from physics to algebra to philosophy to economics.

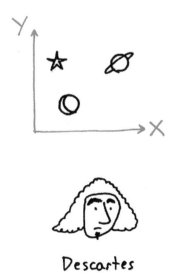

Descartes

◀ Descartes showed that by adding *X* and *Y* coordinates, we could map out pretty much anything.

Forty years later in 1684, Englishman scientist Isaac Newton showed that in our Cartesian universe, simple rules could be used to describe all motion—and indeed could be used to predict the outcome of physical events far in the future or far beyond the horizon. He was also right.

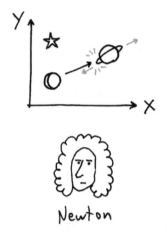

Newton showed us that in ▶ a Cartesian universe, the motion of objects could be understood perfectly, and therefore plotted and predicted with extraordinary foresight.

For the next 250 years, those three models pretty much summarized the physical state of the universe. The universe had a form that was Euclidean, coordinates that were Cartesian, and motion that was Newtonian. The universe was consistent, solid, and predictable. What a relief.

The Euclidean/Cartesian/ ▶ Newtonian physical universe was consistent, solid, and predictable.

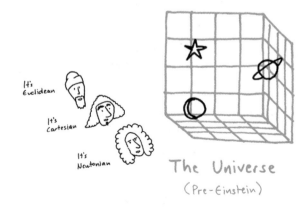

Then in 1905 along came "stupid" Einstein with his special theory of relativity—and messed it all up.

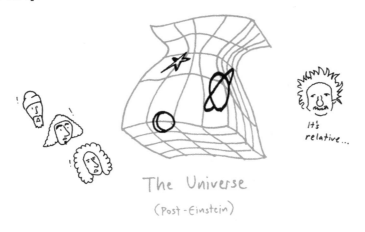

The Universe
(Post-Einstein)

It's relative...

◀ Einstein's theory of relativity shook up the whole universe.

Although Einstein's theory of relativity remains almost impossibly resistant to verbal description, we need look at only two MVPs to understand the essence of what Einstein saw.*

The first multivariable plot illustrates how the universe was believed to work in the centuries before Einstein. It does this by mapping together five variables: three physical objects (for our version I've chosen a hummingbird, a fox, and a ball), time (represented as seconds), and space (represented as distance, here measured in yards).

 FOX   HUMMINGBIRD   BALL   TIME in seconds   DISTANCE in yards

◀ Our five variables: physical objects (a hummingbird, a fox, and a ball), time (in seconds), and distance (in yards).

---

* For that we can thank Dr. Tatsu Takeuchi, assistant professor of physics at Virginia Tech and the author of the breakthrough physics book *An Illustrated Guide to Relativity*. Takeuchi calls his multivariable plots "time-space diagrams" and uses them to introduce nonphysics students to the mind-stretching realities of relativity. Dr. Takeuchi generously gave me permission to reproduce his drawings here, with some modifications.

To create this Newtonian MVP, we lay out distance as the horizontal axis and time as the vertical axis. Then we map in the fox, hummingbird, and ball at a common starting point of zero time and zero distance.

MVP 1: At time zero, the fox, ▶ hummingbird, and ball all share a common location and are not moving.

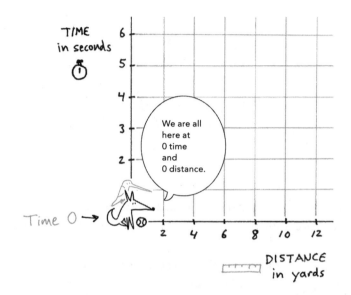

Let's now click a stopwatch, unleash our hummingbird, and throw the ball all at the same time—then wait ten seconds and see what happens.

After ten seconds, our fox hasn't moved an inch (perhaps he's still tired from running through the forest), our hummingbird has flown ten yards, and our ball has traveled twenty yards. We can easily show that in our MVP: we shift everything up on the time axis by ten seconds, shift the hummingbird ten yards to the right, and shift the ball over twenty yards.

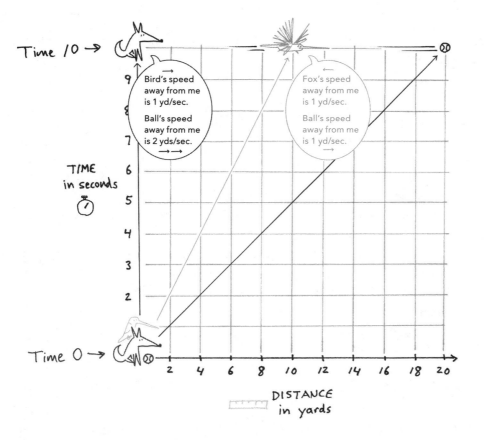

MVP 1 at ten seconds: Everything has moved up the time axis by ten seconds. Along the distance axis, the fox hasn't moved at all, the hummingbird has moved ten yards, and the ball has moved twenty.

This multivariable plot illustrates the predictably stable Newtonian universe. Although the fox and hummingbird have different perspectives on who has moved (the fox sees the hummingbird fly away, the hummingbird sees the fox drift back) they both agree on the speed: one yard per second. *But,* because they are moving at different speeds relative to the ball, they do *not* agree on the ball's speed. To the fox, the ball is moving away at two yards per second, but to the hummingbird, it is moving away at only one yard per second.

Who is correct? Both are—and we can see why: in a Newtonian universe, the fox and hummingbird are moving at different speeds, so of course they each perceive the ball's speed differently.

Now let's use a second multivariable plot to show the universe after relativity. To do that, we need to change just one variable: if we substitute *light* (in the form of a photon) for the ball, the entire universe changes.

Now we add light—and ▶
everything changes.

Einstein knew two funny things about light. First, light is the fastest thing in the universe. Second—and this is the part that troubled him—light's speed remains constant* to any observer, no matter how fast that observer is traveling. Let's use our second multivariable plot to show why that's a problem.

The second MVP starts like the first, but with a couple changes: first, we replace the ball with a photon of light. Second, because the photon is so fast, we'll keep the same time and distance axes but strip off the units. (The numbers get so big they're almost impossible to draw in.) As before, everything starts at time zero and distance zero.

Other than substituting a ▶
photon for the ball and
stripping away the units,
MVP 2 starts just like MVP 1.

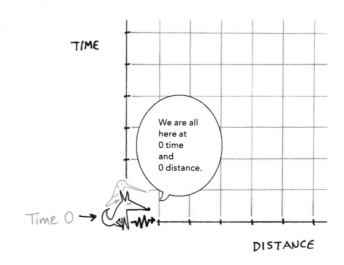

---

* The constancy of the speed of light is why it is given the symbol c in Einstein's famous equation $E = mc^2$. Energy = mass x the speed of light squared.

Just as before, we click a stopwatch, release the hummingbird (who now flies at half the speed of light), and throw the photon (at the speed of light). Then we wait ten seconds. As before, everything moves up the time axis, the hummingbird shifts to the right, and the photon shifts twice as far to the right. But something is wrong: even though the fox and the hummingbird are moving at different speeds, they both see light moving away at the same speed. How can that be?

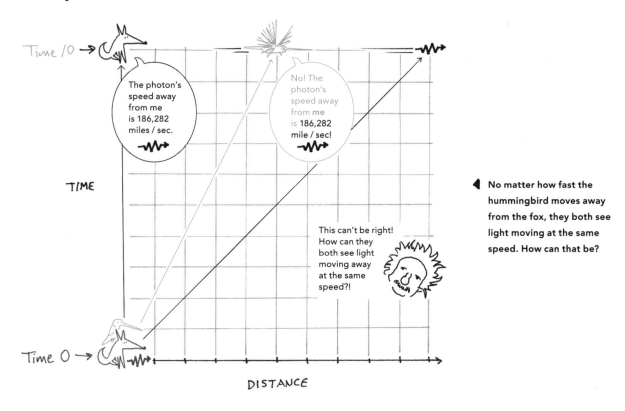

No matter how fast the hummingbird moves away from the fox, they both see light moving at the same speed. How can that be?

How can that be? Einstein had the answer: it can't. And that's where relativity comes into play: the answer, said Einstein, is that the universe tilts. The stationary fox's universe tilts just enough to keep the speed of light constant to him. To the faster hummingbird, however, the universe has to tilt more to keep the speed of light constant. For each observer, time and distance tilt differently. Other than the speed of light, there is nothing stable about the universe at all.

For any observer, no matter ▶ how fast they are going, time and distance tilt just enough so that the speed of light always remains constant.

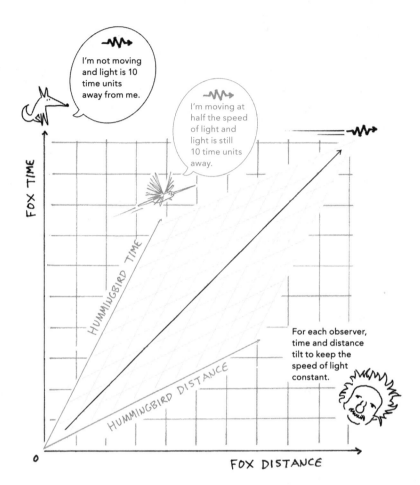

That's it for now. Of course that's just the tip of the relativity iceberg, but it's enough to see the essential form of relativity and how it bends the universe, which is all we need for now. As Einstein said, "All physical theories, their mathematical expressions notwithstanding, ought to lend themselves to so simple a description that even a child could understand them."

The Form Factor

In this one chapter, we just covered a huge range of big ideas: the shape of the earth, computer marketing, tax breaks, late-night TV, the history of money, system dynamics, and the theory of relativity. Because we did it vividly—*when we heard this, we drew that*—we did it without learning a thousand new facts and without having to memorize anything.

That's the power of finding the form of an idea.

CHAPTER 8

F · **O** · R · E · S · T

O Is for *Only the Essentials:* Vivid Ideas Fit in a Nutshell

 he next stop on our tour of the Vivid FOREST is O, which stands for "only the essentials."

Two years ago, I went to Washington to give a talk to the New Policy Committee of the United States Senate. After the talk, the director of

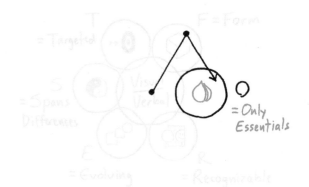

New Policy for the Democrats told me, "The reason the Republicans win on policy is because they always find a way to fit their message into a nutshell. The reason Democrats fail is because we feel compelled to include everything we can think of."

He was right. Vivid Ideas do fit in a nutshell. They have to: With all the things we need to think about to get through the day, there simply isn't space in our minds to let every idea run wild. Sure, with infinite patience, budget, and time, we could fix anything. But we wouldn't: With all that freedom, we would find too many other things to do.

In truth, it's the constraints we face every day that force us to be innovative and creative. If we want our idea to be vivid, our real task is to limit the size of our paper. That doesn't mean we have to edit every idea into a sound bite and jam every concept onto a napkin; *we only have to do that if we want anybody else to pay attention.* "Only the essentials" means we get someone's attention with the basics. Once they're intrigued, we can add all the details we need.

> ◀ "Only the essentials" means we get someone's attention with the basics. Once they're intrigued, we can add all the details we need.

No organization on earth is as focused on efficiency as the U.S. Navy. Everything the navy does, from training to fighting to eating, has to fit on a ship. While the navy's chessboard* is as big as the planet, most of the playing pieces are smaller than a city block. When a few thousand people live and work on such a floating village, efficiency is mandatory: There simply isn't room for anything unnecessary—including words.

I recently led a series of workshops for the navy, helping the Strategic Studies Group at the Naval War College look for ways to utilize simple pictures in strategic planning. The workshops were eye-opening for me, not only because I got to share words and pictures with a roomful of smart and accomplished people but because of what I learned from them: most memorably, how to "BLUF."

BLUF is the military's acronym for how to get your message heard: State the *bottom line up front*. Does an admiral in the midst of battle want to know every detail that every one of her officers knows? No: She needs the bottom line. Does the corpsman need to know every detail of a sailor's medical history to treat a bullet wound? No: He needs the bottom line. The way to get your message heard is to state the *bottom line up front*. This simple approach gets the essentials of the idea across first, leaving it to the recipient to decide whether he or she needs to know more.

BLUF = bottom line up front— ▶
how to get heard in the navy.

BLUF is a great presentation concept, but how do we apply it to our own ideas? After all, isn't stating the *bottom line up front* kind of like putting out a fire before it starts? How

---

* Literally: The floor of the Naval War College dining hall is alternating gray and white tiles. During World War II, some sailor thought the floor looked like the world's biggest chessboard, the ideal place to war-game. Thus it was, by moving model ships around on that cafeteria floor, that the admirals planned the U.S. Navy's World War II island-hopping campaign.

can we know the bottom line until we've been through it? That's precisely the point: We can't state the essentials of an idea until we've run through it ourselves.

Vivid Thinking as Distillation

Every idea starts with many parts—usually more than we can keep track of, and certainly more than anybody else wants to.* To ensure that we understand our own idea well enough to share it with someone else, we have to find a way to distill the idea to its simplest essence: *What is it really about, and why should anyone really care?*

"Idea distillation" is the process of finding the essence of our idea so that we can strip everything else away. It's how we remove everything that distracts from the essentials.

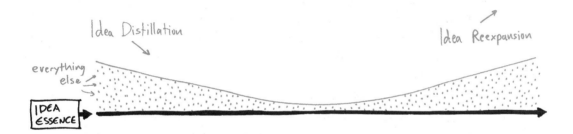

That's how we make BLUF happen: When we begin exploring an idea, we *must* think about and capture everything that comes to mind. At this early stage, we don't want to hold anything back. The thoughts should come fast and furious. But fast and furious is the last thing we want when it comes time to share.

That's where BLUF comes in: When it's time to present the idea, we offer only the essentials.

▲

"Idea distillation" is the process of finding the essence of our idea—so that we can strip everything else away.

---

* It's a sad fact of nature, but nobody will ever be as interested in our great new idea as we are—at least until we've hooked them on the essentials. It's safe to assume that any new idea we want to convey is going to demand a large initial investment of effort on our part as we make it inspiring or interesting for someone else. By limiting our idea to only the essentials, Vivid Thinking takes much of the risk out of that investment.

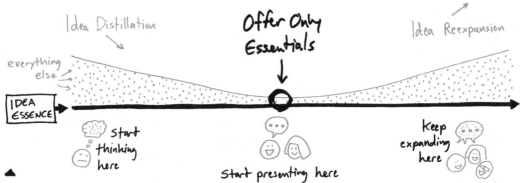

The secret of BLUF is to offer only the essentials at the first meeting. If the essentials are vivid, we'll buy time to expand later.

Details, counter-arguments, variations, possible points of failure, potential unintended consequences—all of these are critical aspects of any idea, but not in the first presentation. If the essentials of our idea are vivid, they will buy us enough time with our audience to get all the other issues heard. It's recognizing that we're looking at trees that matters in this part of the forest.

This is nothing new. The "elevator pitch," the "marketing spin," the "talking points"—they all say the same thing: If we want to quickly share our idea, we must strip away everything that's not essential. That's a great sentiment—except that elevator pitches, marketing spin, and talking points rarely work as well as we hope they will. Because none of them are vivid, they all have an ever-diminishing chance of cutting through.

That's because we've been taught to distill ideas through writing, editing, talking, listening, and note taking; in other words, relying entirely on our fox has become our only option. But our fox alone can't cut the blah-blah-blah anymore. From now on, we're going to have to draft our hummingbird as well. As we balance words with pictures, we're going to actively switch from writing to drawing (and then go back and forth) to force the essentials of our idea to the surface.

The Vivid Two-Step

Here's how "vivid distillation" works. Our fox writes down everything he can think of related to our idea. (So far, nothing unusual.) Hopefully, it's a long list—far too long to quickly summarize with carefully constructed sentences and linear thinking. So (and here's where the *vivid* part kicks in) we then send our hummingbird in to draw a picture visually summarizing what those words signify.

How? By using Vivid Grammar, the Grammar Graph, and the Six Vivid Quick Tricks. We've got the tools now to turn any word into a picture, and this is the time to use them. Our first picture may be a mess (no: it *will* be a mess), but at least we've engaged the part of our mind that sees the whole. Then we hand that picture back to the fox, who writes a description of what that picture shows—and so on. This sifting back and forth becomes the mechanism that distills our idea to its essentials.

Vivid thinking as the "Only Essentials" mechanism:

The handoff from verbal to visual...   again + again...   distills the idea's essence.

Now We Add a Twist . . .

Okay, so we've got this messy vivid process going, words reflecting pictures and vice versa. Our idea is becoming clearer—it might not look like it, but it is—yet at the same time, our paper* is becoming cloudier. What to do? Simple: We stop and reduce the size of our paper by half. And then we start over. What do we carry across? Only the essentials.

▲
Write, draw, write, draw—it doesn't take more than two or three handoffs before the essentials of our idea appear.

---

* Or notebook or whiteboard or collaborative workspace or napkin, etc.

Idea Distillation

Idea Reconstitution

Two or three reductions and we've got the ideal presentation: only the essentials, boiled down on a small sheet of paper. No need to worry about all the other ideas left behind—we haven't lost them; they're just taking the backseat for now. Let's make sure our audience "gets" the essentials first (and can explain them back to us*) before we start the expansion process again. Now when we get into the nuances, we'll have everyone's undivided attention—and if anyone gets lost as we reconstruct the full idea, we just refer back to the essentials to get back on track.

---

* It's been said many times before and is worth saying again: The best way to prove we know something is to be able to explain it to somebody else. If the idea has been distilled down to its essence, that should be a no-brainer.

Coffee Break

Let's take the essentials of coffee as an example. More specifically, let's look at the world of retail coffee sales—and the original specialty coffeehouse in particular. Although the green mermaid of Starbucks now rules the waves, the story of specialty coffee chains in America began back in 1966, when a well-traveled Dutchman opened his first coffeehouse in Berkeley, California. His name was Alfred Peet, and he would change the way the world drinks coffee.

The son of an Old World coffee roaster in Alkmaar, Holland, Alfred traveled the world as a tea buyer for Lipton before finally settling in San Francisco in the 1950s. Ten years later, dismayed at the poor quality of the coffee available in America, he decided to do something about it. Rekindling his father's contacts, Alfred began importing the high-altitude coffee beans of Costa Rica, Guatemala, and East Africa, beans that he knew made the most flavorful cup. With his special dark roast, Alfred's shop became a hit, and before long he had three stores dotted around San Francisco Bay.

That might have been the full extent of Alfred's coffee empire had not two of his biggest fans approached him with expansion plans. English teacher Jerry Baldwin and writer Gordon Bowker, neither of whom knew much about business but both of whom loved Peet's coffee, decided they wanted to open their own coffeehouse one day. Equally inspired by their dedication, Alfred spent hours teaching them the ropes. When their time came, in 1971, Baldwin and Bowker moved to Seattle, set up a commercial contract for coffee beans with Peet's, and opened their own store. They called it Starbucks.

Forty years later, Starbucks had more than sixteen thousand stores worldwide. Peet's had 193.

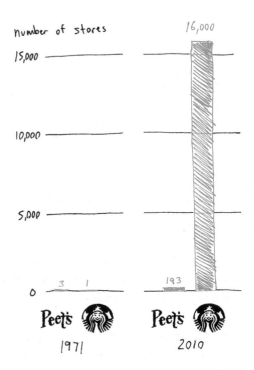

In 1971, the original Peet's ▶
had 3 stores and Starbucks
had 1. In 2010 it was 193 to
16,000.

Although Peet's was the original, Alfred was never interested in growth. His passion was making the best coffee conceivably possible. In that, he was an unquestioned success—his passion is shared today by loyal coffee drinkers everywhere.

But Peet's CEO Pat O'Dea knew that his company had to grow. In 2006, having already made the decision to expand and open new stores, O'Dea needed to solve the paradox of quality and growth. O'Dea recognized that Peet's greatest strength had always been uncompromising quality—something most coffee people considered possible only on a small scale. The challenge for O'Dea and company was how to have both: how to grow without undermining quality and how to find new customers (and make them happy) while keeping existing customers even happier. Now that is a trick.

Distilling the ROP

That year, O'Dea and his team embarked on the journey to quality-focused growth. Their goal: to find a way to open new stores and increase retail channels while improving quality along the way. In a way, it was as if Peet's had to find a way to change nearly everything—while changing virtually nothing. Peet's wasn't just on a business trip; it was on a philosophical journey.

The result was Peet's Retail Operating Philosophy. The ROP, two years of effort by dozens of people throughout the company, was never going to be easy to nail down. First, as the new model for the coffeehouse side of the business, the ROP had to actually *work*: It had to lay out a comprehensive, realistic, sustainable, and scalable vision for the bulk of the company. Second, because it served so many masters, the ROP had to open with *only the essentials*—yet still provide a structure for ready access to thousands of details.

The path to the ROP went like this. First, the leaders put their foxes to work, collecting all the ideas they could find and making lists that they could share.

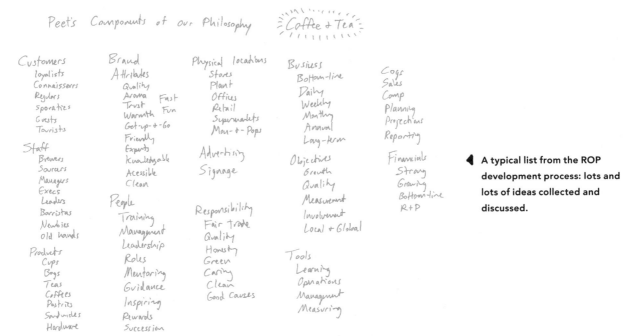

A typical list from the ROP development process: lots and lots of ideas collected and discussed.

Next, the lists were visually compiled into big pictures—not beautiful images, just basic hummingbird maps* that pulled ideas together into common clumps and noted the connections between them.

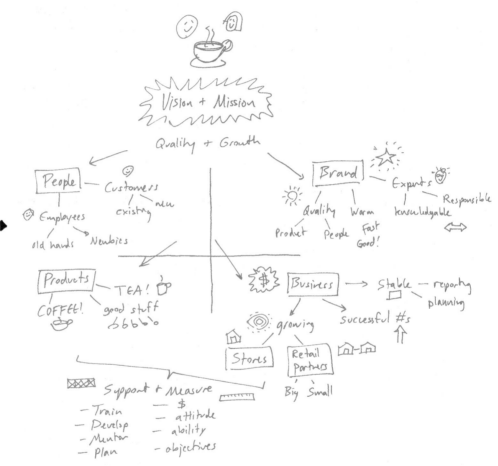

The same list after a go by the hummingbird. Commonalities, clumps, and connections become visible.

---

* Remember that a map—a visual display of the spatial relationships of many items—is the Vivid Grammar response to a list. The Peet's map here is just like the late-night-comedy map of the previous chapter, only this one shows the relationships of ideas rather than people. Same kind of map, though.

Then the fox went back to work. "How would I describe that picture?" he asked himself. And he would answer by saying something like:

*Our vision and mission are clear: quality sits above all else. To support that quality while growing, we might think about dividing our business into four primary areas of focus: people, products, brand, and business. And supporting all that from below is a set of common people and business development tools and measures.**

This process went on for many cycles as linear list met spatial map, each feeding the other with unexpected connections and each unearthing new insights. In the end, the essence of Peet's Retail Operating Philosophy fit on a napkin—an entirely appropriate presentation device for a company that serves hot beverages.

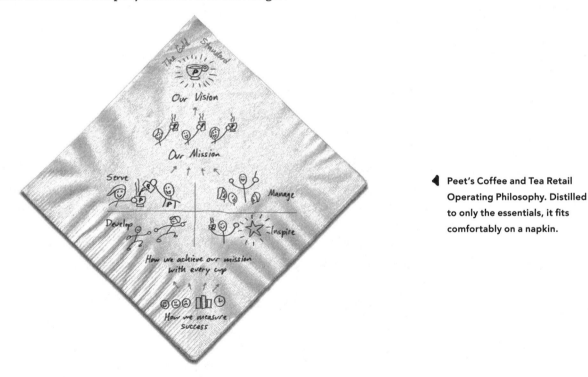

◀ **Peet's Coffee and Tea Retail Operating Philosophy. Distilled to only the essentials, it fits comfortably on a napkin.**

---

* Peet's leadership was kind enough to let me share their ROP process and results, although to protect their business interests I have changed certain aspects and details.

Remember the distillation curve? This essentials-only napkin becomes the midpoint presentation tool. People look at the napkin, they talk it through, and they get it. It's the vivid expression of the big idea.

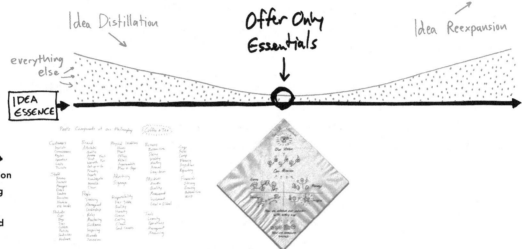

The napkin serves as the "essentials only" introduction to the new Retail Operating Philosophy, all the original ideas distilled into one vivid picture.

Reexpanding the ROP

But wait—there's more: After all, you can't run a company from a napkin. Clear as the essentials are, there remain hundreds of processes, manuals, and supporting materials to put together—not to mention thousands of people who need to use them. Now begins the reconstruction side of the curve. But now that we've found the essence of our idea, that's easy: All we have to do is restore the details. How? Call back in our fox: *Hey, fox— now that we've seen the essentials, would you mind adding your words to explain and expand on this napkin picture?*

Fox: "I'd be delighted. How about this . . ."

Our Vision:

To be the gold standard specialty coffee & tea brand available to the world, with one of the most dedicated and loyal customer followings of any brand.

Our Mission:

To enable and inspire customers to enjoy the daily pleasure of Peet's Coffee & Teas by providing a distinctive, superior product, superior coffee & tea knowledge, and superior service to every customer, every day.

Our Philosophy:

Serve

Clean & Well Organized	Unequaled Quality
Speed of Service	Customer Engagement

Manage

Labor Management	Cost of Goods Sold
Facilities & Inventory	Sales Monitoring

Develop

Unequaled Knowledge	Performance Management
Career Growth	Leadership Training

Inspire

Local Involvement	Global Outreach
Donations & Giving	Rewards & Recognition

Our Tools:

Learning Tools		to build unparalleled knowledge
Operations Tools		to help you run your store every day
Management Tools		to help you manage your business

Our Measures:

 Common Measurements & Standards

▲

The expanded napkin. We start the econstruction process by adding words slowly back in, explaining the essentials in more detail.

From there, we keep expanding, adding layer upon layer to the essentials until we see how they apply to each specific job, role, and task—re-creating whatever materials we need to get the whole message out to the people who need them.

Operations Tools

Shift Planner . . .   Master Task List . . .

Learning Tools

Training Binder . . .

Management Tools

Quarterly Store Plan . . .

The fully reexpanded idea: the essentials applied to all materials. ▶

Role-Based Learning . . .

Measurement Tools

Quarterly Store Assessment . . .

Role Descriptions . . .

And now we've come full circle: from too many ideas to only the essentials and back. Only this time, all the results have something in common: They are vivid.

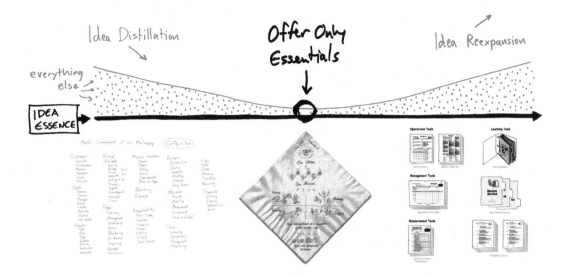

From too many ideas to "only the essence" and back. Only this time, the entire idea is vivid.

That's the lesson of "only the essentials": If we can boil our idea down to its essence, we can introduce it to others in the way they're most likely to accept—and remember.

CHAPTER 9

F · O · **R** · E · S · T

R Is for *Recognizable:* Vivid Ideas Look Familiar

 he third stop in our tour of the Vivid FOREST is *R*, which stands for "recognizable." Vivid Ideas look familiar. When we first hear a Vivid Idea, we don't think, "Wait a minute . . . *What?*" When we first see a Vivid Idea, we think, "Yeah, I know this: *I have seen this before.*"

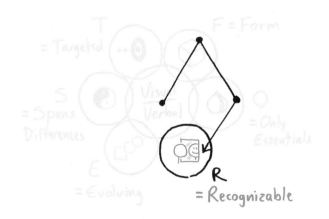

It has long been the domain of psychologists and cognitive scientists to understand how our minds make sense of the world. More recently they have been joined by neuro-biologists and behavioral economists who approach with a whole new set of tools. As all these thinkers start to compare notes, many of their answers boil down to a common rule: When faced with something new, we look for the familiar.

New things cause us stress. Since we don't recognize them, we don't know how to react to them. But once we recognize something familiar in something new, our brains can relax,* because experience tells us what to do. Vivid Ideas take advantage of this by making new and unexpected ideas recognizable.

When we can find the familiar in something new, our brains relax—and we can think better.

Our search for the familiar is a constant process. It's only by recognizing things around us that we are able to navigate the world at all.† For example, when we meet someone new, our mind immediately casts about trying to decide whom he or she looks like. For better or worse, our mind is seeking clues as to how to react based on our experiences with similar-looking people.

When we meet someone new, we immediately compare them with someone we already know.

---

* It doesn't matter whether our reaction to the familiar is positive or negative; either way, our mind takes some comfort in at least knowing what it is looking at.

† The dementias that affect our minds as we age have this trait in common: As our minds lose the ability to recognize (whether faces, places, images, or text), we gradually lose our ability to live.

The same holds true when we see a new machine: We assume it does the same things as a similar-looking old machine. While this assumption can either help us (familiarity with software standards helps us instantly use a new application) or mislead us (thinking that a horseless carriage is just a carriage without a horse can get us run over), the assumption has value in that it gives us a starting point to learn more.

When we see a new machine, ▶ we assume it is like one we already know.

And although we're constantly pulling words from the old to describe the new, our search for the familiar is only tangentially a verbal process. Yes, our fox jumps in, naming names and assigning terms, but his is often a fumbling attempt to define away the stress by nailing it down with familiar words.

The recognition process is actually more of an instant, all-at-once grab for a *visual* metaphor, our mind's attempt to literally answer the question "Where have I *seen* this before?" As much as our fox would love to take credit, recognizing the familiar in the unfamiliar is our hummingbird's domain—and that makes this chapter our hummingbird's favorite. So let's give our fox a break; it's our hummingbird's turn to show off.

This is our hummingbird's ▶ favorite chapter in the whole book—so our fox can take a break and enjoy the show.

Pyramid Power

Our visual mind's desire to see the familiar in the unfamiliar is so compelling that we find recognizable shapes and visual metaphors in new ideas even when the idea's creator never suggested them.*

Among the most frequently used visual metaphors in business and education is the pyramid. Because the image is so familiar and so laden with visual potential, we use the pyramid to describe everything from the sales cycle to project planning to financial management to test scores.

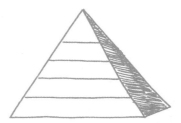

◀ Used in sales, management, project planning, finance, psychology, and education, the pyramid is among the most recognized of visual metaphors.

But nowhere is the pyramid more revered than in marketing, where its hierarchy has come to summarize human motivation—in particular psychologist Abraham Maslow's theories. Born in Brooklyn in 1908, Maslow spent fifty years studying the lives and habits of high-achieving people. The result of his research was a theory he called "The Hierarchy of Needs," a simple model describing the underlying reasons for why we humans do the things we do.

In Maslow's hierarchy, human needs fall into five layers: **physiological** needs on the bottom (breathing, food, water, sex, sleep), **safety** needs next (security, employment, money), **social** needs next (friendship, family, intimacy), followed by **esteem** needs (confidence, achievement, respect), and capped off by **self-actualization** needs (morality, creativity, acceptance of facts).

Based on his hierarchy, Maslow said that the essence of the human condition is a

---

* If we want our idea to be grasped by others in the way we hope, we're often better off providing the "I've seen this before" metaphor right away, rather than have them make up their own.

desire to fulfill our highest needs of self-actualization. However, Maslow also said that people can address their higher needs only when their lower needs are being met. It's easy to see why this model gained such resonance for marketers; Maslow's Hierarchy of Needs provides a clear model for understanding what motivates people to try (and buy) stuff.

But what Maslow did *not* say was that there was a pyramid involved.* In all his works, Maslow never mentioned the word *pyramid* and never drew one. Yet most any reference to Maslow today contains "Maslow's Pyramid." In countless discussions, presentations, and proposals, this immediately recognizable picture of a five-layer pyramid stands in for Maslow's written hierarchy.

The Hierarchy of Needs ▶ pyramid, the most common representation of Maslow's thinking (for pretty much everyone except Maslow).

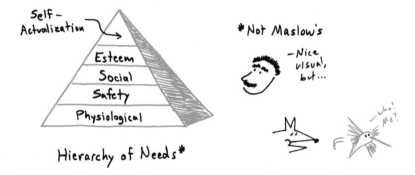

And that's the point: Maslow's greatest idea is essentially a list—and as we know, when we want to make a list vivid, we should draw a map. The map that always gets drawn when someone hears Maslow's list is the familiar, memorable, and understandable pyramid. We will never know whom to thank for drawing the first Maslow pyramid, but it wasn't Maslow.†

---

* There is no mention of "pyramid" (and no drawings at all) in Maslow's defining work *Motivation and Personality,* in which he detailed the Hierarchy of Needs. My search through all his works currently available came up with *no* results for the word *pyramid* and not a single drawing of a pyramid.

† Maslow was a master of coming up with ideas that others made vivid. He is also credited with inventing the Law of the Instrument, otherwise known as the "if I have a hammer, everything looks like a nail" rule. It appears in his last book, *The Psychology of Science: A Reconnaissance,* published in 1970. Where "his" pyramid became the patron icon of marketing strategy, his hammer became the patron icon of technology sales.

Oceans of Opportunity

Recognition—an idea's ability to catch our eye and say, *"Yes, I am new and different—but don't worry, you have seen me before"*—is often the single critical distinction between an idea that rises to the top and a similar idea that remains unnoticed. Nowhere is this more visible than in the business of business books.

Every year, about eleven thousand new business books hit the U.S. market. (To make that number vivid, consider that your average chain bookstore displays about twenty thousand titles on its shelves. Half your favorite bookstore filled with nothing but this year's business books? Yikes.) Of those eleven thousand business books, most will sell fewer than a thousand copies; a few thousand will sell ten thousand copies; a couple hundred "publishing successes" will sell 100,000 copies; and a dozen "blockbusters" will sell a million.

Put another way:

Business Books Sold per Year

sold
— 1 Million
— 100,000
— 10,000
— 1,000

11,000 new business titles

◀ Eleven thousand new business books appear every year. About a dozen of those will sell more than one million copies.

Countless factors contribute to the success of the few. But what's remarkable is how many of those few have titles that are *visually* recognizable.

In 1997, two professors teaching at the INSEAD management school, outside Paris, published an article on business strategy in the *Harvard Business Review*. In the academic language of the business press, authors W. Chan Kim and Renée Mauborgne titled their article "Value Innovation: The Strategic Logic of High Growth." For readers of the *HBR*, that back-to-back lineup of five business terms (*value + innovation + strategy + logic + growth**) meant something meaty, and the article was well received.

The Harvard Business School Press was pleased and suggested that its authors might have a successful book on their hands. For the next seven years, Kim and Mauborgne refined their value-innovation concept, testing it in more than 150 company case studies. When done, they had a book that they believed would sell well to the *HBR* audience.

The authors could have stayed with their original title and, given their stellar academic reputations and the rigor of their research, would probably have achieved publishing success. But Kim and Mauborgne so believed in their concept that they hoped for a blockbuster. They suspected that a more viscerally compelling title than *Value Innovation* might help.

They chose the ocean as a metaphor for their vision. It was a risk. On the surface, an "ocean" has nothing to do with business. But the image is evocatively visual: an ocean is vast, deep, and mysterious—just like the untested markets Kim and Mauborgne explored. And the ocean has always been a symbol of freedom, endless opportunity, and adventure—all catnip to entrepreneurs (who by the way buy lots of books). When they combined this with the solid business term "strategy," a completely original yet perfectly recognizable idea emerged. *Blue Ocean Strategy* hit bookshelves in 2005.

---

* Powerful as these words are for people already steeped in business jargon, none of them are particularly vivid. Just ask a business professional to describe any of them—What is "value"? What makes "innovation" important? What does "strategy" really mean? You'll rarely get a memorable answer. It's not that these words are bad; they just come packaged with a lot of blah-blah-blah. We'd all be better off drawing a picture of them—exactly like Michael Porter did back in Chapter 3.

Business Books Sold per Year

sold

Blue Ocean Strategy

1 Million
100,000
10,000
1,000

11,000 new business titles

It hit like a tidal wave. Kim and Mauborgne's ocean instinct was right. Within weeks their book had achieved bestseller status on every major business book list. Six years after publication, *Blue Ocean Strategy* is still a top-selling business book, with more than two million copies sold in forty-two languages. (That's the most foreign editions of any book in HBSP history.)

There is no question that the authors had a wonderful idea that they researched well and described beautifully. But that's not what made *Blue Ocean Strategy* a blockbuster—after all, thousands of new books have wonderful ideas and good writing going for them. It was the book's title, original yet instantly recognizable, that knocked it off the charts.

To prove it, let's make this story even more vivid. (Since this is about big numbers, we'll add another chart.) Imagine that we wanted to buy *just one* book on business strategy this year. Let's say we went online to see what was available. If we looked up the word "strategy" in the business section of the largest online bookstore, we would find 27,413 titles—an impossible number from which to pick just one. If we looked up "value," we'd find 13,541 titles; "innovation" would give us 9,879. How to choose?

How about being more selective and searching for "value" and "innovation" (the two words in Kim and Mauborgne's original title)? That's better: only 664 books to choose from—but still a lot to slog through. Now imagine that just one of those had "blue ocean" and "strategy" in the title. It would stand out, certainly—and more important, it would trigger our recognition of something new yet familiar. I don't know about you, but I know which book I'm buying.

Number of business books with these <u>words</u> in title:

There are tens of thousands of books with "strategy," "value," and "innovation" in their titles. How many with "blue ocean" and "strategy?" One.

"BLUE OCEAN" + "STRATEGY"	1
"VALUE" + "INNOVATION"	664
"INNOVATION"	9,879
"VALUE"	13,541
"STRATEGY"	27,413

Source: Amazon.com "business and investing" category Feb. 2011

Judge a Book by Its Cover

Is this use of a visual metaphor as a recognizable label an anomaly among new ideas? Not at all. Look over the following page and see if you can find a pattern among the fifteen simple portraits.

Opposite are fifteen simple portraits. See if you can find what they all have in common.

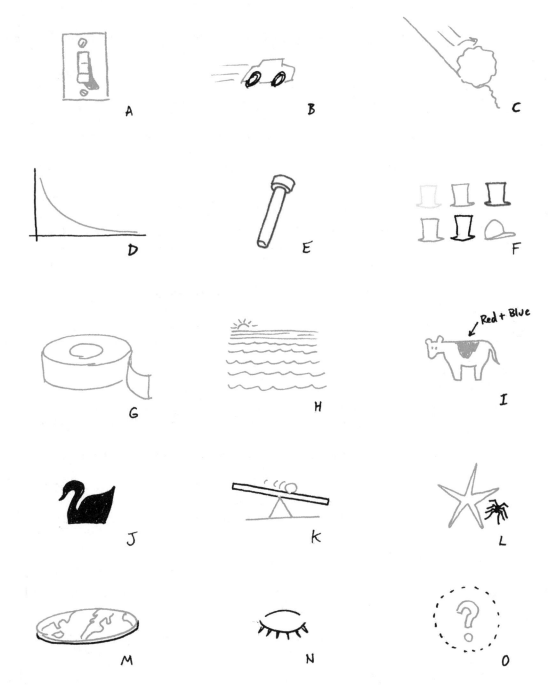

All fifteen are titles of recent blockbuster business books. From the list below, see if you can identify each.

☐	Blink	Malcolm Gladwell	2007
☐	Blue Ocean Strategy	W. Chan Kim and Renée Mauborgne	2005
☐	Drive	Daniel H. Pink	2010
☐	Linchpin	Seth Godin	2010
☐	Made to Stick	Chip and Dan Heath	2007
☐	Purple Cow	Seth Godin	2003
☐	Switch	Chip and Dan Heath	2010
☐	The Black Swan	Nassim Nicholas Taleb	2007
☐	The Long Tail	Chris Anderson	2008
☐	The Six Thinking Hats	Edward de Bono	1999
☐	The Snowball	Alice Schroeder	2009
☐	The Starfish and the Spider	Ori Brafman and Rod A. Beckstrom	2008
☐	The Tipping Point	Malcolm Gladwell	2002
☐	The World Is Flat	Thomas L. Friedman	2007
☐	Your Vivid Idea*	You	?

---

* Why not? You've got an idea and can draw a portrait of it, right? You're already halfway there.

The Difference "Recognizable" Makes

All the books listed here have become influential well beyond the traditional "business" market. (In several cases, bookstores had to come up with new categories just to find a place to put these books.) Notice also that certain authors appear more than once. What do the Heath brothers, Seth Godin, and Malcolm Gladwell know that hundreds of thousands of other idea creators don't? Among (many) other things, they know the power of expressing an original idea through a recognizable visual metaphor.

Visual Metaphors from Nature

Where can we find these visual metaphors? Our hummingbird has a simple answer for that one:

We spend our lives learning to recognize the world around us; where better to look for the essence of our own ideas? Here is a set of recognizable visual metaphors drawn from the natural world, terms we apply to them, and examples of recent ideas they might reflect. (This is our hummingbird's chapter, so let's not say much else. For now, let's roll with her.)

Things we Recognize from nature...

Calm

Ocean, sea.
A new day.
Opportunity.
Potential.

Overwhelm

Tida wave.
Unprepared.
The internet.
Love.

Inspire

Peak.
Ascent.
The guru.
Health care (for some).

Terrify

Tornado.
Chaos.
Anger.
Health care (for others).

Grow

Tree, roots, branches.
Family.
Network.
Facebook.

Shrink

Nut.
Compact.
Hardened.
Politician.

Flow

River, stream.
Fluid.
Ever changing.
Time.

Freeze

Ice.
Cold.
Prone to melt.
North Korea.

Distribute

Leaf, veins.
Transport.
Health.
FedEx.

Constrain

Aphids, disease.
Cancer.
Destruction.
SARS.

Know

Elephant.
Memory, longevity.
Threatened.
Culture.

Ignore

Ostrich.
Gangly.
Willfully unaware.
Wall Street.

Feed

Big fish, little fish.
Cycle of life.
Capitalism.
Microsoft/Yahoo.

Survive

Turtle, shell.
Defense.
Protectionism.
Missile shield.

Work

Beaver.
Industrious.
Endless.
Taxes.

Serene

Swan.
Aloof.
Furious below the surface.
Google.

Visual Metaphors from the World We Make

Things we Recognize from the World we _make_...

Connect

Bridge.
Bring together.
Cross.
Cisco.

Protect

Wall, barrier.
Keep apart.
Limit.
Immigration.

Climb

Stairs.
Ascend. (Descend).
Trend.
Stock market.

Link

Chain.
Strength through numbers.
Weakest link.
The Beatles.

Leverage

Lever, fulcrum.
Influence.
Move the world.
Social marketing.

Expand

Drip.
Ration, allocate.
Influence.
Apple.

Pop

Bubble.
Flexibility.
Surprise.
Housing market.

Distribute

Org chart, family tree.
Patriarchy.
Influence.
Democracy.

If nature doesn't give us what we want or throws a challenge in our way, in the real world we build something to compensate. The same goes for visual metaphors: If we don't see our idea in the natural world, we look for inspiration in the world we create. Here is a series of portraits drawn from our built world.

Balance

Scales.
Yin-Yang.
Tradeoffs.
Red & blue states.

Direct

Compass.
Unseen forces.
Course.
GPS.

Filter

Funnel.
Selection.
Delineate.
Standardized tests.

Move

Boat, sail.
Travel, freedom.
Vulnerable.
NASA.

Fly

Balloon.
Vision.
What goes up . . .
Investors.

Detect

Radar.
Warning.
Stalking.
Customer tracking.

Hide

Mouse hole (& cheese).
Safety.
Temptation.
Financial services.

Measure

Compass, ruler.
Data, numbers.
Uncertain certainty.
Polls.

Heat

Flame, fire.
Energy.
Could get burned.
Nuclear power.

Complicate

Watch.
Mechanism.
The universe.
Economics.

Open

Door.
Willingness.
Potential.
United Nations.

Close

Cage.
Protection.
Trap.
Homeland Security.

When Worlds Collide

Sometimes visual metaphors from the natural world and the built world collide. What happens then?

We get an even better metaphor.

Sometimes visual metaphors ▶ from both worlds collide— making an even better metaphor.

Now What?

Wow, hummingbird, that was an awesome job. Who knew there were so many visual ways to make big ideas look so familiar? From now on, we should all be sure to look for the "recognizable" in every idea we see.

Wow hummingbird!
I had no idea...

— Thanks...

... need...
sugar water...

One last question, though: If the only things we can recognize are things we've already seen before, how does anything truly new ever come along?

Good question—and the answer is the next stop in our forest.

CHAPTER 10

F · O · R · **E** · S · T

E Is for *Evolving*: Vivid Ideas Are Complete—but Not Done

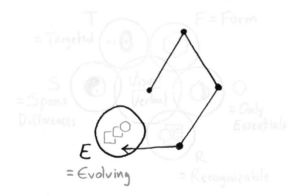

The fourth stop in our forest tour is *E*, for "evolving." Because thinking, leading, teaching, and selling are always fluid, Vivid Ideas are always works in progress. It is true that to be presentable an idea must be complete, but it is also true that for the idea to be adopted, it must also be open to change. "Evolving" reminds us that Vivid Ideas are always complete—but they are never done.

▶ Vivid Ideas are always complete, but they are never done.

The More Things Stay the Same . . .

In 1483, Leonardo da Vinci was thinking about ways people could escape from high castle towers in the event of fire or attack.* Rather than a ladder or a rope (both of which would always be limited in length), he designed the world's first parachute. The way Leonardo saw it, four large triangular sheets of linen sewn together over a wooden frame should do the trick. In the margin of his notebook he drew his concept and specifications:

▶ Leonardo's notebook-margin parachute design, 1483.

If a man is provided with a length of gummed linen cloth with a length of twelve yards on each side and twelve yards high, he can jump from any great height whatsoever without injury.

There it was: the first fully articulated concept of the parachute, complete with description, shape, materials, and dimensions. It wasn't *done,* of course—no one could

---

* Leonardo lived in a time of near-constant civil war in his native Italy and was frequently tasked with designing offensive and defensive weaponry.

be found who was crazy enough to jump from a tower to test it*—but the idea of the parachute was born.

Had nobody ever thought about escaping from a burning tower again, Leonardo's sketch might have been the end of the parachute. But others did think about it, and by adding bits here and changing the materials there, the *idea* of the parachute evolved. It took exactly three hundred more years before anyone became confident enough in the idea to actually jump with one (and live to tell about it). On December 26, 1783, Frenchman Louis-Sébastien Lenormand successfully leaped and landed from the tower of the Montpellier observatory. A working parachute was finally complete. But the parachute still wasn't *done*.

◀ Lenormand's first successful parachute jump took place in 1783, exactly three hundred years after Leonardo's drawing.

In the years since, the parachute has evolved through hundreds of steps. While the dimensions, materials, and details have changed, Leonardo's original idea has proven essentially correct: Jumping with a cloth held overhead can work. (You just need the right cloth.)

---

* It wasn't until 525 years later that anybody jumped using Leonardo's actual design and rode it all the way down. On April 26, 2008, Swiss parachutist Olivier Vietti-Teppa was the first to succeed.

Five hundred years of parachute evolution. Leonardo's original idea was complete, but parachutes will never be "done."

Evolution

Leonardo
1438

Lenormand
1783

Baldwin
1887

Jalbert
1963

They're all crazy if you ask me...

The Vivid Evolution Waddle

We evolve an idea through a combination of breakthrough insight and incremental improvement. In fact, the very process of evolving an idea itself requires two evolutionary steps. The first evolutionary step is *inward*: To make sure our idea is durable enough to become vivid, we must *ourselves* push it right up to within a hair's breadth of completion. The second evolutionary step is *outward*: To make sure other people embrace our idea, we must leave it unfinished enough that they can add their own insights.

First we evolve our idea ▶ inward; then we evolve it outward.

1st step:
Evolve idea **inward**.

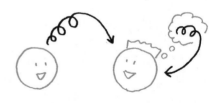

2nd step:
Evolve idea... **outward**.

228 | Blah Blah Blah

Example One: How *Not* to Salt Popcorn

Let's say that I wanted to convince you that salted popcorn is better than unsalted. I could just pour salt on your popcorn and tell you to eat it. You might eat it, and you might even prefer it to unsalted, but you would never forget that salted popcorn was forced upon you. Even as you ate salted popcorn years later, you'd still have that bitter taste in your mouth.

If I try to convince you without your input, I won't convince you.

Example Two: How to *Evolve* Salted Popcorn

Let's try another way. This time I'm going to "evolve" my salted popcorn idea in two steps. First, the inward step: I'm going to try by myself (remember, this step doesn't yet include you) various levels of salt. I'll start with too much, then too little, continually adjusting the quantity until I find what I believe to be the optimal salt-to-popcorn ratio. *No salt = bad. That much salt = bad. This much salt = perfect.* Now I know my salted popcorn idea is well evolved.

First step: I incrementally evolve my idea until I think it's just about right.

The second step is the outward one. (This is when I include you.) I get two bags of unsalted popcorn and give one to you. I make a big production out of salting mine just right, then I put the salt shaker between us. As I enthusiastically enjoy my popcorn, I comment on how much better it is with exactly two shakes of salt.

Evolutionarily, I've done all I can: I've optimized my idea, demonstrated the essentials, and given you all the elements you need: popcorn, salt, instructions, and motivation. The chances are great that you'll now discover the joys of salted popcorn for yourself. And even if you decide you don't like the salt, you'll know it's not because it was forced upon you.

Second step: I let you take the last evolutionary step yourself. Now it's as much your idea as mine. ▶

Inward/outward: My idea becomes your idea—and becomes even better. Salted popcorn aside, this is exactly where most PowerPoint presentations go wrong. When we polish our slides to a high finish, we leave our audience with nothing left to add. Since they can't evolve the idea in their own minds, they never fully engage.

The Essence of Evolution: As We Work on Our Idea, Our Idea Works on Us

As we evolve our idea—iterating, revising, reconsidering, trying options—we modify more than just the idea; we also modify our ability (and the ability of our audience) to think about it. Staying with an idea long enough to see it through to completion* creates

---

* Remember: "Complete" does not mean polished to perfection. There's a reason "unplugged" versions of songs are so popular: Because we hear them as evolving works in progress, we often believe in them more than the perfectly produced studio versions.

a bond between us and the idea that changes both: Our idea gets better, while we get better at thinking about it.

Edwin Land is probably the most famous inventor you've never heard of. Better known by the name of his once unbeatable company, Polaroid, Land acquired more patents in his lifetime than any other American besides Thomas Edison.

America's 2nd
greatest inventor

A Harvard dropout, Land invented polarized sunglasses, targeting devices for the military, the cameras used in America's spy planes, systems for understanding human color recognition, and the original instant camera—fifty years before anyone had ever conceived of digital photography.

Land was a master of both inward and outward evolution. According to those who worked with him, Land's greatest genius was in his ability to capture an idea in his mind's eye and work it ceaselessly until it was near perfect,* then hand it off to teams of assistants with just enough detail so that they could finish it. (This is the same thing people say today about Apple's Steve Jobs.)

Land's approach worked. The more things he invented, the better he got at inventing things. By the time he died, in 1991, Land had 444 patents to his name, for everything from sunglasses to satellite cameras.

---

* Land became so involved in his work that he had to be reminded to eat. While solving a problem involving polarization, Land once worked for eighteen days straight without stopping to even change his clothes. (Yeah, I know . . .)

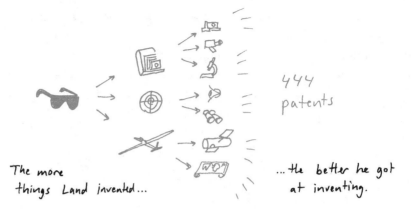

The more things Land invented, ▶ the better he got at inventing.

The more things Land invented...

444 patents

...the better he got at inventing.

Above all, Land understood two things: First, while truths don't change (people throughout history have sought ways to "take pictures" of each other and then share them), the mechanisms for achieving those truths change all the time (the "camera" will always evolve). Second, if you want an idea to stick, give the people who use it the last few steps to fill in for themselves. That was the genius of the Polaroid instant camera in the era before digital photography: You got to join in the last step of the process by watching the photo magically appear in your hand.

"Clara" and the Clear Idea

To see how Vivid Thinking helps us evolve an idea, let's do the popcorn exercise again, only this time with an entire organization.*

Imagine that you and I work for a growing social media company called Clara. "Clara" is an acronym that stands for *"Clean Living and Responsible Action."*† Our mission is to use social media tools to spread the word about responsible product purchasing. (Rather

---

* This case study is loosely based on a real company I worked with. Since the company is developing a game-changing social business model, I can't mention their name or actual strategy. Instead let's look at "Clara," a completely fictitious organization with some parallels.

† To the best of my knowledge, there is no "Clean Living and Responsible Action" Clara out there. If you do happen to run such an organization, please consider this a free marketing lesson.

than buying any old product, we all benefit by choosing a product that is better for us and better for the planet.)

Our founder chose the symbol of a tree as our logo because it represents nature, networks, and sustainable growth. Now it's up to you and me to convey our mission in a vivid way.

◀ Clara: Clean Living and Responsible Action. Our mission: Use social networking to help consumers make better purchasing decisions.

Let Your Fingers Do the Walking (Inward Evolution)

Evolving a Vivid Idea means stepping back and forth between words and pictures, actively guiding the idea's direction while simultaneously watching the unexpected unfold. Here's how we start: Hold up two fingers in the "V for victory" sign. The first finger means "words." The second finger means "pictures." This is our vivid evolution tool.

◀ Make a V with your fingers. One finger means "words," the other means "pictures." Put them together and V = "vivid."

Now point your hand downward, rest your two fingers on this book, and start walking.

Vivid
Evolution
words

Now let your fingers do the
walking. Words—pictures—
words—pictures: the perfect
path for an evolving idea.

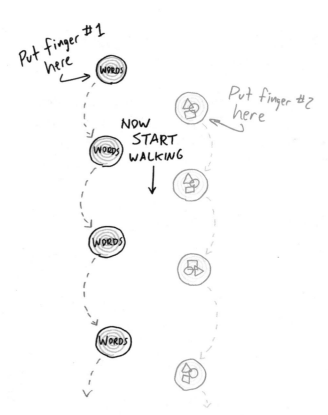

Put finger #1
here
WORDS

Put finger #2
here

NOW
START
WALKING

WORDS

WORDS

WORDS

Sure, it's an ungainly waddle, but this waddle means everything. When we write down an idea, we think about it one way. When we draw the same idea, we think about it another way. Shifting from one to the other forces both views to the surface; over time, a better view inevitably emerges.

Evolving Clara: From Mission Statement to Vivid Idea

(WORDS) Back at Clara, we start with the words—and thanks to our boss, they've already been given to us:

At Clara, we use social media tools to spread the word about responsible product purchasing.

(PICTURE) Next we draw a picture. That's also been given to us: a tree.

Okay: We've got some words and a picture of a tree. Where's the "evolution"? Let's keep V-walking to find out.

(WORDS) Our next word step is to use words to describe the tree:

A tree is a natural network, a collection of distinct components (bark, wood, branches, leaves, and seeds) all working together to create a single growing organism. A tree represents hope, stability, longevity, and growth. The tree is the perfect metaphor for our mission.

(PICTURE) And now let's create a simple portrait to describe that:

(WRDS) Let's tie the tree portrait back to social media:

Social media is like the tree because a single person is like a seed. Small but potentially powerful, that single person (with the right care and resources) becomes the starting point of an entire forest. With the technologies of today, Clara can help anyone become that seed.

(✎) Now let's draw a couple of parallel timelines to describe that comparison: seed versus person.

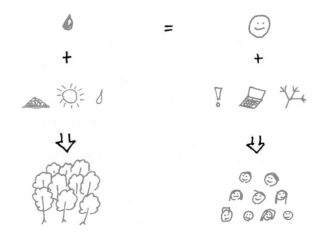

Putting them together  + we've now got a vivid mission statement:

Clara is your arborist: By providing you with fertile ground (a good idea with deep meaning and access to an established network), resources (social media tools, messaging concepts, a library of images), and the potential to grow (a limitless global audience), Clara helps you create your own forest of responsibility and opportunity.

The waddle has paid off. By stepping back and forth from words to pictures, we've used inward evolution to create a visceral, memorable, and clear vision for Clara. And that's not even the best part.

Connect the Dots (Outward Evolution)

We've come up with a vivid message for Clara—and, like our salted popcorn, we evolved it until we knew it was good. But also like our salted popcorn, our vivid message won't mean anything if it doesn't appeal to anyone else. Now it's time for the second evolutionary step: outward. We've done everything we can; now we've got to find a way to let everyone else see Clara's potential for themselves.

What could be better than providing a framework and the tools necessary for our audience to finish it for themselves?

Conceptually, we're all familiar with this idea. Back when we were kids, many of us loved connect-the-dots pictures. The most engaging pictures in our coloring books weren't the fanciest; they were the ones that we had to complete ourselves. Someone had laid out a sequence of dots and we connected them, revealing a hidden image.

The best part of connect the dots was our feeling of ownership of the picture—and we didn't even have to be any good at drawing.

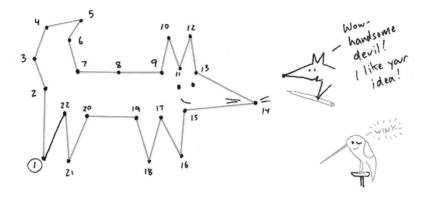

What might happen if we applied the same approach to engaging audiences with our Vivid Idea?

Game Theory

When Will Wright was young, he built lots of models: "ships, cars, planes—I loved to do that," he told an interviewer in 2006. When he got older, Wright's fascination with building models stayed with him, and he began to imagine what it might be like to use computers to create a living model of a city. No such city-building game existed, so Wright decided to create one. He called it *SimCity*.

Unlike most games at the time, *SimCity* gave the player tools to build things rather than destroy them. Although *SimCity* debuted quietly in 1989, the game's you-finish-it approach caught on, and it earned more than $230 million.

With that success behind him, Wright focused deeper into his simulated cities. Now he imagined what it might be like to let players create a single home and then manage the lives of people who lived in it. This time his you-finish-it approach caught fire. *The Sims* was released in 2000 and went on to become the best-selling game in PC history.

Game Boss
Will Wright

Twice emboldened, Wright began work on the game he'd dreamed of since he was a kid. *Spore* gave the player the tools not just to create a city or a house but to create life. Although the game reflected many of Wright's favorite concepts—the evolution of organisms, life on other planets, interstellar travel—his greatest design insight was that the game would be best if he left it up to the players to create most of it by themselves. Because he gave players an underlying game framework and several simple creation tools, Wright didn't need to finish it; the players would.

Spore launched in September 2008. Within six months, players would upload more than ninety million pieces of user-created content. Once again, Wright was right: When people have the ability to finish a nearly complete idea themselves, the success of the idea not only is more likely—it often becomes inevitable.

Connecting the Dots with Clara

When last we left Clara, we had inwardly evolved our idea until we had a vivid verbal + visual mission statement. Now let's engage a potential Clara member by letting her connect the dots as we introduce the concept step by step—in six steps.

Step 1: First we expand our mission statement picture into an almost fully evolved map. We do this by adding necessary details—and, more important, by removing any specific references to our member. (These she will fill in herself.) Thus we begin our introduction with a map outlining the essential framework of our idea—and a blank circle where we invite our potential member to imagine herself. We give this incomplete map to the potential member.* *(Go ahead—draw yourself in!)*

My clara network

> ◀ Outward evolution Step 1: We almost complete the tree picture—then remove audience-specific references.

Step 2: Now we explain that the purpose of Clara is to help the members connect the right products to the right people. We let the potential viewer select from a range of sample products, draw them in, and connect the dots back to herself.

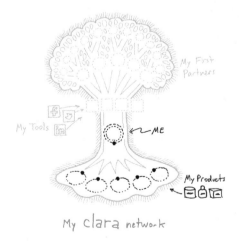

My clara network

> ◀ Step 2: We invite the viewer to select sample products and connect the dots back to herself.

---

* If this was a face-to-face meeting (unlikely for a social networking site, but you never know), we would simply hand our potential member a printout that she could fill in. Online, this would be a digital file she could print or electronically complete.

Step 3: We introduce the social networking tools that Clara uses to spread the word about products. We let the member select her preferred tools, draw them in, and connect those back to herself.

Step 3: The viewer selects her preferred social networking tools and connects herself to them. ▶

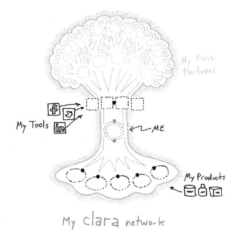

Step 4: Since the goal of Clara is to help our member to connect the right products to the right people, we invite her to draw in her own contacts and connect the entire tree from bottom to top.

Step 4: The member draws in her own contacts and connects the tree from bottom to top. ▶

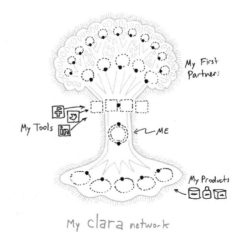

Step 5: Our potential member has now completed her own diagram of her own Clara network. Because she "evolved" it herself, Clara is now vivid in her mind. She not only understands the essence of Clara; she now sees exactly where she fits in it.

My clara network

Step 5: Because she "evolved" it herself, our potential member now has a vivid image of Clara.

But that's not the last step. As we know, Clara is all about social networking, using online tools to create an ever-expanding network. As a last picture, we show our potential member what happens to her network when her own contacts join: Her single "tree" becomes an entire "forest." When she connects those dots, the potential of Clara becomes . . . well, vividly clear.

My **clara** network
^
Growing

Enter Lady Gaga

One last thought on Edwin Land and Polaroid. Master of evolution though he was, not even Land could see the digital photo *revolution* coming. Long after Land's death and after years of struggling to counter digital technology, the Polaroid Company finally failed and declared bankruptcy in 2001.

But that's not the end of the Polaroid story. In 2010, a reborn Polaroid company announced that it was hiring pop sensation Lady Gaga as creative director. In a way, it's the perfect next step: The company founded by the man who invented dark sunglasses gets taken over by the woman who is (currently) most famous for wearing them.

The evolution continues.

America's 2nd greatest inventor

1948

1969

1972

1976

2001

2011

50 years of Polaroid evolution

CHAPTER 11

F · O · R · E · **S** · T

S Is for *Span Differences:* Vivid Ideas Include Their Opposite

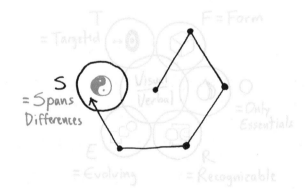

S o far, each stop in the forest has shown us how to make our idea more vivid. But what if our idea feels incomplete? How does a Vivid Idea account for options we haven't yet considered, variables that might undermine it, and the differing opinions of others?

Vivid Ideas address those opposing ideas by spanning outward to include them. The second-to-last stop is *S*, which stands for "span differences." This stop shows us that ideas become most vivid when they openly account for their own opposites, differences, and limitations.

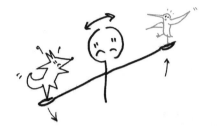

Ideas are most vivid when we span their differences. ▶

This isn't a new idea. F. Scott Fitzgerald, America's favorite Jazz Age author, wrote in *Esquire* magazine in 1936 that "the test of a first-rate intelligence is the ability to hold two opposed ideas in the mind at the same time, and still retain the ability to function."

Vivid Ideas do just that: They show us one idea more clearly by showing us the opposite. If the original idea is sound, illustrating its limitations doesn't undermine it—on the contrary, it makes the idea even stronger.

Yin and Yang

That was far from a new concept even back in the Jazz Age. It's just the restatement of an ancient idea, an idea dating back two thousand years to the oldest of classic Chinese texts, the *I Ching* and *Tao Te Ching*.* Among many other ideas, those texts described the essence of all things as yin and yang—two opposites that must fit together to make a single whole.

Originally represented as the sun passing over a valley, *yin* literally translated as "shady place" and described the cool area in the mountain's shadow, while *yang* translated as "sunny place" and described the warm valley below.

---

* *I Ching* translates approximately as "Book of Changes" and introduces the concept that a balance of simplicity, variability, and persistency underlie the universe. *Tao Te Ching* translates approximately as "The Classic Way of Virtue" and describes the necessary balance of yin (female) and yang (male) in all things.

陰 陽
Yin Yang

◀ In the original translation, *yin* meant "shade" and *yang* meant "sun."

Most famously represented by the *taijitu* symbol (or "the diagram of ultimate power"), yin and yang are simply the most vivid description of a truth we all know yet all too often forget: For any idea to be effective, it must include and compensate for its opposite.

Taijitu

(Diagram of Ultimate Power)

◀ Something old and something new: the *taijitu*, the most vivid description ever of the need to span differences.

While the *taijitu* is a wonderfully vivid representation of a concept that transcends time and culture, what does it have to do with creating Vivid Ideas today?

How to Make an Electric Car Go

Most problem solving today begins with the assumption that solutions are always a trade-off. In the auto industry, for example, for a hundred years it's been gospel that a car has to trade power for efficiency. You could either build a car with lots of power or you could build a car that got great gas mileage, but you could not accomplish both. Every car being made proved the point: A Hummer H1 could uproot a tree but drove only six miles on a gallon of gas, while a Smart car drove almost six times that far—but barely carried two people.

The traditional auto industry tradeoff of performance vs efficiency: A Hummer could uproot a tree but got terrible mileage; a SmartCar got incredible mileage but could barely carry two people. ▶

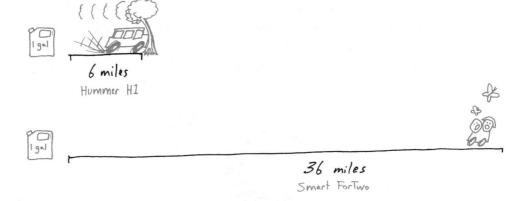

The Tesla Roadster bypasses the tradeoff completely: It has the power of a supercar while running nearly five times more efficiently than a SmartCar. ▶

Vivid Ideas start from a different assumption: Like our fox and hummingbird, a Vivid Idea straddles a balance. It doesn't begin with a tradeoff—it begins with a what-if.

◀ Vivid Ideas don't begin with a tradeoff—they begin with a what-if.

In 2000, two engineer friends with several successful technology start-ups behind them were looking for a new business to enter. They both liked cars but hated the tradeoff of power versus efficiency. So Martin Eberhard and Marc Tarpenning asked each other, "Why can't a car be both as powerful as an SUV and as efficient as a hybrid?" They knew the answer was found in the limitations of the internal combustion engine. Because that traditional engine burns gas to create energy (a relatively inefficient way to make something go), it was the original reason that all cars were designed around the Hummer-versus-Smart-car tradeoff.

Knowing that was a pretty silly answer, given the power and efficiency of modern electric engines, Eberhard and Tarpenning decided to start an electric-car company. While looking for the simplest electric engine designs to work with, Eberhard and Tarpenning came across the original plans for a powerful alternating-current electric motor created in 1882 by the eccentric Serbian-American scientist Nikola Tesla.

Eberhard and Tarpenning were so impressed by the possibilities of this 120-year-old design that they decided to name their company after the mad scientist who'd designed it, and Tesla Motors was born.

As of last year, Tesla had sold more than 1,500 pure-electric Roadsters, each with the performance of a supercar and fuel efficiency five times higher than even the Smart car. Because the Tesla was designed around performance *and* efficiency (not performance versus efficiency), the company has become a business success in a way no previous electric car ever had.

135 miles
Tesla Roadster

The Mad Scientists' Club

Well before Tesla (the man or the car), the central idea of modern chemistry was born when another scientist decided he didn't like tradeoffs either. The youngest of seventeen children* born to a rural Siberian family in the 1830s, Dmitri Mendeleyev became known for two things: his wild beard (which he trimmed only once a year) and his ability to see patterns that "normal" people could not. Mendeleyev was crazy, all right, but he was crazy like a fox—and a hummingbird.

World's Greatest Chemist

Dmitri Mendeleyev: crazy like a fox (and a hummingbird). ▶

Prior to Mendeleyev, scientists had listed the earth's chemical elements in two unrelated ways. The first list arranged the elements† according to their chemical properties: They were acidic or basic, gaseous or metal, etc. The second list arranged the elements by atomic weight, a complexly calculated number that compared each element's weight relative to a single gram of oxygen.

These two lists were useful for keeping track of elements in a rudimentary way.

---

* It might have been fourteen. Records in early-nineteenth-century Siberia weren't known for being the most accurate. Either way, his mom was a wonder. To make sure her youngest got the best education possible, she hitchhiked a thousand miles across nineteenth-century Siberia to get Dmitri to school on time in St. Petersburg.
† There were about fifty elements known at the time Mendeleyev began looking for patterns.

Using the first list, a chemist could see that hydrogen was a gas and aluminum was a metal, for example. Using the second, unrelated list, a scientist could see that a given number of aluminum atoms weighed more than the same number of hydrogen atoms—which was interesting to know if you were a chemist but didn't mean much to anybody else.

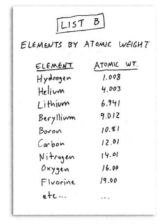

Prior to Mendeleyev, scientists sorted chemicals according to two unrelated lists. Mendeleyev did not like it.

These two *either/or* lists bothered Mendeleyev. Since both listed the same elements, he was convinced there must be a way to combine them. Copying both lists onto cards, he unleashed his hummingbird. According to legend, Mendeleyev occupied his hours of train rides across the endless Russian steppe by playing with his cards, sorting them this way and that, looking for patterns.

On long rail journies across Russia, Mendeleyev played with his chemical cards. ▶

Eventually he noticed that when he placed the elements in order horizontally according to their number of protons* and vertically according to their properties, a repeating pattern emerged.

In the end, he found several recurring patterns among all the elements. He called these "periods." ▶

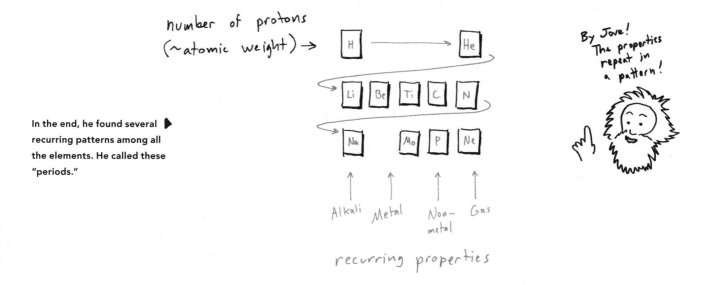

_____

* A simple single number that roughly approximated the unwieldy digits of atomic weight and was much easier to count.

He called these repeating patterns "periods" and mapped out the whole thing on a single sheet of paper, creating what became the world's greatest organizational chart: the periodic table of the elements.

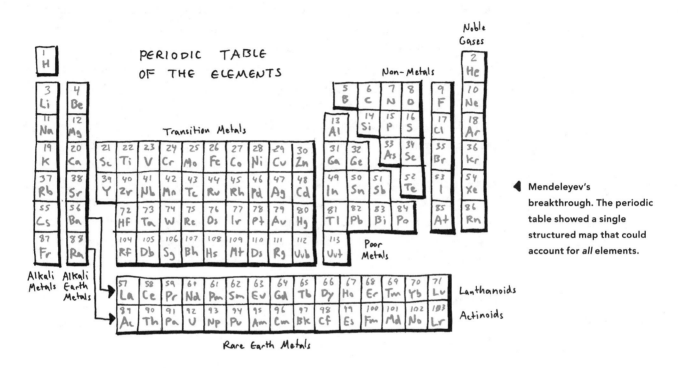

Mendeleyev's breakthrough. The periodic table showed a single structured map that could account for *all* elements.

World's Greatest Org Chart

By *not* making a tradeoff between element number and element property—but rather by intentionally searching for a way to combine them—Mendeleyev revealed the underlying pattern of all elements. The pattern had been there all along; it just took someone willing to *span differences* to find it.

Watching the Meltdown

We shouldn't be surprised by this "Hey, you got chocolate in my peanut butter!"* approach, but we always are. Throughout the economic meltdown of the past few years, the most frequent defense from the bankers and regulators who should have seen it coming was "Sorry, but the system got too big and complex. Nobody really knew what was going on."

According to Michael Lewis, in his 2010 book *The Big Short: Inside the Doomsday Machine,* that's not true. At least one person knew exactly what was going on: Michael Burry. Like Mendeleyev spanning differences in chemistry, Burry spanned differences in the finance industry and saw precisely what was coming. Burry was up-front with his investors and the big banks about what he saw. And while his investors made a lot of money from his insights, the big banks failed, taking much of the economy with them.

The differences that Burry spanned were two wildly divergent financial tools: "shorting" and mortgages. Traditionally, these two investment approaches have had nothing to do with each other. Shorting is how savvy investors bet against companies, the ultimate tool of the financial pessimist. Mortgages are how banks loan people money to buy a home, the ultimate tool of the eternal optimist. These two opposites were Burry's chocolate and peanut butter.

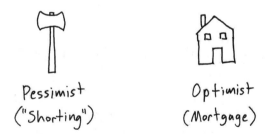

Pessimist
("Shorting")

Optimist
(Mortgage)

---

* In the 1970s, the Hershey Company famously advertised Reese's Peanut Butter Cups candy by having two people—one eating chocolate, the other eating peanut butter—bump into each other. The product slogan was "Two great tastes that taste great together."

To understand what Burry saw that the banks didn't requires only a couple of simple pictures. Not surprisingly, the words-only way the economic story usually gets told makes it appear deceptively complicated.* Vivid grammar can clear most of it up. Had the bankers drawn pictures of what they were doing, I suspect they could have avoided their biggest mistakes.

BURRY'S YIN: "SHORTING"

The first piece of Burry's *taijitu* was shorting. Shorting is a way for investors to make money by betting that a business is going to fail. A complex and risky strategy, it is typically practiced only within the domain of large investors. (Unlike buying stocks in the hopes that their value will rise—something any of us with a few extra dollars can do—shorting requires a lot of money up front and enough guts to keep that money in play for a long time.) Because shorting involves betting against individual companies (or bonds), it had traditionally been limited to the stock and bond markets.

---

* It is the way the financial-meltdown story was described *while it was happening* that was the biggest problem. There was nothing especially complex in what occurred. But since financial institutions have always thrived on obscuring what they do, it was the intentional opacity of their language that made it difficult to see what was going on. As Lewis points out, "The subprime-mortgage market had a special talent for obscuring what needed to be clarified."

BURRY'S YANG: MORTGAGES

Mortgage

The second piece of Burry's *taijitu* was the good old-fashioned mortgage. (Actually, not so old-fashioned, as Burry saw.) Since houses have always cost more money than people actually possess, home loans have long been the cornerstone of retail banking. Home loans were good for consumers (if we could prove a stable income, we could borrow the amount we needed to buy a home), good for the economy (high home ownership statistically drives a whole slew of other positive economic indicators), and good for the banks (the more banks loan, the more they earn—and home loans earn the most). As a win-win-win, the traditional mortgage was always viewed as the basis of a solidly growing economy.

Our dream!

These two pieces represented the extremes of the finance world that Burry entered in 2000. On the one hand, he saw shorting: risky, adventurous, and pessimistic. On the other hand, he saw the mortgage: solid, conservative, and optimistic. There had never been a better set of opposites to put together.

BURRY SPANS THE DIFFERENCES

By 2004, having spent years reading the fine print that banks passed out with their home loans, Burry became convinced that the banks had lost their minds. In a mad rush to offer new loans to new housing customers, banks were giving away up-front money for free—even inventing new mortgages specifically designed for people without any visible means of support. While Burry could see a bubble the size of the entire country building up, he didn't see anybody in the finance world trying to slow it down.

Knowing what he did about shorting, he put two and two together: "What would happen," asked Burry, "if I could find a way to *short* those crazy mortgages?" With so many loans about to go bad, it was an unprecedented opportunity to bet against the insanity of the entire financial services industry.* Burry knew it was impossible, of course: While there were lots of bundled-mortgage bonds called "CDOs" being traded among the big financial players,† there was no way to short individual mortgages, no matter how bad they might be.

But then the lightbulb went off, the yin and yang slid together, and Burry spanned the opposites: Why not short the mortgage bundles?

◀ Hmm: What would happen if you could "short" mortgages?

It was an audacious idea. Burry's greatest insight was to realize it could be done at all, through a financial tool called a "credit default swap." Invented only a decade before as a way for big financial players to hedge against potentially bad loans they made to big companies, credit default swaps could be traded like stocks—and if you can short a stock, why not a CDO-mortgage-bond-credit-default swap?‡

---

* It was also a bet against any homeowner who had been overenthusiastic about his buying power, customers dazzled by the bank hype of zero-interest loans, and most anyone who had succumbed to good old greed.

† CDOs are "collateralized debt obligations," huge piles of good and bad mortgages that can be traded as one bundle. While not necessarily dangerous by themselves, the problem was that CDOs were rated as a better credit risk than they actually were. Since these bundles contained some good mortgages, they were rated as a "solid" investment, in spite of containing billions more dollars of potentially bad mortgages—those that would later be called "toxic assets."

‡ A *CDO-mortgage-bond-credit-default swap*? See what I mean about the blah-blah-blah language of finance?

With the pieces in place, Burry founded an investment company called Scion Capital and went to work.

Mortgages + CDOs + credit default swaps = all the pieces needed to short the housing market. ▶

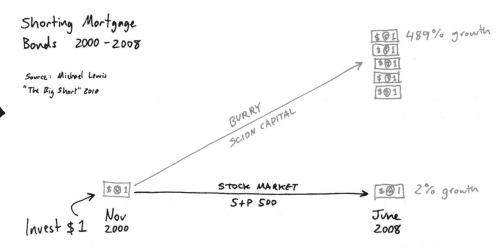

It worked. Buying up and selling credit default swaps between the big financial houses (few of whom seemed to care what Burry was doing), Burry made a mint for his investors. If you had invested one dollar with Scion Capital in 2000, by 2008 it would have been worth nearly five dollars. If you had invested that same dollar at the same time in the stock market, by 2008 it would have been worth . . . $1.02.

Shorting Mortgage Bonds   2000 – 2008

Source: Michael Lewis "The Big Short" 2010

Shorting the housing market ▶ worked for Burry and his investors, earning five dollars for every dollar. (Meanwhile, the stock market earned essentially zero.)

BURRY
SCION CAPITAL

489% growth

Invest $1   Nov 2000

STOCK MARKET
S+P 500

2% growth

June 2008

Burry didn't invent the crazy mortgages, didn't force banks to lower their lending standards, and didn't coerce homebuyers to borrow more than they could afford. He didn't even invent the tools he used, the CDO and the credit default swap. But it was his ability to see how opposite pieces fit together that heralded the collapse of Wall Street. Love him or hate him, Burry's secret wasn't so much that he looked at everything differently; he just really looked.

TRIZ

Yin and yang remind us of the need to account for opposites, but they don't offer any practical advice for finding them. For the *how-to,* we need another set of "difference-spanning" tools. The best set ever written comes from another Russian* scientist, one whose work remains largely unknown in the West.

Born in 1926, Genrich Altshuller was trained as an engineer and pilot by the Soviet navy. When the Second World War broke out, Altshuller was tasked with reviewing patent ideas coming from within the Soviet armed forces. As thousands of ideas poured across his desk, Altshuller increasingly noticed recurring patterns among them.†

After the war, Altshuller reviewed his notes and distilled them into a list of "forty principles for discovering new ideas." All forty relied on looking at problems in specific ways, and all were highly visual. This list included such insights for innovation as:

- *Segmentation*: See what happens when you divide a single object up into individual parts.

---

* Altshuller was born to a Jewish family in Tashkent, Uzbekistan, which actually makes him a Jewish Uzbek Soviet. His work is known today primarily by engineering students in Russia and Europe, although in recent years TRIZ-style thinking has begun to spread in American engineering schools.

† Ironically, this is the same job (albeit in a different country and during a different war) that Einstein occupied when he collected the notes that would soon become the special theory of relativity.

- *Asymmetry*: If an object is symmetrical, see what happens when you make it asymmetrical.

- *Merge*: See what happens when you bring together similar parts.

- *Universality*: See what happens when you make one part perform multiple functions.

Taken together, Altshuller's forty principles formed the basis of a tool set he called TRIZ.* Although TRIZ itself is highly theoretical,† Altshuller's essential idea is brilliantly

---

* For a complete list of Genrich's 40 Principles, visit the Web site triz-journal.com.

† TRIZ is a Russian acronym for "The Theory of Inventive Problem Solving." The formal application of TRIZ to a problem demands a highly structured approach and a dogmatically rigorous adherence to process, making it challenging to apply in a nonengineering setting.

simple: The best way to invent something new is not to sacrifice one capability at the expense of another but instead to look for a way to span both capabilities.*

This is exactly what Eberhard and Tarpenning did with Tesla, Mendeleyev did with elements, and Burry did with the finance industry—and this is what Vivid Thinking does for us.

The Vivid Stretch Test

By forcing us to span both the verbal and the visual, Vivid Thinking exposes unexpected connections and illuminates innovative ideas. "Spanning differences" stretches the possibilities of an idea far beyond what first occurs to our fox. To put our hummingbird to practical use, we can use the "Vivid Stretch Test."

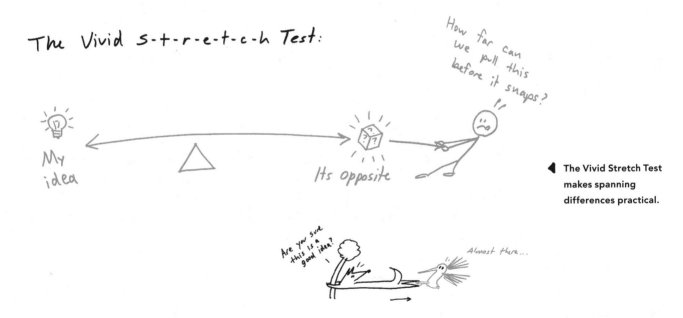

The Vivid Stretch Test makes spanning differences practical.

---

* Unfortunately for Altshuller (and the Soviet Union), when he and his colleagues proposed using his ideas to help rebuild the devastated postwar Soviet infrastructure, he was thrown into the Arctic gulag at Vorkuta for four years. So much for "spanning differences" in the Soviet Union.

Here's how the Vivid Stretch Test works. (It's kind of like mental Pilates or conceptual yoga.)

THE VIVID STRETCH TEST, STEP 1: FIND THE FORM

Let's say we've got the beginnings of a good idea—our GPS-enabled mobile phone from Chapter 5, for example—and in the hopes that we can come up with something really innovative, we want to see how far we can stretch it. (As a reminder, we started with a lost user, a GPS-enabled mobile phone, and a mapping application.)

A vivid reminder of our ▶
GPS-enabled mobile
phone from Chapter 5.

Recalling the essentials of everything we've covered so far, we use Vivid Grammar to find the form of our idea. In this case, we draw a timeline. (Depending on the essence of our idea, we could draw any picture from the *Grammar Graph*: a portrait, a chart, a map, a flowchart—even a multivariable plot.)

There it is, the essential form of our idea: A lost user pulls out his phone, sees his location, and isn't lost anymore.

Here is the vivid form of ▶
our idea: a simple timeline
showing how a user becomes
un-lost.

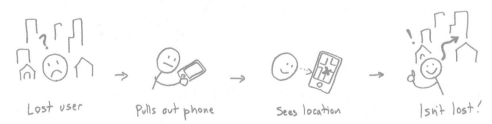

Looks good. Now let's stretch it.

THE VIVID STRETCH TEST, STEP 2: PICK ANY ESSENTIAL ELEMENT AND DRAW ITS OPPOSITE

The next step in the Vivid Stretch Test is to pick any single element in the form of our idea and find its opposite. Flip the element around, turn it upside down, imagine it doesn't exist at all—whatever it takes to see the element differently. This is where our hummingbird excels, so now is the time to let her go.

Looking for opposites is when we unleash our hummingbird.

In this case, let's start with the first element, the lost user. What might be the opposite?

☐ A user who *isn't* lost? (Good opposite, but we've already solved for that problem, so no need to include it.)

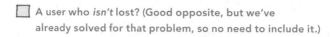

Isn't lost!

☐ A user who isn't alone?

A lost user who <u>isn't</u> alone.

☐ A user who *wants* to be lost?

A user who <u>wants</u> to be lost.

☐ A user without a phone?

A lost user <u>without</u> a phone.

☐ A user who doesn't exist?

A user who <u>doesn't</u> exist.

Yes, this feels a little crazy, but don't worry: That is precisely the point—to see how many new ways of looking at our idea we discover by simply asking, "What is the opposite of my idea?" Any one of these could lead to a new—and potentially better—idea.

For this example, let's pick the second opposite, *the user who isn't alone,* to continue the test.*

THE VIVID STRETCH TEST, STEP 3:
DRAW A PICTURE THAT ACCOUNTS FOR BOTH

Now that we've got an original element (a lost user with a phone) and one possible opposite (a *group* of lost users), the next step is to find a way to account for both. To do that, we refer back to our original elements . . .

And add the new one . . .

---

* If this was a real test, it might make sense to continue the next step with all the opposites. Why not? Even a brief glance at each reveals a whole slew of new possibilities for GPS-enabled phones.

And now we've got something even more interesting than we started with: a GPS-enabled phone location application that allows you to find other users. In other words, by spanning differences, we've gone from a single-user mapping application to a socially networked friend finder. Now *that* is a Vivid Idea.*

A social-network
location application!

---

* Just ask Foursquare. Foursquare is a socially networked GPS-based friend finder that launched in 2009 and within a year was awarded the Tech Leader of the Year award by the World Economic Forum.

CHAPTER 12

F · O · R · E · S · **T**

T Is for *Targeted:*
Vivid Ideas Matter to Me

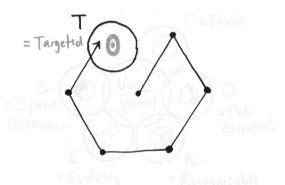

T he last stop on our journey through the forest is the one that prepares us for our way out. *T* stands for *"targeted"*—and targeting helps us get ready to return to the world of blah-blah-blah. In the forest so far, we've been refining our idea mostly by ourselves. Targeting helps us look at our idea from everyone else's perspective.

The fact that we need to "target" our ideas is the result of a simple truth of human nature: An idea aimed at no one is an idea no one sees.

An idea aimed at no one is an idea no one sees. ▶

There are only three points in every PowerPoint presentation at which we can absolutely guarantee that everyone is awake: the beginning, the end, and the slide that shows how everyone is going to get paid.* Why? Because the things we notice most are the things pointed *personally* toward us. That's what targeting is about: helping other people see our idea as vividly as we do—by pointing it toward *them*.

Vivid Ideas have a target. ▶

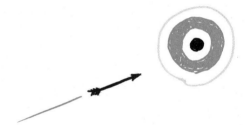

The Killer Cloud

We started this forest tour with *F*, for "form." We said that many ideas are like clouds just passing by: fluffy, vague, nondescript, and easy to forget. To fight that—to make our ideas visceral and memorable—we learned to give them form. Now we end our tour with another way: We give them a target.

As a teenager in the early 1980s, I learned to fly a small plane. One day, on a solo flight across the mountains of Montana, I did exactly what my instructor had told me a

---

* For students, substitute "how everyone is going to be graded."

hundred times never to do: I flew into a cloud. Fluffy and nondescript from the outside, the moment I flew in, I knew that cloud wanted to kill me. As I bounced around within solid walls of gray, that cloud got *personal*. From the second it targeted me, my sole purpose in life was to fight it. I fought it and I finally flew out, shaken but in one piece. To this day I've never forgotten that cloud.

◀ **The cloud that targeted me is the one I will always remember.**

Was that particular cloud any different from the hundreds of others floating through the sky that afternoon? No. Do I remember any of those other clouds? No. Do I remember the one that targeted me? Absolutely.

I told you about clouds.

Now who's "dumb"?

◀ **Thanks hummingbird. Lesson learned.**

Vivid Targeting: Two Steps

We've worked through all the steps of the forest to make our cloud stand out. We've made this idea of ours as clear, visceral, and memorable as we can. Now we have to share it. Whether our goal is to offer people a new idea, to try to change people's minds, or to change people's actions, we can't know what people are willing to do until we know something about them. The first step in vivid targeting is to get to know our audience.

We do that by either talking about them (good); or talking with them (even better) *and* drawing them. We'll call this the **"dramatis personae"** side of vivid targeting.

Once we know something about our audience, we can begin to make educated guesses about the best way to approach them. The second step of vivid targeting means using what we know about our audience to deduce how they will likely see our idea. We do that by looking at our audience through the **Vivid LENS**.

Making a list and checking it twice: idea targeting via dramatis personae and the Vivid LENS. ▶

Dramatis Personae

The ancient Latin term *dramatis personae ("persons of the drama")* first appeared in English usage three hundred years ago as the name for the list of characters that appear in a play. Since then it has become the standard opening element of any dramatic script. By listing all the players (with name and brief description) up front, the dramatis personae introduces us to all the characters we are about to meet before the action begins. As we saw when trying to make sense of a complex story,* having this list up front helps us create a mental map of who is who before we get lost in the drama of all the goings-on.

---

* A dramatis personae is precisely the list we prepared when mapping out Bill Carter's late-night-comedy book.

The opposite is also true: Creating a dramatis personae not only helps us see who plays what role in our idea; it also helps us anticipate who is likely to be in our audience.

Creating a useful audience list involves more than just writing down a bunch of names: We need to get our hummingbird involved as well; after all, she recognizes far more people than our fox ever will. We create vivid dramatis personae using our now familiar process of alternating words with pictures.

First Come the Names . . .

First, we write down as many audience categories and members as we can anticipate. If we're going to give a formal speech, we ask the sponsor what sorts of people we can expect to be there. If we're going to introduce our idea in an in-person or virtual meeting, we send out a note in advance to see who is planning to attend; if we're going to introduce our idea among a small group of colleagues, we already know who is coming.

When our audience list is complete, it should include as many categories of attendees as we can nail down (roles, organizational level, industry, expertise, the CEO, the janitor, etc.), as well as all the names we know (James the manager, Molly from HR, Pradesh from the client, etc.). Looking over the list, we should feel that we have a reasonable sense of whom we'll likely be talking to.*

---

* While these lists reflect a "formal" presentation, we should go through the same exercise whenever we hope we might one day share our idea. Knowing our potential audience in advance always pays off down the line.

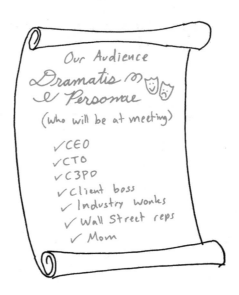

Our completed audience dramatis personae includes names, categories, industries—anyone we can think of whom we're going to need to present to. ▶

Then Come the Pictures . . .

Our written list complete, we unleash our hummingbird—yes, we're going to *draw* a portrait of the key members of our audience. This is important: The act of picturing someone's face forces us to think about that person in far more vivid detail than simply writing his or her name. If we *really* want to know what it will mean to have the CEO in the room, for example, we *really* do need to create a picture of her. At a minimum, we need to conjure up her face in our mind's eye; better still, we should sketch a quick portrait of her on a sheet of paper.*

---

* Like all portraits, we don't need much detail, just enough to trigger our mind to see her: How does she keep her hair? Does she wear glasses? How does she dress? Recalling even just the basics brings her to life in a way a name alone does not.

Taking a minute to create a portrait of our attendees (even if only in our mind's eye) forces us to think about them as fully realized people, not just names on a page.

Yes, that is hard. Yes, that takes time. And yes, that is the point: If this meeting really matters, then the time is worth it—if for nothing other than to prepare ourselves for how we will react when we see the most important people in the audience.

But what if we don't know any of the people personally—how on earth are we going to draw everyone? Simple: We don't. We profile. We pick a few faces (known, expected, hoped-for, dreaded) and draw only those. They become our surrogate targets. If we can mentally see a handful of potential audience members well enough to draw them—even if only as stereotypes—then the exercise will prepare us well for when we meet the real audience.*

The public speaker's oldest trick in the book: We don't talk to a hundred people; we talk to three. And thanks to the vivid dramatis personae we've created, we've "seen" them before.

---

* This is an old trick from public speaking. Although we may be presenting to a room of thousands, we never really speak to everybody. In reality, we pick just a few faces and talk directly to them. This is the same drill, only done vividly.

The Vivid LENS

Once we've identified whom we're likely to meet, we then take a careful look at them through the Vivid LENS. The Vivid LENS is a conceptual looking glass composed of four separate lenses, each of which tells us something important about whom we will be presenting to.

The Vivid LENS is our ▶ conceptual looking glass. It helps us understand our audience in four critical ways.

The four lenses reflect four distinct attributes of any audience. Each of the four helps us anticipate audience reaction and thus prepare the most effectively targeted presentation in advance. The four lenses are:

L for *leadership* level
E for *expertise* level
N for *numeracy* level
S for *sympathy* level

The four lenses: leadership, ▶ expertise, numeracy, sympathy.

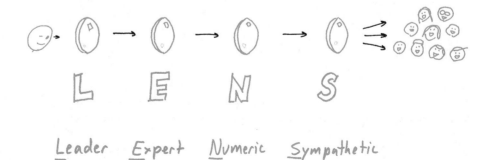

Each of the four lenses maps to a unique sliding scale of opposites: *Leader* opposes *doer; expert* opposes *newbie; numeric* opposes *emotional;* and *sympathetic* opposes *antagonistic*. These four sliding scales work because they offer a quick yet comprehensive checklist* of key audience hot buttons.

Leader	Expert	Numeric	Sympathetic
?	?	?	?
Doer	Newbie	Emotional	Antagonistic

By looking at our audience according to these four criteria, we build a deep understanding of who we are really show-and-telling to and what they are really willing to look-and-listen to. Let's quickly look at each of the four and the types of vivid pictures most effective for each.

L = LEADER OR DOER

Lens 1 indicates whether our audience target is someone who *primarily* leads or does. The leader is responsible for setting the vision, the doer the one responsible for making it

---

* There are certainly many more audience criteria worth considering—and myriad combinations of just these four are possible—but for a rapid-fire "I've got to get onstage in fifteen minutes" checklist, this Vivid LENS is pretty unbeatable.

happen. The leader wants to see a picture of where we're going—so we'd better show them a portrait or a map. The doer wants to see the picture of how we're going to get there, so we'd better show them a timeline or a flowchart.

E = EXPERT OR NEWBIE

Lens 2 shows us whether our audience target is an expert or a newbie. An expert already knows more than we do about our idea (or thinks he does), so his tolerance for simplicity will be limited. A newbie, on the other hand, knows next to nothing about our topic, so he won't tolerate initial complexity. When introducing our idea to an expert, it's better to err on the side of complexity (at least at first), if only to establish our credibility.* When we introduce our idea to anyone else, initial simplicity always rules the day.

N = NUMERIC OR EMOTIONAL

The third lens helps us determine whether our audience is moved more by numbers or by emotions. The more numeric among us—the "quants," analysts, and accountants—

---

* This is the one exception to the "distillation curve" model. When we face an expert who initially questions our competence, we need to quickly establish that we do know and respect the nuances of his world. After establishing our street cred, we can quickly fall back on the simple to get the real essence of our idea across.

always like to start with the cold, hard numbers. Yet relying on those very same numbers to introduce our idea is the fastest way possible to ensure that the more emotional audiences—those motivated by intuition, feeling, and empathy—check out quickly, and with a grudge. When introducing our idea to a numeric audience, we start with a chart. When introducing our idea to an emotional audience, we start with a portrait.

S = SYMPATHETIC OR ANTAGONISTIC

The final lens helps us prepare for love or war. If we face an audience already on our side, we're lucky: Barring any major screwup on our part, we can introduce our idea freely without fear of immediate rejection. But if we know that our audience is predisposed against us, we have our work cut out for us. While there are hundreds of approaches for dealing with a hostile audience,* the one that works best in a vivid presentation is simple: We just make sure our first picture includes them.

◀ There is no faster way to disarm a hostile audience than to vividly show we understand their perspective.

---

* Dozens and dozens of books and videos are available with helpful strategies. Let us focus only on the one that takes the most advantage of Vivid Thinking.

There is no faster way to disarm a potentially difficult audience than to show we are aware of their concerns—and the best way to show that is to create the picture that vividly illustrates those concerns. We don't have to pander or change our own idea; just by *vividly* showing an audience that we've taken their concerns into account *up front*, we've done enough to buy their attention for a while. And if our idea really is good and really is vivid, that should be enough to get them on our side.

USING THE VIVID LENS

Whenever we're about to step back into the world of blah-blah-blah, it pays to first scan the crowd with the Vivid LENS. The more we know about the people we're likely to run into, the more likely we'll be seen and heard.

Whenever we step back into ▶ the world of blah-blah-blah, we should first make a quick scan with the Vivid LENS.

Back to the Blah-Blahmeter

Let's wrap up this Vivid FOREST tour where we began so many chapters ago: with five famous people trying to convey five different ideas with five varying levels of success. This time, as we review the words of Obama, Petraeus, Sully, Coke, and Madoff, we'll use the Vivid LENS to see how well they did or did not target their audience.

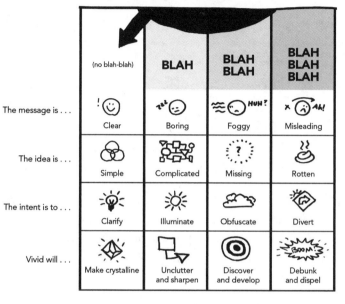

The Blah-Blahmeter

	(no blah-blah)	BLAH	BLAH BLAH	BLAH BLAH BLAH
The message is . . .	Clear	Boring	Foggy	Misleading
The idea is . . .	Simple	Complicated	Missing	Rotten
The intent is to . . .	Clarify	Illuminate	Obfuscate	Divert
Vivid will . . .	Make crystalline	Unclutter and sharpen	Discover and develop	Debunk and dispel

◀ **Back to the Blah-Blahmeter one more time.**

SULLY KNOCKS IT OFF THE SCALE

We'll start with Captain Chesley "Sully" Sullenberger, who successfully landed stricken US Airways Flight 1549 in the Hudson River, saving all aboard. Remember his only communication with his passengers?

> *This is the captain. Brace for impact.*

How effective was Sully's targeting of that idea? Let's set the Vivid LENS and take a look.

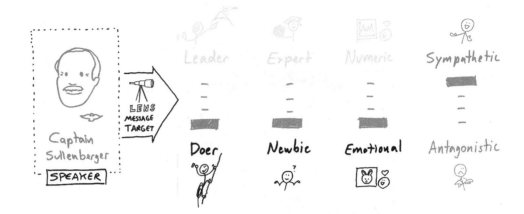

How about 100 percent? *"This is the captain"*: Sully was the leader, and everyone else was going to do exactly what he said; there was no doubt about that. Sully also knew he was sharing his idea with a group of emotionally wrought newbies* who wanted nothing more than to believe in him. *"Brace for impact"*: simple, direct, vivid—it's hard to imagine a clearer delivery of a clear idea.

MADOFF IN THE EXTREME

At the extreme end of the Blah-Blahmeter is Bernie Madoff, Wall Street tycoon and financial charlatan. Remember the quote from his firm's business prospectus?

> *Typically, a position will consist of the ownership of 30–35 S&P 100 stocks, most correlated to that index, the sale of out-of-the-money calls on the index and the purchase of out-of-the-money puts on the index . . .*

---

* There was one passenger aboard who was an "expert" in surviving emergencies. Before boarding Flight 1549, Maryann Bruce had lived through a tsunami, an earthquake, an avalanche, a hurricane, and the first World Trade Center bombing. Maryann was one of the few on the plane who knew she was going to live.

Bernie scored a perfect *blah cubed:* an intentionally misleading expression of a rotten idea meant to divert his audience from the truth. (The truth being that he was running a pyramid scheme.)

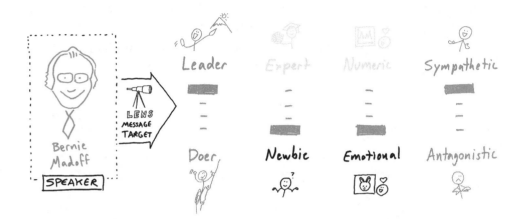

Madoff set his targeting lens differently. Since his clients tended to be leaders in their own fields, he used intricate-sounding technical language to appeal to their sense of confidence. Most of his investors were relative newbies to hard-core investing, so the actual lack of meaning in his language was lost on them—and although many Madoff clients believed themselves to be great numbers people, their emotional attachment to his miraculous winning streak blinded them to reality. Lastly, most of Madoff's biggest investors considered themselves personal friends of Bernie. They were sympathetic to him to a fault—making his treachery even more shocking.

Reprehensible as his intention was, his delivery was perfect—an unbeatable illustration of the dangers of perfectly targeted blah-blah-blah.

VITAMINWATER FOOLS US ALL

On a similar note, but less shocking, because—as Coca-Cola's lawyers themselves said—"no reasonable consumer could have been misled," is the VitaminWater blah-blah.

Specially formulated with nutrients that enable the body to exert physical power by contributing to structural integrity of the musculoskeletal system, and by supporting optimal generation and utilization from food.

On the Blah-Blahmeter, VitaminWater scored at *blah squared:* an intentionally foggy description of a nonexistent idea intended to obfuscate the truth. Why do marketers do this kind of thing? Because although it's only blah-blah, it's really well-targeted blah-blah.

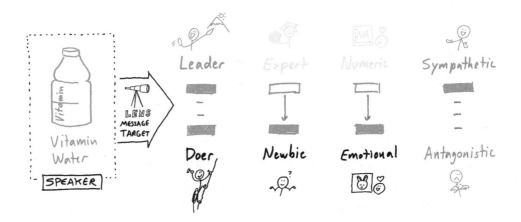

Customers of VitaminWater could be leaders or doers; the important thing is that they want to believe they're taking care of themselves. The bottle's marketing language appeals to the health expert who is really a newbie, the by-the-numbers nutritionist subconsciously seeking sugary comfort. Good marketing does just that: It takes a potentially antagonistic audience and makes them sympathetic. Score 100 percent on the Vivid LENS for Coca-Cola.

PETRAEUS AND THE WAR OF PERCEPTION

General Petraeus knows that when he goes to war, he has two battles to fight: one against the enemy and one for perception. He knows that to win both, his messages to the American people need to be just as targeted as his instructions to his troops.

> We sought to . . . build an oil spot that would encompass the six central districts of [Afghanistan] and then to just keep pushing that out, ultimately to connect it over with the oil spot that is being developed around Kandahar City.

Petraeus has a tricky audience every time he speaks to Congress and the press: leaders and doers, experts and newbies, number types and emotionals, sympathizers and hostiles. The genius of this description of his strategy is how vivid it is. Although he didn't physically draw a picture, his use of the "oil spot" metaphor makes the idea recognizable and gives his plans clear form.

Petraeus does a masterful job of complex message targeting. His clarity appeals to leaders and doers, experts and newbies alike. His calm delivery of a metaphorical yet rational image assures the numbers people while keeping emotions at bay, and by remaining vivid, he effectively straddles the line between those who support him and those who would oppose him.

OBAMA AND THE HARDEST SALE EVER

We'll end our look at vividly targeted ideas—indeed, our entire tour through the Vivid FOREST—with a final look at the most challenging political sales job ever: President Obama and the reform of American health care. Whether good or bad, the right thing to do or the worst, if there was ever an idea that needed to be vivid, this was it.

It wasn't.

> *We defined it fairly clearly in terms of what we thought would work best. What I said was that it shouldn't be something that's simply a taxpayer-subsidized system that wasn't accountable but rather had to be self-sustaining through premiums and that we had to compete with private insurers.*

On rereading, that's not that complicated an idea. But it didn't catch on. The first problem is that the idea isn't vivid: "Health care reform" had no form, hadn't been boiled down to its essentials, wasn't recognizable, didn't (in the end) evolve with full participation, and didn't span cultural differences.

The second problem was that health care reform wasn't targeted. The same messages were delivered to everyone. Remember: A message aimed at no one is a message no one sees. Given all the battling constituencies, maybe there was no way to target effectively—but that's no way to make a sale.

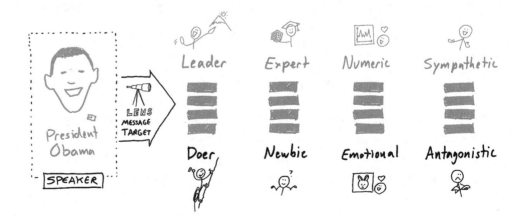

The lesson: With a complex idea, talking is never enough; it pays to make every message vivid.

In the End . . .

In the end, great ideas are great for two reasons: They make sense to the broadest range of people yet matter most to the smallest number, namely *me*. Vivid Ideas aren't just inspired, well thought through, cleverly worded, and brilliantly illustrated. Vivid Ideas matter because they combine all of those things in the service of targeting me—with a difference *that I can see*.

PART 4

Conclusion

CHAPTER 13

Bye-Bye, Blah-Blah-Blah

e made it. We're out of the forest. We found form, offered only the essentials, recognized metaphors, evolved our thinking, spanned differences, and targeted our ideas. Wow, fox and hummingbird: That was one impressive performance. You guys deserve a round of applause.

◀ Thanks, you two. That was impressive.

I think we're done with you for now—go ahead and take a break. But don't go too far: We'll need you later . . . oh, never mind.

Shhhh! We better let them rest for now: We're going to need them again before long . . . ▶

Bad News, Good News

For the rest of us, here's the bad news: Now we've got to return to the land of blah-blah-blah. That's where everyone else is, so that's where we're going to have to make our ideas work.

But here's the good news: Blah-blah-blah isn't going to look the way we remember. Instead of a place where we can't hear anyone else and they can't hear us, in this new land people are going to find our ideas so vivid that they will put down everything else to look and listen. Even better, now that we have our Blah-Blahmeter, Vivid Grammar, and a map of the forest, everyone else's ideas are going to be a lot clearer to us as well.

Time to pack up our tools . . . ▶

With our new tools and understanding, going back to blah-blah-blah won't be all that traumatic. On the contrary—knowing what we now know, we are going to make waves, kick butt, and change the world.

Our Treasure Map

The Forest and the Trees

Our path.

Look out blah-blah-blah!

The Land of Blah-Blah-Blah

VIVID

Our destination.

◀ . . . and head back to blah-blah-blah. (Only it won't be the same blah as before.)

Tactics and Strategies: Eight Rapid-Fire Ways to Put Vivid Thinking to Work

As we close out our journey away from blah-blah-blah and begin our return, let's conclude with eight simple ways to make vivid real: four tactical tips for applying our new tools immediately and four long-term strategies for revitalizing how we think and communicate.

THE TOP FOUR TACTICAL TIPS FOR BECOMING MORE VIVID *RIGHT NOW*

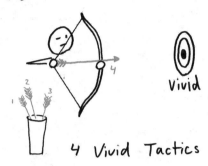

4 Vivid Tactics

We'll start with the tactics. Here they are: four things we can do *right now* to become more vivid.

Tactical Tip No. 1: Use the Vivid Checklist

When boiled down to their essence, all the tools in this book serve as a Vivid Idea checklist. Whether we're listening to someone else's idea or sharing our own, running through the checklist helps us make sure that we're seeing the idea clearly, "getting" it, and vividly thinking about what it means.

At a high level, the short vivid checklist looks like this.*

---

* The full Vivid Checklist complete with all questions and actions is included as Appendix C at the back of the book.

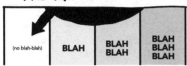

The Blah-Blahmeter

(no blah-blah) | BLAH | BLAH BLAH | BLAH BLAH BLAH

Use the Blah-Blahmeter

- ☐ If the idea has no blah-blah-blah ▶ No changes needed.
- ☐ If the idea is boring (1 blah) ▶ *Unclutter* and *sharpen*.
- ☐ If the idea is foggy or befuddling (2 blahs) ▶ *Discover* and *develop* the idea's essence.
- ☐ If the idea is misleading (3 blahs) ▶ *Debunk* and *dispel*.

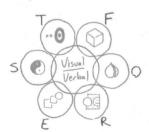

The Vivid Grammar Graph

PORTRAIT

CHART | MAP | TIMELINE

M.V. PLOT | FLOWCHART

Use Vivid Grammar

- ☐ When I hear a noun ▶ Draw a portrait.
- ☐ When I hear an adjective of quantity ▶ Draw a chart.
- ☐ When I hear a preposition ▶ Draw a map.
- ☐ When I hear tense ▶ Draw a timeline.
- ☐ When I hear a complex verb ▶ Draw a flowchart.
- ☐ When I hear a complex sentence ▶ Draw a multivariable plot.

The Vivid FOREST

T F
S Visual/Verbal O
E R

Use the Vivid FOREST

F: Does the idea have <u>form</u>? *(Do I see the underlying shape of the idea?)*

O: Can it be explained with <u>only the essentials</u>? *(Has it been distilled to its essence?)*

R: Is the idea <u>recognizable</u>? *(Do I know where I have seen the idea before?)*

E: Can the idea <u>evolve</u>? *(Does it leave room for someone else's ideas?)*

S: Does the idea <u>span differences</u>? *(Does it account for opposites?)*

T: Is the idea <u>targeted</u>? *(Does the idea matter to me?)*

I designed the order of the three tools in this book (**Blah-Blahmeter, Vivid Grammar, Vivid FOREST**) to help us *get out* of blah-blah-blah. To get back in (so we *can* change the world), we should use the tools in reverse order. In other words, to better understand our own ideas and make sure we're ready to share them, we run the Vivid Checklist backward.

- ☐ I first run my own idea through the Vivid FOREST to make sure it is clear, simple, and memorable.
- ☐ Next, I use Vivid Grammar to add the simplest and most direct visuals as I prepare my presentation.
- ☐ Finally, I run my own idea through the Blah-Blahmeter to make sure it is free of blah-blah-blah *before* I present it to others.

Tactical Tip No. 3: Create "Who Maps" for Books, Reports, and Presentations

More than anything else, our minds are interested in other people. We want to know what others are thinking, doing, and dreaming. Since the days of Oog and Aag, we've

been social animals—and we've developed the facial recognition capabilities to match. We're attracted to people whose look we like, repelled by those whose look we don't, intrigued by those with a new look, and bored by people we've been looking at too long.

For this reason, any complex problem can be clarified enormously simply by looking at *who* is involved with it. In fact, the hardest part of solving most problems is simply keeping track of who the players are. If we can make a vivid list of the players—who they are, what they look like, how many there are, how directly or indirectly involved they are—we will have solved half the problem. Once we know who the people are (including ourselves—let's not forget that as far as our brain is concerned, if there is a problem that we're involved in, we're by definition in the center of it), all that remains is to anticipate how they are likely to act.

This holds true for any complex story. Try this: The next time you read a book involving more than two characters, take a sheet of paper and write down the names of the characters as they appear. Keep the list up to date as more characters appear. As the players interact, draw lines between them showing who is related to whom. Fairly quickly, a map will appear. By referring back to the map when the plot gets thick and by watching the progress of the characters across it, we will engage with the story in a powerful and memorable way.

This "who mapping" process works wonders for anyone trying to understand a complex novel, a legal brief, a mathematical word problem, or even a business meeting: There really is no better way to get the big picture than drawing out the people.

Tactical Tip No. 4: Draw Out a Premeeting Picture (*and Get Ahead of the Blah*)

Every meeting has "*the* picture"—the one central image, whether drawn out or imaginary, intentional or accidental—that imprints itself most clearly on the memories of all who were there. Knowing before the meeting begins what that picture might look like goes a long ways toward guiding how the meeting will end.

Before going into any meeting that we are leading (or in which we expect to play a major role), we should take the time to create "*the* picture" of what we most want to share. By vividly mapping out in advance the one thing we hope people will remember, we focus our own mind and give everyone else the benefit of at least one clear idea to discuss.

Put bluntly, the person who walks into the meeting with the clearest picture in mind is the one most likely to guide the outcome. Using the tools in this book, we now have the means to create that picture.

By sketching out our idea in advance using Vivid Grammar or the Vivid FOREST as a guide (depending on our idea and the goals for the meeting, it could be any vivid picture), we will be preparing ourselves for success. Once the meeting begins, we should go up to the erasable board and draw it out. Whether or not this was "our" show, the moment we draw the defining picture, we will own the meeting.

Subtip: The "Boss Test"

If you are the boss, sharing your idea verbally and visually ensures that everyone knows your thoughts—which in turn reaffirms your right to *be* the boss. That's great on both counts. Now disregard the following paragraphs.

If you are *not* the boss, use your next picture as the "boss test." When you begin drawing your picture in the meeting, your boss will either love it or hate it.

If your boss loves it, you can be pretty sure that you have an expansive, confident, open-minded boss who appreciates the effort you've made to think through your idea in an innovative way. Such a boss will appreciate your desire to make your idea clear—even if (especially if) your picture disagrees with her thinking. (At a minimum, at least your boss will have your picture to use as a clear illustration of what she is *not* thinking.)

If, on the other hand, your boss hates your picture, you can be pretty sure that you have a small-minded boss who is frightened of change, does not like making waves, and does not appreciate real innovators shaking things up in the office. In this case, act accordingly and start working on your exit plans.

(Either that or your drawing was *really* off-base—in which case you might want to go back and reread this book.)

THE BIG PICTURE: THE TOP FOUR STRATEGIES FOR LONG-TERM VIVID THINKING

We'll conclude with the strategies. Here they are: four long-term ways we can improve the ways we think and communicate.

Strategy 1: Become Double-Minded

Becoming vivid reminds us that we're better thinkers than we thought. There is no idea, no matter how complex, that cannot be described in an engaging and understandable way when we put our whole mind to it. When we put our idea in a form that people *want* to learn, they will. When we share our idea in a way people *want* to understand, they will.

Strategy 2: Make *Vivid* the First Step of *Viral*

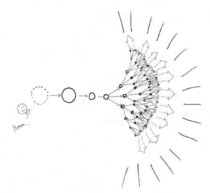

The most amazing thing about Vivid Ideas is that once we send them out into the land of blah-blah-blah, we don't have to keep talking. If our idea really is that clear, simple, and clarifying, it will do most of its work on its own.

The one thing that all our feverish communications channels demand is ideas.

Whether we're talking about the Internet, the blogosphere, the twitterverse, the social graph—yes, even network-enhanced "traditional" media like magazines, books, and broadcast—they don't mean a thing if they don't have good ideas to share. And nothing is easier to share than a Vivid Idea.

A Vivid Idea has everything it needs to go viral: It's simple, it's clear, it's compact. By taking the time to make our ideas vivid, we've given other people everything they need to help it go viral. We all want to spread ideas that make us look smart—and nothing makes us look smarter than passing along an idea that people understand.

Strategy 3: Appoint Your CSO (Chief Simplicity Officer)

The real job of the boss is to know all the complexity of vision, execution, and operations but to retain the ability to keep it simple for others.

Every organization of more than two people has a natural tendency to add more complexity. In scientific circles this is known as the law of entropy: Everything naturally moves to a state of disorder—more details, more nuances, more items on the agenda. We need someone dedicated to keeping things *off*. The most brilliant example I saw of this was a set of two-day meetings I had with the head of an innovative hedge fund in New York. Although I know nothing about the nuances of financial planning, risk management, or "fundamental" market approaches versus "quants," the boss could describe it all in a series of simple pictures, taking me from hedge fund neophyte to conceptual expert in less than eight hours.

Portrait of the Chief Simplicity Officer.

Why not create a new executive-level position called the *chief simplicity officer*? Every company worth its brand has a chief marketing officer who ensures that every time the brand is mentioned it's mentioned the right way. From now on, companies should have someone making equally sure that every message delivered and every customer interaction is guided by the rule "*Keep it simple.*"

The CSO's job description? Easy: Run every idea through the Vivid FOREST, Vivid Grammar, and Blah-Blahmeter *before* it leaves the house.

Strategy 4: Believe in Your Hummingbird (She's More Bazooka Than Bambi)

Remember our fox and our hummingbird? (How could we forget, right?) Our fox is our verbal mind, and we've trained him and given him tools our entire life. Our hummingbird is our visual mind—and we've given her pretty much nothing.

It makes sense. A fox is clever and makes a good show of himself in a meeting: linear, logical, and persuasive—who wouldn't want him on their side? Meanwhile, a hummingbird is a disaster in the boardroom: flighty, scattered, and hyperactive—who would want her there at all?

But think about this. Who really sees the big picture: the fox or the hummingbird?

Seven hundred years ago, the Aztecs, the mightiest nation of the Americas, sought out a symbol to represent their warrior spirit. Of all the animals of the forest—the jaguar, the snake, the eagle—they wanted the fastest, fiercest, and most omniscient creature of all to become their warrior god. Which animal do you think they chose to lead them into battle?

You got it: the hummingbird. Under the guidance of *Huitzilopochtli,* the Aztecs dominated Mexico and Central America for three hundred years.

Let us never again underestimate ▶ the power of our hummingbird.

— Next time, don't count me out.

Yes'm!

So next time we think our hummingbird isn't a force to be reckoned with, we should think again. If you're struggling to find the right words, maybe you should stop looking for words alone; add pictures to make your message vivid. If nobody remembers what you said, maybe you're using the wrong bazooka.

Final Thought: Go Change the World

The single greatest challenge to leaders today (and that includes thinkers, teachers, managers, presidents, parents, CEOs, designers, salespeople, students—all of us) is this: We have to make *more* increasingly complex ideas *more* clear, *more* quickly and *more* persuasively than ever, to *more* audiences who are *more* informed and have *more* access to *more* information than ever.

Whew. No wonder it's tough to be a leader today.

Want to make a difference? Don't blah-blah-blah. Be vivid.

ACKNOWLEDGMENTS

It takes many people to make a book. I want to thank you all.

There is a mistaken impression that writing a book is a lonely task. Yes, there are many long lonely moments, but in reality the entire process is a team endeavor. Put simply, the number one rule of creating a book is that it cannot be done alone. I could go on with a long list of who did what on this book (and it would be a long list), but I worry that might come across as too much blah-blah-blah. So let me thank the whole cast in a more vivid way.

The home team.

 Isabelle
 Sophie
 Celeste

My publishing team.

 Ted Weinstein
 Adrian Zackheim
 Courtney Young
 Eric Meyers
Will Weisser

My clients & business friends team.

 Pat O'Dea
 Laila Tarraf
 Todd Spaletto
 Jeff DiDomenico
 David Rich

 Guy Kawasaki
 Sunni Brown
 Nancy Duarte
 Alex Osterwalder
Sean Murphy

My timeless support network.

 Dan Thomas
 Nancy Beckman
 Dr. Tony Jones
 Gordon Evans
 Darcy Dapra
 Karen Graham

 Dave Gray
 Leslie Flores
 David Yager
 Maria Mahar
 Tom Strich
 Ken Schaefer

Mom
RIP 2010

 Karl

 Mike

 Dad

 Lilli

 Napa
Fox

Tweets

My promotion team.

 Mark
Fortier

 Elizabeth
Hazelton

 Amanda
Pritzker

 Jamie
Jelly

 Tom
Neilssen

 Les
Teurk

 Marge
Hennessy

 Freya
Joy

 Christina
Teichmann

 Mark
Mullen

 Roger
Barnett

 Dr. Michel
Fuller

 Marci
LeFevre

 Nancy
Napier

 Elise
Olding

 Morgen
Newman

 Marianne
Wilman

 Carmine
Gallo

 Macon
Phillips

 Goh
Ai Yat

 Brandon
Hoe

 Tim
West

 Ken
Cornelius

 Hugh
Forrest

Corey
McGuire

 Eric
Eislund

 Linda
Eislund

 Martin
Michaud

 Andy
Grogan

 Lynn
Carruthers

 Kristina
Halvorson

 Mark
Schar

 Elliot
Eisner

 Kim
Sealey

 Anna
Wachter

 John
Lally

 Kate
Rutter

 Larry
Minney

 Geoff
Badner

 Xavier
Fan

 Bob
Morris

x

Acknowledgments | 303

APPENDIXES

APPENDIX A
How We Lost Half Our Mind

The Test

The SAT is the standard high school aptitude test in the United States. It is taken by nearly every teenager hoping to attend college, and nearly every higher-learning institution requires an SAT score for admission. As the primary nationally standardized measure of intellectual ability, SAT scores are considered the single most reliably consistent predictor of academic fitness. (The other two measures considered by application boards are grade-point average and extracurricular activities.)

In many ways, a young adult's SAT score is the number-one determinant of his or her academic future. A high score significantly increases the chances of acceptance to a good university, whereas a medium or poor score virtually guarantees nonacceptance. It's not an overstatement to say that for most college-bound students, the three hours and forty-five minutes they spend taking the SAT will have more impact on their educational future than anything else they do in their first sixteen years.

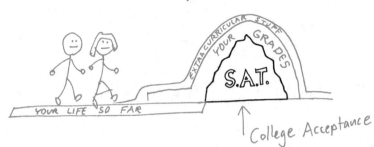

For most young Americans, the SAT is the single most important determinant of future educational opportunity. ▶

Given the extraordinary impact this test has on young people's future (and the future of the country), you might think that the SAT would include sections on logical deduction, multidimensional problem analysis, creative problem solving, mechanical-conceptual-physical reasoning, and visual-spatial processing. You'd be wrong. The SAT contains none of these.

What does the SAT actually test? ▶

What the SAT does contain is three sections, one each for math, critical reading, and writing. That's all. Our student's future is determined 66 percent by his or her ability to read and write and 33 percent by his or her ability to correctly answer structured math questions. For the test creators and college acceptance boards, that makes sense: These are all critical skills that can be taught, tested, and, most important, *measured*. But for the rest of us, that's absurd: None of these sections actually proves our ability to solve anything.

A Tale of Two Studies

That the SAT remains the critical deciding factor in the lives of so many young people tells us more about the conceptually impoverished nature of our educational system than it does about our future leaders' abilities to meet the challenges of today and tomorrow. We used to know that a solely verbally taught and verbally measured mind is missing half its thinking capability. Today we know more than that: We know that a solely verbally taught and verbally measured mind is in many ways worse.

That's right: Using words alone to discover, develop, and share ideas blinds us to entire worlds of possibilities. All fox and no hummingbird does not a great problem solver create.

Two studies give a glimmer of what does. (Note the ages of these studies: Both are more than twenty years old. Hey, educators: *This is not new stuff.*)

STUDY NO. 1: THE PICTURE SUPERIORITY EFFECT

The Picture Superiority Effect

In 1984, two business scholars conducted a series of tests aimed at understanding what makes consumers remember brands. The result was what they called "The Picture-Superiority Effect on Consumer Memory." In their studies, Terry Childers and Michael Houston verified that "visual imagery is a rich mnemonic device that enhances learning and retention of material over such techniques as sentence elaboration or rote rehearsal."

If the purpose of education is to "enhance learning and retention of material," that finding by itself is a pretty damning commentary on tests like the SAT. But that's just the beginning. Childers and Houston's study revealed three ways in which images provide a richer and more memorable experience than words:

(1) Incidental Redundant Cues. "When imaging a stimulus, a large number of incidental cues are contained within the image . . . The redundant cue explanation argues that imagery involves a form of elaboration that yields stored semantic information beyond that contained in the original stimulus. Thus for verbal material to be remembered as well as pictures, it would have to be processed at a semantic level and be of a form that generated additional information that resulted in multiple retrieval paths."

(2) Relational Organization. "Imaginal processing of paired items [such as can be seen in a picture] allows the individual to find a connective relationship between the items. [This] suggests that for verbal-only material to be learned as well as pictures, processing at a semantic level is necessary. Furthermore, the verbal material should be of a form that promotes cohesion within it."

(3) Stimulus Differentiation. "The stimulus differentiation argument suggests that imagery results in a *more distinctive, more isolated* single memory code . . . The essence of the stimulus differentiation hypothesis is that imagery is a more *reliable* encoding process than verbal encoding."

Childers and Houston conclude their study with two hypotheses:

H1: "Pictorial material conveying brand-product-class associations is recalled better than corresponding verbal-only material when each is processed at a sensory level."

H2: "Greater sensory discrimination of pictures improves their recall over corresponding verbal-only material when each is processed at a sensory level."

What does all this tell us? When we want to remember something, a visualized picture is more useful than a bunch of memorized words.

STUDY NO. 2: VERBAL OVERSHADOWING

Verbal Overshadowing

In 1990, two cognitive psychologists conducted a study that looked at the visual-versus-verbal balance from another direction—and came up with the same answer. In their study "Verbal Overshadowing of Visual Memories: Some Things Are Better Left Unsaid," Jonathan Schooler and Tonya Engstler-Schooler used six experiments to determine whether talking about a visual memory improved the accuracy of the memory. They found the opposite: Their studies consistently showed that when we talk about something we've seen (faces and colors were the objects used in the tests), we actually lose our ability to accurately remember what the original object looked like.

In other words, when our verbal mind processes something seen by our visual mind, our verbal side not only takes over; it distorts our recollection of what we saw. Our verbal mind overshadows our visual mind to the point that it blinds us to what we saw.

In the words of Schooler, "the verbalization of a visual memory can foster the formation of a nonveridical [non-reality-based] verbally biased representation. Access of this verbally biased representation can then interfere with subjects' ability to make use of their intact visual code. Verbalization impairs memory for a variety of different nonverbal stimuli; in each case the nonverbal stimuli cannot be adequately recalled in words."

In plain English, that means that a witness to a crime who is asked to verbally describe the perpetrator is *less likely* to identify the real criminal in a lineup than the witness who said nothing.

Two studies, complementary results. First: Pictures are a better way to remember a sensory stimulus. Second: Applying words degrades our ability to accurately recall the reality of that stimulus. The SAT mostly measures our ability to think with words. What truth is that test really measuring?

What Happened on the Way to the SAT?

How has it come to pass that we have so successfully purged our visual mind from our understanding of intelligence? No matter where we look in human history, recorded language started with pictures. What happened? (And what have we lost along the way?)

THE CLAN OF THE CAVE BULL

Long, long before any words were ever written, people believed in the power of pictures. Thirty-two thousand years ago, Oog and Aag* walked into a cave in what is today southern France. They picked up a couple of pieces of charcoal and started drawing a bull. We don't know anything about Oog and Aag except that they could draw beautiful bulls, horses, and rhinos. We don't know why they chose to draw these animals, whether they were spiritual leaders among their people or bored loners, or whether their pictures were part of a language or were purely decorative—we don't even know why they chose to draw their animals in the darkness of a cave.

What we do know is that their pictures are the oldest discovered images ever made by a human hand. In the entire sweep of history, Oog and Aag's bull is the beginning of the *whoosh*. When we look back from our vantage point today and try to imagine who might have been the first person to pick up a pencil and record a vision of the world, we end up with Oog and Aag and their bull.[†] And what a beautiful bull it is.

---

* Remember Oog and Aag from Chapter 3? Here we get to meet them again, a million years later. To be fair, we have no idea whether it was Oog or Aag (or both) who walked into the cave, but for me it's a nicer image to think that they were working together.

† Many people are familiar with the cave drawings found at Lascaux, France. Oog's drawings are found on the walls of another cave not far away on a map but twenty thousand years away on a timeline. The Chauvet Cave was discovered in 1993, and its earliest drawings have proven to be more than twice as old as Lascaux's.

THEN CAME THE EGYPTIANS

Now we jump forward in time twenty-seven thousand years. (Yes, this is a sequence—we'll get to the *timeline* that makes it vivid in a moment.) Five thousand years ago, another group of people, thousands of miles away from Oog and Aag's cave, also started to draw bulls. In the cliffs along the Nile River in what is now Egypt, a scribe named Heptep* picked up a stick and on a wet mud brick drew his version of a bull. It looked a lot like Oog and Aag's.

Heptep's bull: Although drawn twenty-seven thousand years later and thousands of miles away, it looks a lot like Oog and Aag's.

At first, Heptep and his people drew the bull to represent . . . well, a bull. Bulls were important to the commerce of ancient Egypt, and drawing them gave traders a way to record transactions. Before long, Heptep's drawings evolved to become a complete visual system useful for recording economics, politics, and history—as well as the sacred texts for keeping track of the hundreds of gods that ruled life along the Nile. Thus, hieroglyphics were born—the world's second writing system.†

---

* The name is fake, but his gender is real: We do know that the scribes of ancient Egypt were mostly men.

† Cuneiform, the written language of ancient Mesopotamia, was first by a whisker—but frankly, who cares? Although written cuneiform predates full hieroglyphics by maybe a hundred years, in both cases the writing started with pictures. But because the pictorial elements of cuneiform quickly fell away, to be replaced by chicken scratches, cuneiform lost any hold on our cultural imagination. When we look at it, we see nothing our modern mind can grab on to. On the contrary, the visual splendor of hieroglyphics to this day stimulates endless fascination.

The problem for Heptep and his fellow scribes was that people said a lot more, a lot faster, than they could record with their elaborate pictures. (Look at that: Just a few centuries after introducing the first language-recording system, it was already overwhelmed with blah-blah-blah. Let this be a lesson to us all.) So Heptep decided to make some of the pictures represent sounds. For example, when Heptep drew an owl, he didn't mean the bird (although owls existed along the Nile, they did not figure prominently in Egyptian life); he meant the sound "M"—which sounded like the ancient Egyptian word for "owl." This was huge. Not only was there now a written way to convey ideas; there was a written way to convey words.

Pictogram versus phonogram: ▶
Heptep's bull means "bull,"
but his owl stands for the
sound "M."

Pictogram   Phonogram

That proved to be the great puzzle of hieroglyphics. Sometimes the "words" in hieroglyphics are *pictograms,* meaning that the pictures really do represent the things they look like. But sometimes the "pictures" in hieroglyphics are *phonograms,* meaning they represent sounds that have nothing in common with the picture.

The fact that hieroglyphics are *both* pictorial and phonographic is precisely the reason it took so long for Europeans to decode their meaning. For a thousand years, word-centric European scholars could not believe that a language as visually resplendent as hieroglyphics was really a written language at all. It took a self-educated (and probably dyslexic) Frenchman to prove them wrong.

After years of laborious effort, Jean-François Champollion, a man who himself struggled to distinguish the difference between pictures and words in his native French, discovered the binary *picture-and-sound* structure of hieroglyphics. The key lay in not only comparing the parallel hieroglyphic and Greek texts found on the Rosetta Stone* but in

---

* Discovered by Napoleon's troops during their 1799 conquest of Egypt, the Rosetta Stone is a yard-square block of granite into which was carved the same inscription in three different scripts: Greek, demotic, and hieroglyphic. By comparing the three side by side, Champollion and his contemporaries ultimately decoded ancient Egyptian.

recognizing that the same pictures appeared to represent both objects and sounds. Ironically, part of Champollion's revelation was triggered by a contemporary's insights into the world's other great pictographic language, Chinese.

Through Champollion's work, Europeans finally came to recognize that a language could be both pictorial and verbal. In other words, the first written languages were vivid.

THEN CAME PHONETICS

But that's not the end of the story. Around two thousand years after Heptep drew his bull, seafaring merchants from the far eastern shores of the Mediterranean saw his pictures and liked them. As the world's greatest traders, these Phoenicians also needed a written language to keep track of who owed whom what. They adopted Heptep's picture for use in their own writing and for a brief time used his bull's head to represent *alf*, the Phoenician word for "ox."

$$= \text{"Alf" (ox)}$$

But the bull didn't last long. These Phoenicians had a different idea about writing. They weren't interested in using pictures to represent *things* the way the Egyptians often did. The Phoenicians wanted their picture to represent *only* sounds.* This is the crucial turning point in our story, because it marks the beginning of the end for pictures in European languages. There are many possible reasons why the Phoenicians dropped pictures—maybe drawing took too long or was too difficult for the rapidly growing population of writers; maybe drawings weren't specific enough or flexible enough for the

---

* Phoenicians weren't the first to purge pictographic imagery from writing. Although the Mesopotamians' cuneiform began as a pictographic language, the pictures quickly became so abstracted that any semblance to the original image was lost. Even the Egyptians, recognizing that their increasingly cryptic hieroglyphics were tricky for anyone but the most educated scribe to write and read, developed a simplified "phonetic" form for use in day-to-day writing, called "demotic." This was the third script found on the Rosetta Stone.

countless details the Phoenicians needed to document. We'll never know exactly what this new generation of scribes was thinking, but we all live with the result.

Sometime around 1000 B.C.E., by simplifying and rotating the bull (perhaps to make it easier to draw quickly), the Phoenicians created a letter that no longer meant "ox" but represented only the sound "alf."

The Phoenicians called this new letter *aleph* and made it the first letter in the *alphabet* they were creating. (And this is why today we call any language that uses symbols for sounds "phonetic.")

It only took another six hundred years for another Meditteranean seafaring people, the Greeks, to pick up that symbol, further simplify it, rotate it again, and make it their own. Thus arrived the Greek letter *A,* and the rest, as they say, is history.

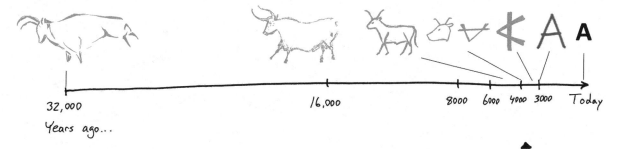

32,000
Years ago...

16,000

8000 6000 4000 3000 Today

▲
Thirty-two thousand years of writing: a long road from pictures to words.

There we have it: the thirty-two thousand years of European writing history, a straight line from Oog and Aag to Heptep to us; from our original cave pictures to the "vivid" writing system of ancient Egypt to our purely verbal system today.

While the sound-based writing system we Westerners use today is efficient, straight-forward to learn, and easy to duplicate, the long road to get here has taken its toll on our visual mind. Our hummingbird, once central to all thinking, is no longer called upon when writing. For all educational, political, and practical intents, she has died. Our words killed her.

APPENDIX B

Connections Back to The Back of the Napkin

I've always been a believer in the power of pictures. Whenever I speak with clients, colleagues, friends, or family, I encourage everyone to draw. On napkins, whiteboards, book margins, dusty tabletops, and frosted windows, our pictures appear. It doesn't matter what surface we draw on, nor does the "quality" of our pictures matter; what matters is that we draw. The more we draw, the more our ideas become visible, and as they become visible they become clear, and as they become clear they become easier to discuss—which in the virtuous cycle of visual thinking prompts us to discuss even more.

When I began *The Back of the Napkin* five years ago, I started by asking myself, "If simple visuals are so powerful, why don't more people use them?" I assumed the answer was a lack of tools and instruction, so my goal in that book was to provide a handful of well-structured yet simple ways for anyone to become a good visual problem solver.

The book was a hit. Published by Portfolio in 2008, *The Back of the Napkin* won many business innovation and creativity awards and became a bestseller in twenty languages. Yet something unexpected happened amid all that success: I realized my starting question was only half-right.

The question isn't "Why don't more people think with pictures?" We *do* think in pictures, all of us, all the time. The real question is "Why have we forgotten that?"

Blah-Blah-Blah is my answer. The tools in this book—the Blah-Blahmeter, Vivid Grammar, and the Vivid FOREST—serve the same purpose as those in *The Back of the Napkin:* they make it easier for us to think about and share complex ideas. But where the *Napkin* tools focused almost entirely on the pictorial, the tools in this book work to help us combine our visual and verbal minds.

To me, it's the differences between the two sets of tools that make them interesting, but it's the parallels that make them fascinating.

The 6x6 Rule

I wrote the core of *The Back of the Napkin* around one essential visual-thinking tool: the **6x6 Rule.*** This rule says that since there are six essential pathways along which our brains process imagery, there are six equivalent essential pictures we can draw to visually explain anything.

In other words, our brain has evolved to become a highly efficient visual processing machine. To handle the overwhelming amount of information coming in through our eyes, our brains break the visual world into a set of six discrete types of information. These types map almost directly to the old "six W's" taught in English composition class: *who and what, how much, where, when, how,* and *why.* (Yes, there are actually seven— I combine *who* and *what* into a single common information type—and how ends with *w* rather than starts with it, but that's close enough.)

---

* There is a second tool in *The Back of the Napkin* called the SQVID, a mnemonic device that helps us remember the five essential questions to ask when creating a picture: simple versus elaborate, qualitative versus quantitative, vision versus execution, individual versus comparison, and difference versus status quo. Since the SQVID does not play any direct role in this book, that's enough said. For more details, please take a look at *Napkin.*

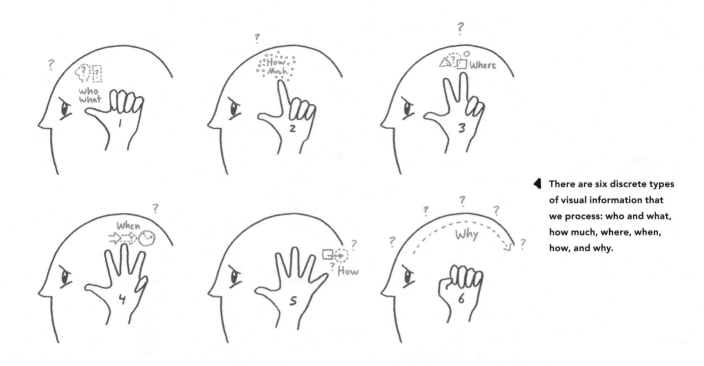

There are six discrete types of visual information that we process: who and what, how much, where, when, how, and why.

My 6x6 Rule simply adds another step to this internal processing system: If our brains see the world in six ways, then it stands to reason that we can draw just six pictures (one for *who* or *what* and one each for the remaining five W's) to create an illustration of any idea our brain can conceive of.

Put in pictures, the 6x6 Rule looks like this:

The 6x6 Rule: six ways we see = ▶ six pictures to explain anything.

To me, the beauty of the 6x6 Rule is that it is both immediate and comprehensive. The immediacy part is important from a survival perspective. Let's say we're suddenly faced with a new problem or idea. Instead of panicking, we simply do what our visual brain is hardwired to do: We break the idea into its essential component elements, process them individually, and then stitch them together to create the richness of the whole. Presto: instant visual problem solving.

The comprehensive part of the 6x6 is equally important. Because the six essential questions map to the major rational* processing capabilities of our higher brain, if we can address all six, we can be pretty sure we've covered just about everything there is to know about an idea.

---

* The one big missing piece in the 6x6 is emotion: what we *feel* about an idea. Emotions are mainly processed in what is called our "limbic brain," a central core sitting below our cortex. As we all know, our emotional response to something frequently trumps our ability to think about it. Part of the purpose of the 6x6 is to remind us that we need to intentionally *think* about big ideas and problems if we really want to solve them. Which is the unspoken beauty (and challenge) of visual problem solving: Because pictures so readily provoke an emotional response, we can easily skew our perception of an idea by the choice of pictures we make to represent it.

The Origins of Vivid Grammar

The 6x6 Rule is the original genesis for the *Vivid Grammar* I describe in this book. How the one became the other is, in hindsight, blindingly obvious. One day about a year after the publication of *The Back of the Napkin*, I gave a presentation on visual thinking to a roomful of middle school teachers. Knowing from experience that most of them would not rely on pictures in their teaching (primary teachers do rely on pictures to describe ideas, but by middle school most of the pictures have been banished in favor of written descriptions), I thought it might be useful to make a parallel between the pictures of the 6x6 Rule and verbal grammar.

I'd never thought of it before, but as I heard myself saying that a "who-and-what portrait" could be thought of as a visual version of a noun and a "how-much chart" a visual version of an adjective, everything clicked: The six types of pictures mapped perfectly to the main elements of speech. I suppose the symmetry shouldn't have been such a surprise: Grammar is a reflection (and evolution) of the essential thinking processes of our verbal mind, so why shouldn't visual grammar be a similar reflection of our visual mind?

In any case, if you find the *Vivid Grammar* structure a useful way to think about a verbal-and-visual way to describe your idea, you might want to refer back to *The Back of the Napkin* for more details on the neurobiology and cognitive science behind it.

The Origin of the Vivid FOREST

The 6x6 Rule also served as a guide for creating the *Vivid FOREST*—as well as the tool for validating it. It's not by chance that the forest is composed of six variations on the visual-and-verbal idea: Each one of the variations maps to one element of the 6x6 Rule. The connection is best seen if we first lay out the two tools side by side. Here they are, the 6x6 Rule and the *Vivid FOREST*.

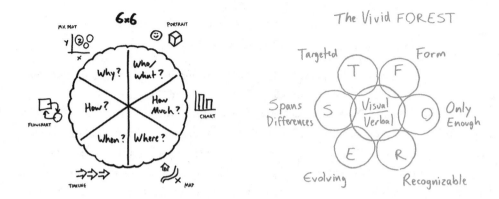

When placed side by side, ▶ **the similarities between the 6x6 Rule and the Vivid FOREST begin to emerge.**

Both are composed of a single "whole" divided into six surrounding elements (a pie chart for the 6x6 and a Venn diagram for the forest), and in both cases those six surround the core in a sequential (clockwise) circular direction. That's true, but there's more to their relationship than just conformational similarities: Superimposing the *forest* on the 6x6 reveals that both answer the same six elemental questions of cognition, just in slightly different ways.

Superimposing the Vivid ▶ **FOREST on the 6x6 reveals that both address the same six cognitive questions, but provide answers in slightly different ways.**

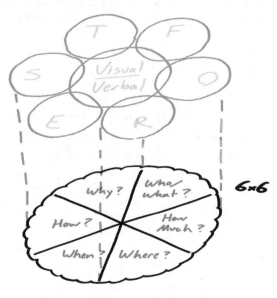

This table shows the overlap between the two tools.

ESSENTIAL COGNITIVE QUESTION	6X6 RULE	VIVID FOREST
Who and What		Form (What does my idea look like?)
How much		Only Essentials (How much should I show?)
Where		Recognizable (Where have I seen this before?)
When		Evolving (When do I pin it down?)
How		Spans Differences (How does this idea work?)
Why		Targeted (Why does it matter to me?)

In other words—and in closing—when we apply any of the tools, we're doing the same thing: We're helping our brain find an easier way to think about (and share) complex ideas. If we ask the six essential questions, we're helping our verbal mind. If we use the 6x6 Rule, we're helping our visual mind. If we use *Vivid Grammar* and the *Vivid FOREST*, we're helping both our verbal and visual minds. And most important, we're helping them work together.

APPENDIX C
The Complete Vivid Checklist

Just getting our fox and hummingbird to work together is a huge step toward smarter, clearer, and more memorable ideas. We don't have to use every vivid tool for every idea; often we may find that our idea snaps into focus before we've dived into the Grammar Graph or made it halfway around the Vivid FOREST. But just to be safe, it makes sense to quickly run through the complete checklist—you never know if we might find one more great idea.

The Complete Vivid Checklist (Long Version)

MY IDEA IS VIVID [MANDATORY]

- [ ] I created it using words and pictures.
- [ ] It contains words and pictures.
- [ ] I can explain it *to any audience* using words and pictures.

I CHECK MY IDEA USING THE BLAH-BLAHMETER

The Blah-Blahmeter

| (no blah-blah) | BLAH | BLAH BLAH | BLAH BLAH BLAH |

- [ ] If the idea has no blah-blah-blah ▶ No changes needed.
- [ ] If the idea is boring (1 blah) ▶ *Unclutter* and *sharpen*.
- [ ] If the idea is foggy or befuddling (2 blahs) ▶ *Discover* and *develop* the idea's essence.
- [ ] If the idea is misleading (3 blahs) ▶ *Debunk* and *dispel*.

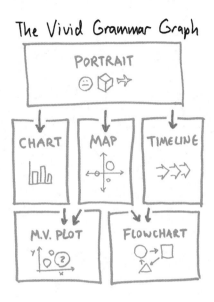

The Vivid Grammar Graph

I USE VIVID GRAMMAR TO CREATE WORDS AND PICTURES THAT EXPRESS MY IDEA

☐ When I hear a noun ▶ I draw a <u>portrait</u>.

☐ When I hear an adjective of quantity ▶ I draw a <u>chart</u>.

☐ When I hear a preposition ▶ I draw a <u>map</u>.

☐ When I hear tense ▶ I draw a <u>timeline</u>.

☐ When I hear a complex verb ▶ I draw a <u>flowchart</u>.

☐ When I hear a complex sentence ▶ I draw a <u>multivariable plot</u>.

The Vivid FOREST

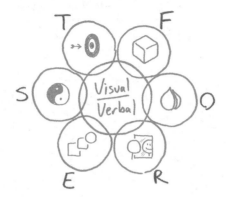

I WALK MY IDEA THROUGH THE VIVID FOREST

☐ **F:** My idea has *form*.

I used the Six Vivid Quick Tricks and determined that the idea's form is:

☐ A **noun** (a *who* or a *what*) made vivid with a **portrait**.

☐ An **adjective of quantity** (a *how much*) made vivid with a **chart**.

☐ A **preposition** (a *where*) made vivid with a **map**.

☐ **Tense** (a *when*) made vivid with a **timeline**.

☐ A complex **verb** (a *how*) made vivid with a **flowchart**.

☐ A complex set of **nouns** (a *why*) made vivid with a **multivariable plot**.

☐ **O:** My idea can be expressed with *only the essentials*.

I used the distillation curve to:

☐ Begin my idea with every useful insight I could think of.

☐ Distill my idea down to its essence. *(This is how I will first present my idea.)*

☐ Expand my idea back up to include its details. *(For those still interested.)*

☐ **R:** My idea is *recognizable*.

☐ I have identified where I have seen my idea before.

☐ I have utilized a visual metaphor from nature to represent my idea.

or

☐ I have utilized a visual metaphor from the built world to represent my idea.

- [ ] **E:** My idea *evolves*.
  - [ ] I utilized "inward evolution" (the verbal-visual waddle) to *nearly* complete my idea.
  - [ ] I left something unfinished for my audience to complete: "outward evolution" (connect the dots).
- [ ] **S:** My idea *spans differences*.
  - [ ] I used the Vivid Stretch Test to make sure I explored *(and included as necessary)* the opposite of my idea.
- [ ] **T:** My idea is *targeted*.
  - [ ] I used the Vivid LENS to make sure I know who my audience is and what vivid image they need:
  - [ ] A **leader** wants to see where we are going ▶ I create a *portrait* or a *map*.
  - [ ] A **doer** wants to see how we are going to get there ▶ I create a *time line* or a *flowchart*.
  - [ ] An **expert** wants more complexity ▶ I create a more *elaborate* explanation.
  - [ ] A **newbie** wants more simplicity ▶ I create the *simplest* possible explanation.
  - [ ] A **numeric** person wants quantities ▶ I create a *chart*.
  - [ ] An **emotional** person wants feelings ▶ I create a *portrait*.
  - [ ] A **sympathetic** person wants to support me ▶ I can use a vivid explanation to push ideas even further.
  - [ ] An **antagonistic** person wants me to fail ▶ I can use a vivid explanation to show them that I know their concerns and I include them in my idea.

AT THE END OF THE DAY, MY IDEA SATISFIED BOTH MY FOX AND MY HUMMINGBIRD

NOTES

Page

5 **"Some weeks we have four books"**: NPR "More from Jon Stewart's *Fresh Air* Interview," NPR, October 22, 2010. Retrieved February 3, 2011, from http://www.wbur.org/npr/130704771/more-from-jon-stewarts-fresh-air-interview.

6 **"We all read it and have no idea"**: David Carr, "Condé Nast Futuregram: No Magazines, but Lots of 'Consumer Centricity,'" *New York Times Media Decoder* blog, October 28, 2010. Retrieved October 29, 2010, from http://mediadecoder.blogs.nytimes.com/2010/10/28/conde-nast-futuregram-no-magazines-but-lots-of-consumer-centricity.

8 **"I'm not going to live"**: Dana Priest and William M. Arkin, "A Hidden World, Growing Beyond Control," *Washington Post Top Secret America* project, July 19, 2010. Retrieved October 23, 2010, from http://projects.washingtonpost.com/top-secret-america/articles/a-hidden-world-growing-beyond-control.

16 **By the time he died**: *Publishers Weekly*, "Bestselling Childrens Books of All Time (Hardcover)." Infoplease.com, 2002. Retrieved October 27, 2010, from http://www.infoplease.com/ipea/A0203049.html.

18 **They revealed that kids preferred**: J. Hersey, "Why Do Students Bog Down on the First R?" *Life*, May 24, 1954: 136–50.

19 **Looking at the lists**: L. Menand, "Cat People." *The New Yorker*, December 23, 2002.

40 **This text was cited in a lawsuit**: Center for Science in the Public Interest, "Lawsuit Over Deceptive Vitaminwater Claims to Proceed," July 23, 2010. Retrieved October 10, 2010, from http://www.cspinet.org/new/201007231.html.

42   **"It's a proprietary strategy"**: E. E. Arvedlund, "Don't Ask, Don't Tell." *Barron's*, May 7, 2001.

59   **"These thoughts did not come"**: Andrew Robinson, *Einstein: A Hundred Years of Relativity* (Bath, England: Palazzo, 2005).

60   **Until he was eight, Albert**: ibid., p. 33.

61   **Since the time of Oog and Aag**: Leonard Schlain, *The Alphabet Versus the Goddess: The Conflict Between Word and Image* (New York: Penguin Compass, 1998), pp. 17–23.

62   **"the brain can be divided"**: John Medina, *Brain Rules* (Seattle: Pear Press, 2008), p. 77.

62   **All vertebrates have a bi-lobed brain**: Leonard Schlain, *The Alphabet Versus the Goddess: The Conflict Between Word and Image* (New York: Penguin Compass, 1998).

64   **By assigning names to the things it saw**: Steven Pinker, *The Stuff of Thought: Language as a Window into Human Nature* (New York: Viking, 2007).

68   **One day, when he was working**: Richard P. Feynman, *The Pleasure of Finding Things Out* (New York: Perseus Publishing, 1999).

69   **The problem was that Harvard Business School**: Walter Kiechel, *The Lords of Strategy: The Secret Intellectual History of the New Corporate World* (Boston: Harvard Business School Press, 2010), pp. 113–30.

71   **"most famous business school professor"**: Michael Porter, *Competitive Strategy: Techniques for Analyzing Industries and Competitors* (Boston: Free Press, 1980).

179   **Donella Meadows and her colleagues**: Donella H. Meadows, *Thinking in Systems* (White River Junction, VT: Chelsea Green, 2008).

201   **The son of an Old World coffee roaster**: G. Raine, "Coffee Pioneer Alfred Peet Dies," *San Francisco Chronicle*, September 1, 2007.

213   **In Maslow's hierarchy**: Abraham H. Maslow, *Motivation and Personality* (New York: Addison Wesley Longman Inc., 1954).

215   **Every year, about eleven thousand**: Publishing Central, "Bowker Reports U.S. Book Production Declines 3% in 2008, but 'On Demand' Publishing More Than Doubles." *Publishing Central*, May 19, 2009. Retrieved February 7, 2011, from http://publishingcentral.com/blog/book-publishing/bowker-reports-us-book-production-declines-3-in-2008-but-on-demand-publishing-more-than-doubles?si=1.

215   **In 1997, two professors**: Renée Mauborgne, "Value Innovation: The Strategic Logic of High Growth." *Harvard Business Review*, January–February 1997: 103–12.

217   **Six years after publication**: W. Chan Kim and Renée Mauborgne. "W. Chan Kim." *Blue Ocean Strategy*, 2010. Retrieved February 7, 2011, from http://www.blueoceanstrategy.com/aut/chan_kim.html.

226   **"If a man is provided with a length of gummed linen cloth"**: Leonardo da Vinci, from the *Codex Atlanticus*, c. 1478–1518; in the Biblioteca Ambrosiana, Milan, Italy.

231   **Land was a master of both**: Peter C. Wensberg, *Land's Polaroid: A Company and the Man Who Invented It* (New York: Houghton Mifflin, 1987).

239 **When Will Wright was young:** J. Seabrook, "Game Master," *The New Yorker,* November 6, 2006.

246 **"the test of a first-rate intelligence":** F. Scott Fitzgerald, "Handle with Care," *Esquire,* April 1936.

253 **He called these repeating patterns:** Bill Bryson, *A Short History of Nearly Everything* (London: Black Swan, 2003).

258 **It worked. Buying up and selling:** Michael Lewis, *The Big Short: Inside the Doomsday Machine* (New York: W. W. Norton, 2010).

259 **Born in 1926, Genrich Altshuller:** Larisa D. Komarcheva, "Genrick Saulovich Atlshuller English Introduction." *G. S. Altshuller Foundation,* October 15, 2003. Retrieved March 1, 2011, from http://www.altshuller.ru/world/eng/index.asp.

259 **"forty principles for discovering new ideas":** Ellen Domb, "40 Inventive Principles with Examples," *TRIZ Journal,* July 1997. Retrieved March 1, 2011, from http://www.triz-journal.com/archives/1997/07/b/index.html.

310 **"The Picture-Superiority Effect on Consumer Memory":** T. L. Childers, "Conditions for a Picture-Superiority Effect on Consumer Memory." *The Journal of Consumer Research,* September 1984: 643–54.

311 **"Verbal Overshadowing of Visual Memories":** J.W.S. Schooler, "Verbal Overshadowing of Visual Memories: Some Things Are Better Left Unsaid." *Cognitive Psychology* 22 (1990): 36–71.

314 **After years of laborious effort:** Andrew Robinson, *The Story of Writing: Alphabets, Hieroglyphs & Pictograms* (New York: Thames & Hudson, 1995).

BIBLIOGRAPHY

Arvedlund, E. E. "Don't Ask, Don't Tell." *Barron's*, May 7, 2001.

Bellis, T. J. *When the Brain Can't Hear: Unraveling the Mystery of Auditory Processing Disorder.* New York: Atria Books, 2002.

Boyle, C. "Flight 1549's Charmed Passenger," *The Week,* January 22, 2009. Retrieved March 24, 2011, from http://theweek.com/article/index/92523/flight-1549s-charmed-passenger.

Bryson, B. *A Short History of Nearly Everything.* London: Black Swan, 2003.

Calaprice, A. *The New Quotable Einstein (Enlarged Commemorative Edition).* Princeton, NJ: Princeton University Press, 2005.

Carr, D. "Condé Nast Futuregram: No Magazines, but Lots of 'Consumer Centricity,' " *New York Times Media Decoder* blog, October 28, 2010. Retrieved October 29, 2010, from http://mediadecoder. blogs.nytimes.com/2010/10/28/conde-nast-futuregram-no-magazines-but-lots-of-consumer -centricity.

Carr, N. *The Shallows: What the Internet Is Doing to Our Brains.* New York: W.W. Norton & Company, 2010.

Carter, B. *The War for Late Night.* New York: Viking, 2010.

Center for Science in the Public Interest. "Lawsuit Over Deceptive Vitaminwater Claims to Proceed," July 23, 2010. Retrieved October 10, 2010, from http://www.cspinet.org/new/201007231.html.

Childers, T. L. "Conditions for a Picture-Superiority Effect on Consumer Memory." *The Journal of Consumer Research*, September 1984: 643–654.

Dehaene, S. *Reading in the Brain: The New Science of How We Read.* New York: Penguin Books, 2010.

Domb, E. "40 Inventive Principles with Examples," *TRIZ Journal,* July 1997. Retrieved March 1, 2011, from http://www.triz-journal.com/archives/1997/07/b/index.html.

Ferguson, E. S. *Engineering and the Mind's Eye.* Cambridge: The MIT Press, 1992.

Ferguson, N. *The Ascent of Money.* New York: Penguin Books, 2008.

Feynman, R. P. *The Pleasure of Finding Things Out.* New York: Perseus Publishing, 1999.

Fitzgerald, F. S. "Handle with Care." *Esquire,* April 1936.

Gordon, K. E. *The Transitive Vampire: A Handbook of Grammar for the Innocent, the Eager, and the Doomed.* New York: Times Books, 1984.

Hersey, J. "Why Do Students Bog Down on the First R?" *Life,* May 24, 1954: 136–150.

INSEAD. "Blue Ocean Strategy Interview with the Authors," *INSEAD Alumni Newsletter,* February 2005.

Johnson, S. "Grace Hopper—A Living Legend." *All Hands,* September 1982: 3–6.

Johnson, S. *Where Good Ideas Comes From: The Natural History of Innovation.* New York: Riverhead Books, 2010.

Kiechel, W. *The Lords of Strategy. The Secret Intellectual History of the New Corporate World.* Boston: Harvard Business School Press, 2010.

Kim & Mauborgne. "W. Chan Kim." *Blue Ocean Strategy,* 2010. Retrieved February 7, 2011, from http://www.blueoceanstrategy.com/aut/chan_kim.html.

Komarcheva, L. D. "Genrick Saulovich Atlshuller English Introduction." *G. S. Altshuller Foundation,* October 15, 2003. Retrieved March 1, 2011, from http://www.altshuller.ru/world/eng/index.asp.

Kranowitz, C. S. *The Out-of-Sync Child: Recognizing and Coping with Sensory Processing Disorder.* New York: Perigee Books, 2005.

Kuhn, M. "The Land List: An Ongoing Project in Cataloging Polaroid Cameras." *Landlist,* February 9, 2008. Retrieved March 10, 2011, from http://www.rwhirled.com/landlist/landhome.htm.

Lattman, P. "Michael Lewis's 'The Big Short'? Read the Harvard Thesis Instead!" *WSJ Blogs Deal Journal,* March 15, 2010. Retrieved March 2, 2011, from http://blogs.wsj.com/deals/2010/03/15/michael-lewiss-the-big-short-read-the-harvard-thesis-instead.

Lester, T. *The Fourth Part of the World.* New York: Free Press, 2009.

Lewis, M. *The Big Short: Inside the Doomsday Machine.* New York: W. W. Norton & Company, 2010.

Maslow, A. H. *Motivation and Personality.* New York: Addison Wesley Longman Inc., 1954.

Maslow, A. H. *The Psychology of Science: A Reconnaissance.* Washington, DC: Henry Regnery Co., 1970.

Mauborgne, R. "Value Innovation: The Strategic Logic of High Growth." *Harvard Business Review,* January–February 1997: 103–112.

Meadows, D. H. *Thinking in Systems.* White River Junction, VT: Chelsea Green, 2008.

Medina, J. *Brain Rules.* Seattle: Pear Press, 2008.

Menand, L. "Cat People." *The New Yorker,* December 23, 2002.

Neffe, J. *Einstein: A Biography.* Baltimore: The Johns Hopkins University Press, 2005.

NPR. "More from Jon Stewart's 'Fresh Air' Interview." NPR, October 22, 2010. Retrieved February 3, 2011, from http://www.wbur.org/npr/130704771/more-from-jon-stewarts-fresh-air-interview.

Pinker, S. *The Stuff of Thought: Language as a Window into Human Nature.* New York: Viking, 2007.

Porter, M. *Competitive Strategy: Techniques for Analyzing Industries and Competitors.* Boston: Free Press, 1980.

Priest, D., and W. Arkin. "A Hidden World, Growing Beyond Control," *Washington Post Top Secret America* project, July 19, 2010. Retrieved October 23, 2010, from http://projects.washington post.com/top-secret-america/articles/a-hidden-world-growing-beyond-control.

Publishing Central. "Bowker Reports U.S. Book Production Declines 3% in 2008, but 'On Demand' Publishing More Than Doubles." Publishing Central, May 19, 2009. Retrieved February 7, 2011, from http://publishingcentral.com/blog/book-publishing/bowker-reports-us-book-production -declines-3-in-2008-but-on-demand-publishing-more-than-doubles?si=1.

Raine, G. "Coffee Pioneer Alfred Peet Dies." *San Francisco Chronicle,* September 1, 2007.

Rich, B. R. *Skunk Works: A Personal Memoir of My Years of Lockheed.* New York: Bay Back Books, 1996.

Robinson, A. *Einstein: A Hundred Years of Relativity.* Bath, England: Palazzo, 2005.

Robinson, A. *Sudden Genius? The Gradual Path to Creative Breakthroughs.* Oxford: Oxford University Press, 2010.

Robinson, A. *The Story of Writing: Alphabets, Hieroglyphs & Pictograms.* New York: Thames & Hudson, 1995.

Schlain, L. *The Alphabet Versus the Goddess: The Conflict Between Word and Image.* New York: Penguin Compass, 1998.

Schooler, J. W. S. "Verbal Overshadowing of Visual Memories: Some Things Are Better Left Unsaid." *Cognitive Psychology* 22 (1990): 36–71.

Seabrook, J. "Game Master." *The New Yorker,* November 6, 2006.

Shubin, N. *Your Inner Fish.* New York: Pantheon Books, 2008.

Surowiecki, J. "Soak the Very, Very Rich." *The New Yorker,* Financial Page, August 16, 2010.

Takeuchi, T. *An Illustrated Guide to Relativity.* New York: Cambridge University Press, 2010.

Weekly, P. "Bestselling Childrens Books of all Time (Hardcover)." Infoplease.com, 2002. Retrieved October 27, 2010, from http://www.infoplease.com/ipea/A0203049.html.

Wensberg, P. C. *Land's Polaroid: A Company and the Man Who Invented It.* New York: Houghton Mifflin, 1987.

Whitehall, H. *Structural Essentials of English.* New York: Harcourt, Brace and Company, 1951.

INDEX

Blah-blah-blah (*cont.*)

   information problem, degrees of, 4–8

   negative impact of, 1, 22, 28, 36

   root cause of, 73

   Treasure Map out of, 10–14, 139

Blah-Blahmeter, 30–56

   clear message filter, 30, 37–38

   full form diagram, 31

   functions of, 2, 30–31

   "idea is" component, 45–47

   "intent is" component, 47–49

   "message is" component, 31–43

   misleading words filter (duplicity), 30–31, 41–42

   misused words filter (foggy), 34–35, 40–41

   overused words filter (boring), 34–35, 38–39

   quotations, measuring, 32–35, 37–42

   scale of, 30–31

   subjectivity and user, 39n

   Vivid Checklist for, 328

   Vivid Thinking component, 50–56

BLUF, 196–98

Books, Who Maps for, 294–95

Book titles, visual metaphors as, 216–20

Boring. *See* Overuse of words (boring)

Boss test, 296–97

Bottom line up front (BLUF), 196–98

Bowker, Gordon, 201

Brafman, Ori, 220

Brain

   balanced thinking. See Balanced thinking; Vivid Thinking

   evolutionary view, 35–36, 61–62

   limbic brain, 63n

   reptilian brain, 63n

   split brain theory, 62–63, 65n

   visual-verbal mind, 66–71

   See also Thoughts/thinking

Bruce, Maryann, 280n

Burry, Michael, 254–59, 261

Business model, Five Forces, 70–71

Carter, Bill, 169

Cat in the Hat, The (Seuss), 19–20

Cause-and-effect, understanding, flowchart for, 127–28, 177–81

Cave paintings, 312

Cerf, Bennett, 19–20

Champollion, Jean-François, 314–15

Charts, 115–18

   creating, best way, 117

   form of idea, finding, 164–68

   important role of, 116

   numbers, understanding with, 164–68

   problem related to, 116n–17

   verbal parts represented by, 115

   and Vivid Thinking, 104

Chauvet Cave, 312n

Chief simplicity officer (CSO), 299–300

Childers, Terry, 310

Citizens' School Study Council, 17

Clear message

   Blah-Blahmeter filter, 30, 37–39

   ideas expressed by, 46

   intent expressed by, 48

   power of, 27–28

   presenting, efforts in, 45n

   Vivid Thinking enhancement of, 51, 53

Coca-Cola Company

   Blah-Blahmeter in quote from, 34–35, 40–41

   targeting by, 281–82

Collateralized debt obligations (CDOs), 257–58

Columbus, Christopher, 154

Tactile tips, for Vivid Thinking, 292–97

Taijitu, 247, 255–56

Takeuchi, Dr. Tatsu, 187n

Taleb, Nassim Nicholas, 220

Tao Te Ching, 246n

Targeting, 267–85

    audience, understanding, 268–78

    by Coca-Cola Company, 281–82

    by General Petraeus, 283

    by Madoff, 280–81

    by Obama, 284

    purpose of, 267–68

    by Sullenberger, 273–74

Tarpenning, Marc, 249, 261

Tense of verbs, 99–100

    visual representation of. *See* Flowcharts;
        Timelines

Tesla, Nikola, 249

Tesla Motors, 248–49

Thoughts/thinking

    all-at-once path, 65, 72, 83

    balanced in. *See* Balanced thinking; Vivid
        Thinking

    connection to language, 63–64, 68–69

    descriptive thinking, 61n

    evolutionary view, 35–36, 61–64

    Feynman's definition, 68–69

    piece-by-piece path, 63–64, 72, 83

    split brain theory, 62–63, 65n

    visual versus verbal mind. *See* Verbal mind;
        Visual mind

Timelines, 123–25

    for economic crisis (2008), 174–77

    form of idea, finding, 173–77

    history, understanding with, 173–77

    for leaders/doers, 276

    sequential part of, 124

    verbal parts represented by, 123

    and Vivid Thinking, 104

Townsend, Chuck, 6

Treasure Map, 10–14, 139, 291

Trees, Vivid FOREST, purpose of, 141

Trigger phrases, 157–58

TRIZ (Theory of Inventive Problem Solving),
    259–61

Universality, in TRIZ, 260

Universe, theories of, multivariable plot for,
    184–92

Unplugged music, 230n

U.S. Navy, 195–96

Verbal Grammar, 98–103

    components of, 99

    picture of, 100

    Vivid Grammar representation for, 104

Verbal mind

    balance with visual. *See* Vivid Thinking

    combined with visual, power of, 86–91

    development of, 63–64, 92

    dominance of, 67n, 77–78, 86, 91–93

    fox and hummingbird analogy, 80–95

    manifestation in business, 89

    Verbal Grammar, 98–103

    view of forest by, 84–85

    versus visual mind, examples of, 66–71

Verbal overshadowing, 311

Verbs, 99–100

    complex, visual representation of. *See*
        Flowcharts

    simple, visual representation of. *See* Portraits

Viral, Vivid Ideas going, 298–99

Visual metaphors, 216–24

    for book titles, 216–20